# KITCHENER'S ARMY

# KITCHENER'S ARMY

## RAY WESTLAKE

SPELLMOUNT
Staplehurst

In memory of my late mother-in-law, Mrs Harriet Wilcox, a young girl at the time of the First World War, but who remembered vividly the men from her home in the Rhondda Valleys going off to war with the 38th (Welsh) Division

By the same author:
Collecting Metal Shoulder Titles (1980)
The Rifle Volunteers (1982)
The Territorial Battalions (1986)
The Territorial Force (1988)
British Battalions on the Somme 1916 (1994)
English and Welsh Infantry Regiments (1995)
British Regiments at Gallipoli (1996)
British Battalions in France & Belgium 1914 (1997)

British Library Cataloguing in Publication Data:
A catalogue record for this book is available
from the British Library

ISBN 1-86227-212-3

First published by Spellmount Ltd in the UK in 1989

This paperback edition published in the UK in 2003 by
Spellmount Limited
The Old Rectory
Staplehurst
Kent TN12 0AZ

Tel: 01580 893730
Fax: 01580 893731
E-mail: enquiries@spellmount.com
Website: www.spellmount.com

1 3 5 7 9 8 6 4 2

The right of Ray Westlake to be identified
as the author of this work has been asserted by him
in accordance with the Copyright, Designs
and Patents Act 1988

Printed in Singapore

# CONTENTS

# FOREWORD

In August 1914 Kitchener started on his duties as Secretary of State for War with the great asset of enjoying the confidence of almost the whole of the British Empire, from King George V to the most junior native soldier. He has been criticised for not making use of the Territorial Army for recruiting, but the association of his great reputation with the new armies may have had a valuable effect on their morale. Lloyd George, no great admirer of Kitchener, referred to the new recruits in a Cabinet Memorandum as 'Kitchener Armies', as did the French General Joffre in his General Orders.

Kitchener was one of the very few people in authority who foresaw a long war, and this made him resist a strong demand from GHQ in France for the soldiers he needed as instructors in England. Winston Churchill described this as the greatest of all the services Kitchener rendered to the nation.

Kitchener's other important contribution to the ultimate success of the BEF was his visit to Paris at the end of August 1914, when he persuaded the Commander-in-Chief, Sir John French, to abandon his plan to retreat. The BEF was then able to play its part in the decisive victory at the Battle of the Marne.

**The Earl Kitchener TD DL**

# ACKNOWLEDGEMENTS

I would like to thank the following for allowing me to use photographs from their collections; their help has been invaluable: Dave Ashwin, David Barnes, Stuart Barr, Peter Blagojevic, Peter Bronson, Chris Coogan, Andrew Gavaghan, Peter Howling, The Imperial War Museum, Mike Ingrey, Clive Lewis, John Lowe, Brian Nevison, Lt Bryn Owen FMA, RN, Geoff Archer Parfitt, Peter Scott, The Shropshire Regimental Museum, The Ulster Museum Belfast, The Welch Regiment Museum, Denis Wood, Tom Wylie.

Copies of illustrations credited to the IWM are available for purchase from its Department of Photographs, Imperial War Museum, Lambeth Road, London SE1 6HZ. The archive is open to visitors by appointment.

# INTRODUCTION

The purpose of this book is to set out in pictures a record of the men and divisions that existed during the First World War, and were known as Kitchener's Army. An attempt has also been made to provide the reader with an outline history of each division, together with an order of battle showing which units served in each formation.

In the narrative for each division emphasis has been given to the movements of its infantry; although it must be appreciated that the artillery, engineers, transport, medical and other divisional personnel all played an important and necessary role and were as much a part of the division as the battalions that fought in the forward positions.

Every unit of Kitchener's Army, from the small field company of engineers to the division itself, could justify a complete history in its own right. Indeed, the services of many divisions and battalions have been published. As the average divisional history often runs to several hundred pages, it would of course be impossible to record a complete account of service in the space available. Instead, mention of only the more important movements, battles and engagements has been made and enough detail given, it is hoped, to encourage further study.

Turning to the order of battle lists given with each division, only units allotted as part of the division up until the signing of the Armistice on 11 November 1918 are mentioned. There were in all divisions a number of formations attached but these were not on the permanent establishment. As the main reason for including an order of battle is to inform the reader as to which units served in each division, I have not listed obvious groups where their title alone would indicate a higher formation. For example: the 34th Divisional Ammunition Column, 35th Divisional Signal Company, etc should all be apparent, as would be the machine gun battalions which, after March 1918, all bore the same number as that of the division in which it served.

The titles used for the infantry are those which were currently in use in 1914. Each battalion would have had in addition the word 'Service' in brackets, but this, for the sake of brevity, has been left out. Pioneer battalions also indicated their role within their full titles. The use of Roman numerals to identify artillery formations was introduced at the beginning of the war, *viz*: 113th Field Brigade of the 25th Division would be known as CXIII Field Brigade. Only the original numbers have been used throughout this work.

The sub-titles associated with a number of infantry battalions often varied in their make-up, and occasionally a unit was only known locally by its special name. Almost all of the infantry of the Fourth and Fifth New Armies were known as 'Pals' battalions, *viz*: 'Liverpool Pals', 'Birmingham Pals', but these titles were not official. Only approved titles, appearing in the Army List and other official publications, have been used.

When locally raised battalions began to form, a number of individuals would have been involved, and consequently the person given credit as being responsible for the formation of the unit often differs at a local level. Once again only official lists giving the names of persons or organisations have been quoted.

Forming part of the history of each New Army division are records of the uniforms and badges, also the equipment used. These are all major studies in their own right and consequently only the briefest of reference has been made in this work to these subjects.

As the title of this book implies, a photographic history is being offered, and it is my sincere wish that the illustrations chosen represent a visual study of what must surely be one of the most interesting periods in the history of the British soldier. The sacrifice made by these men should never be forgotten, I hope this book helps to keep their memory alive.

Ray Westlake
August 1989

# 1
# FORMATION OF THE NEW ARMIES

When war was declared on 4 August 1914 the British Army consisted of the Regular Army, with its Reserve and Special Reserve, and the Territorial Force. In 1914 the strength of the Regular Army, or First Line, stood at around 235,000 men of which almost half were serving overseas, usually in India. Those units stationed in the UK subsequently formed the British Expeditionary Force of six divisions and one cavalry division, having been brought up to war establishment by drafts from the Reserve.

Turning to the Territorial Force, there were in 1914 fourteen divisions and an equal number of mounted brigades, each trained to a high standard and organised much the same as the Regular Army. However, these were intended for home defence, a Territorial not being liable for overseas service, unless as a volunteer. The TF, of course, did subsequently serve abroad and its fine record is now a matter of history.

At the outbreak of war the Prime Minister, Mr Asquith, was also acting as Secretary of State for War, a post that he subsequently passed on to Field-Marshal Earl Kitchener of Khartoum on 5 August. On the same day that he assumed his duties, Lord Kitchener asked Parliament to authorise an additional 500,000 men for the Army. It was his opinion that the war would not be, as generally thought, a brief affair, and that the country should prepare itself for a three-year period in which some seventy divisions would be required.

Lord Kitchener had been opposed to the concept of the Territorial Force from its creation in 1908 and was not prepared to use its framework as a basis for his planned massive expansion. His plan was to raise a completely new army which would be made up of volunteers, each being required to enlist as a regular soldier for three years or the duration, and to undertake a commitment of service anywhere.

On 11 August Kitchener's now famous proclamation headed 'YOUR KING AND COUNTRY NEED YOU. A CALL TO ARMS' was published and called for some 100,000 men aged between 19 and 30 to enlist. Within two weeks the required number had come forward and on 21 August Army Order 324 approved of the addition to the Army of six divisions and Army Troops.

*Field-Marshal Rt Hon H. H. Earl Kitchener of Khartoum.*

*Lord Kitchener's Notice, August 1914 – 'A CALL TO ARMS'.*

Included in this Army Order were details of the composition and nomenclature of the new units and formations, a matter in which Kitchener himself expressed indifference, as all he wanted were the men. The new battalions were to be raised as additional battalions of the regiments of Infantry of the Line, receiving numbers following on consecutively from the existing battalions of their regiments. They were to be further distinguished by the word 'Service' after the number, *eg*: 8th (Service) Bn The Royal Welsh Fusiliers.

These first six divisions were to form the First New Army, soon referred to as Kitchener's Army and by some simply as K1. By the time of the Army Order of

Your King and Country Need You.

## A CALL TO ARMS.

An addition of 100,000 men to his Majesty's Regular Army is immediately necessary in the present grave National Emergency.

Lord Kitchener is confident that this appeal will be at once responded to by all those who have the safety of our Empire at heart.

### TERMS OF SERVICE.

General Service for a period of 3 years or until the war is concluded.

Age of Enlistment between 19 and 30.

### HOW TO JOIN.

Full information can be obtained at any Post Office in the Kingdom or at any Military Depot.

### God Save the King!

## THE LATE
# LORD ROBERTS' STIRRING WORDS
## TO LONDON'S SPECIAL SERVICE BATTALION:

"I respect and honour you more than I can say. My feeling towards you is one of intense "admiration.

"HOW VERY DIFFERENT IS YOUR "ACTION TO THAT OF THE MEN "WHO CAN STILL GO ON WITH "THEIR CRICKET AND FOOTBALL

"as if the very existence of the country were not "at stake!

## "THIS IS NOT THE TIME TO PLAY GAMES

"We are engaged in a life and death struggle, "and you are showing your determination to do "your duty as soldiers, and, by all means in your "power, to bring this War to a successful result. "GOD BLESS AND WATCH OVER YOU ALL."

# CAN YOU READ THIS UNMOVED?

---

# UNIVERSITY & PUBLIC SCHOOLS BRIGADE
## 5000 MEN AT ONCE

The Old Public School and University Men's Committee makes an urgent appeal to their fellow Public School and University men

to at once enlist in these battalions, thus upholding the glorious traditions of their Public Schools & Universities.

### TERMS OF SERVICE.

Age on enlistment 19 to 35, ex-soldiers up to 45, and certain ex-non-commissioned officers up to 50. Height 5 ft. 3 in. and upwards. Chest 34 in. at least. Must be medically fit.

#### General Service for the War.

Men enlisting for the duration of the War will be discharged with all convenient speed at the conclusion of the War

#### PAY AT ARMY RATES.

and all married men or widowers with children will be accepted, and will draw separation allowance under Army Conditions.

### HOW TO JOIN.

Men wishing to join should apply at once, personally, to the Public Schools & Universities Force, 66, Victoria Street, Westminster, London, S.W., or the nearest Recruiting Office of this Force.

## GOD SAVE THE KING!

---

*Recruiting poster for the Sportsmen's Bn, Royal Fusiliers.*

*Recruiting poster for the University and Public Schools Bde, (18th, 19th, 20th, 21st Royal Fusiliers, 1914).*

*Notice of a public meeting in Cardiff in aid of the formation of the 16th Bn, Welsh Regt.*  Welch Regt Museum

*Later version of Lord Kitchener's recruiting poster.*  Welch Regt

---

## SPECIAL NOTICE.

### Cardiff City Battallion.

A

# PUBLIC MEETING

WILL BE HELD AT THE

### CLARENCE ROAD SCHOOLROOM

## THIS EVENING,

### Tuesday, November 24th,
FRIDAY
At 8-15 p.m.  27

TO FURTHER THE ABOVE MOVEMENT

Come in crowds to hear
MAJOR GASKELL,
who has just returned from the Front wounded.

The Cardiff Stationery Company, Limited, Docks.

---

21 August, the original six regular infantry divisions had been augmented by a seventh, its formation commencing at Lyndhurst by the end of the month. This meant that K1 would enter the order of battle as the 8th to 13th Divisions. In addition to its number, each division held a title, the 8th (Light), indicating its formation from battalions of Rifle and Light Infantry regiments, and the 9th (Scottish), 10th (Irish), 11th (Northern), 12th (Eastern), 13th (Western), all showing their main areas of recruitment.

By the beginning of September 1914 the formation of another regular division was well under way, its battalions having been recalled from various overseas stations, *viz*: India (3), South Africa (1), Aden (1), Egypt (3), Malta (3) and Bermuda (1). This division was subsequently designated as 8th, thus requiring the 8th (Light) Division to renumber as 14th.

Under the same Army Order which amended the

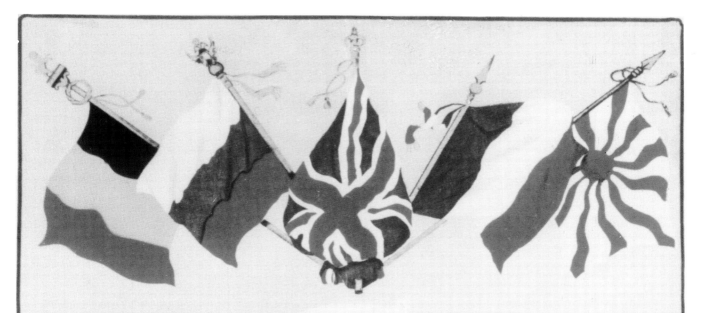

**DON'T IMAGINE YOU ARE NOT WANTED**

EVERY MAN between 19 and 38 years of age is WANTED!

Ex-Soldiers up to 45 years of age

"YOUR COUNTRY NEEDS **YOU**"

**MEN CAN ENLIST IN THE NEW ARMY FOR THE DURATION OF THE WAR**

**RATE OF PAY:** Lowest Scale 7s. per week with Food, Clothing &c., in addition

**1. Separation Allowance for Wives and Children of Married Men when separated from their Families** (Inclusive of the allotment required from the Soldier's pay of a maximum of 6d. a day in the case of a private)

| | | |
|---|---|---|
| For a Wife **without** Children | - - | 12s. 6d. per week |
| For Wife with One Child | - - | 15s. 0d. per week |
| For Wife with Two Children | - - | 17s. 6d. per week |
| For Wife with Three Children | - - | 20s. 0d. per week |
| For Wife with Four Children | - - | 22s. 0d. per week |

and so on, with an addition of 2s. for each additional child.

Motherless children 3s. a week each, exclusive of allotment from Soldier's pay

**2. Separation Allowance for Dependants of Unmarried Men**

Provided the Soldier does his share, the Government will assist liberally in keeping up, within the limits of Separation Allowance for Families, any regular contribution made before enlistment by unmarried Soldiers or Widowers to other dependants such as mothers, fathers, sisters, etc.

**YOUR COUNTRY IS STILL CALLING. FIGHTING MEN!       FALL IN!!**

**Full Particulars can be obtained at any Recruiting Office or Post Office.**

numbering of the Light Division (AO 382 of 11 September 1914) an additional six divisions were authorised. Kitchener had, on 28 August, asked for another 100,000 men to come forward, a request that was met with even greater response than his previous one. Hence the Second New Army (K2) was born, its divisions being recruited along the same lines as K1 and assuming the designations 15th (Scottish), 16th (Irish), 17th (Northern), 18th (Eastern), 19th (Western), and 20th (Light). The formation of the Third New Army (K3) followed fast on the heels of the Second, its six divisions receiving no titles but known simply by their numbers: 21st to 26th.

Turning now to the construction of a wartime division in 1914 we find that each contained three numbered infantry brigades. The numbering of brigades within the New Armies began at 26 and continued on through the divisions in the order that they were numbered: 26th, 27th, 28th Brigades were part of the 9th (Scottish) Division; 29th, 30th, 31st

Brigades with the 10th (Irish), etc. A simple way to determine what brigades were with what division is to take the number of the division and multiply this by three. The answer represents the number of the middle brigade in each division, *eg* 9 by three: 27, 10 by three: 30. There were twelve infantry battalions in each division – four per brigade.

Each division contained, in addition to its infantry battalions, the required number of divisional troops. In 1914 this represented, mainly, four brigades of field artillery, each with its own ammunition column; two, later three, field companies of engineers; a signal company; three field ambulances; a mobile veterinary section; and transport and supply train. A number of Army Troops battalions (units attached for training) also formed part of each division. Later, trench mortar batteries, machin gun companies, pioneer battalions and mounted troops were also added.

As the war went on, a number of changes in the establishment and organisation of divisions took place. Those of special interest were in February 1918 when each division on the Western Front was reorganised on a nine-battalion basis, three per brigade; and in the following March when brigade machine gun companies were withdrawn and formed into battalions of the Machine Gun Corps.

The proposals to form a Fourth New Army were first put forward in Army Order 389, issued on 14 September 1914 and later approved in another issued in November. Personnel for the infantry of the 'original' Fourth New Army, as it became known, were to be found from the now duplicated reserve battalions of line regiments. These men had in fact come forward in August and September 1914 to join the first three new armies but, due to the great response, had been placed in reserve.

*Taking the Oath at the Central Recruiting Depot, Whitehall.*

*Recruits training in civilian clothes.* B. Nevison

*The University and Public Schools Bde being inspected by Maj-Gen Sir Francis Lloyd before leaving for Epsom, Hyde Park, Sept 1914.*

*17th Bn, Royal Fusiliers (Empire) being inspected by Maj-Gen C. L. Woollcombe. Green Park London, 1914.*

Upon formation, the order stated, the Fourth New Army would consist of the 27th to 32nd Divisions. However, a number of Regular Army battalions withdrawn from overseas garrisons in India, China, Hong Kong, Singapore and Egypt, and one Territorial Force battalion, were eventually formed into three divisions that received the numbers 27th, 28th and 29th. Subsequently, when the Fourth New Army was formed in November 1914, its six divisions received the numbers 30th to 35th.

The training centres selected for the field artillery and infantry were at Cannock Chase, Prees Heath, Oswestry, Rhyl and Clipstone. The ammunition columns and heavy batteries were at Woolwich, the engineers and signals assembled at Buxton and Shrewsbury, and the field ambulances at Llandrindod Wells.

On 16 January 1915 it was notified that the engineer field companies in each of the New Army divisions would be increased from two to three. This resulted in the twelve companies then on the establishment of the Fourth New Army being removed and placed with the 21st to 26th Divisions. It was intended to form three new companies for each of the six divisions in the Fourth New Army but this was never carried out.

On 10 April 1915 the six divisions of the original Fourth New Army were broken up, the idea being that its battalions could be used as reinforcements for the First, Second and Third New Armies. In consequence, the infantry brigades of the 'original' Fourth New Army were designated as Reserve Infantry Brigades (numbered 1st to 18th) and at the same time their battalions became known as 2nd Reserve Battalions. At this time each regiment had at least one reserve battalion, the old Militia, which was used to train and supply drafts for the regular battalions. Later on the Fifth New Army was redesignated as Fourth and its six divisions (37th to 42nd) were renumbered 30th to 35th. Hence the need for the distinction 'original' when referring to the Fourth New Army and its divisions prior to 10 April 1915.

The composition of the 'original' Fourth New Army was as follows:

### 30th Division (Original)

*89th Brigade (later 1st Reserve Infantry Brigade)*
15th Bn The Northumberland Fusiliers. Formed at Darlington.
11th Bn Alexandra, Princess of Wales's Own (Yorkshire Regt). Formed at West Hartlepool.

16th Bn The Durham Light Infantry. Formed at Durham.

17th Bn The Durham Light Infantry. Formed at Barnard Castle.

*Members of the University and Public Schools Bde boarding hired London buses for Epsom, 18 Sept 1914.*

*The University and Public Schools Bde in Epsom High Street, 19 Sept 1914.*

**90th Brigade (later 2nd Reserve Infantry Brigade)**

13th Bn The Prince of Wales's Own (West Yorkshire Regt). Formed at York.

9th Bn The East Yorkshire Regt. Formed at York.

11th Bn The King's Own (Yorkshire Light Infantry). Formed at Hull.

11th Bn The York and Lancaster Regt. Formed at Harrogate.

*91st Brigade (later 3rd Reserve Infantry Brigade)*
9th Bn The Lincolnshire Regt. Formed at Lincoln.
11th Bn The Duke of Wellington's (West Riding Regt). Formed at Halifax.
14th Bn The Sherwood Foresters (Nottinghamshire and Derbyshire Regt). Formed at Lichfield.
14th Bn The Manchester Regt. Formed at Lichfield.

The divisional field artillery consisted of the 118th to 121st Brigades. The 118th later served with the 1st Canadian and 11th (Northern) Divisions while the remaining three joined the 38th (Welsh) Division. The two field engineer companies (97th and 98th) transferred to the 21st Division in January 1915 and the three field ambulances (90th, 91st and 92nd) later became part of the new 32nd Division.

**31st Division (Original)**

*92nd Brigade (later 4th Reserve Infantry Brigade)*
14th and 15th Bns The King's Royal Rifle Corps. Formed at Sheerness.
14th and 15th Bns The Rifle Brigade (The Prince Consort's Own). Formed at Southend.

*93rd Brigade (later 5th Reserve Infantry Brigade)*
9th Bn The Queen's (Royal West Surrey Regt). Formed at Gravesend.
9th Bn The Queen's Own (Royal West Kent Regt). Formed at Chatham.
14th Bn The Duke of Cambridge's Own (Middlesex Regt). Formed at Gravesend.
15th Bn The Duke of Cambridge's Own (Middlesex Regt).

*Special badge worn by the University and Public Schools Bde in civilian clothes.*

*Members of the University and Public Schools Bde at Epsom 1914. Note the round badges being worn in the lapels.*

*The University and Public Schools Bde erecting huts at Epsom, 1914. Note the band of cloth being worn by the NCO, bottom right.*

*Special shoulder titles for the 1st, 3rd and 5th City Bns, Manchester Regt. There were eight City Bns and the remaining five wore similar titles, but with the relevant numbers.*

*94th Brigade (later 6th Reserve Infantry Brigade)*
10th Bn The Norfolk Regt. Formed at Walton-on-the-Naze.
10th Bn The Suffolk Regt. Formed at Felixstowe.
9th Bn The Bedfordshire Regt. Formed at Felixstowe.
11th Bn The Loyal North Lancashire Regt. Formed at Felixstowe.

The Division's 122nd Field Artillery Brigade transferred to the 38th (Welsh) Division while the

*Mr Frank Lawrence, Signwriter, being kept busy at one of the new camps set up for the New Army at Winchester, 1914.*
B. Nevison

*Men from several regiments constructing billets.* B. Nevison

remaining three (123rd, 124th and 125th) joined the 37th Division. The two field engineer companies (99th and 100th) became part of the 22nd Division and the three field ambulances (93rd, 94th and 95th) transferred to the new 31st Division.

## 32nd Division (Original)

*95th Brigade (later 7th Reserve Infantry Brigade)*
9th Bn The Buffs (East Kent Regt). Formed at Dover.
14th and 15th Bns The Royal Fusiliers (City of London Regt). Formed at Dover.
10th Bn The East Surrey Regt. Formed at Dover.

*96th Brigade (later 8th Reserve Infantry Brigade)*
10th Bn The Leicestershire Regt. Formed at Portsmouth.
13th Bn The Hampshire Regt. Formed at Parkhurst.
9th Bn The Oxfordshire and Buckinghamshire Light Infantry. Formed at Portsmouth.
9th Bn Princess Charlotte of Wales's (Royal Berkshire Regt). Formed at Portsmouth.

*97th Brigade (later 9th Reserve Infantry Brigade)*
12th Bn The Royal Warwickshire Regt. Formed at Parkhurst.
13th Bn The Royal Warwickshire Regt. Formed at Golden Hill.
10th Bn The Royal Sussex Regt. Formed at Dover.
13th Bn The Highland Light Infantry. Formed at Gosport.

Only one (the 126th) of the four artillery brigades was formed. This transferred to the new 37th Division. The 101st and 102nd Field Companies, Royal Engineers went to the 23rd Division and the three field ambulances (96th, 97th and 98th) became part of the new 32nd Division.

## 33rd Division (Original)

*98th Brigade (later 10th Reserve Infantry Brigade)*
9th Bn Prince Albert's (Somerset Light Infantry). Formed at Plymouth.
12th and 13th Bns The Worcestershire Regt. Formed at Plymouth.
13th Bn The Sherwood Foresters (Nottinghamshire and Derbyshire Regt). Formed at Plymouth.

*Service battlion of the Welsh Regt leaving Cardiff, 1914.*
Welch Regt Museum

*99th Brigade (later 11th Reserve Infantry Brigade)*
10th Bn The King's Own (Royal Lancaster Regt). Formed at Saltash.
10th Bn The East Lancashire Regt. Formed at Plymouth.
10th Bn The South Staffordshire Regt. Formed at Plymouth.
10th Bn The Prince of Wales's (North Staffordshire Regt). Formed at Plymouth.

*100th Brigade (later 12th Reserve Infantry Brigade)*
11th Bn The Devonshire Regt. Formed at Exeter.
11th Bn The East Surrey Regt. Formed at Devonport.
14th Bn The Highland Light Infantry.
14th Bn Princess Louise's (Argyll and Sutherland Highlanders).

Both the 14th HLI and 14th Argylls were intended for the 100th Brigade but had not joined by the time the Division was broken up. The four artillery brigades were not formed, the engineer companies (103rd and 104th) went to the 24th Division and the three field ambulances (99th, 100th and 101st) joined the new 33rd Division.

## 34th Division (Original)

*101st Brigade (later 13th Reserve Infantry Brigade)*
12th Bn The Cameronians (Scottish Rifles). Formed at Nigg.
11th Bn The Black Watch (Royal Highlanders). Formed at Nigg.
10th Bn Seaforth Highlanders (Ross-shire Buffs, The Duke of Albany's). Formed at Cromarty.
8th Bn The Queen's Own Cameron Highlanders. Formed at Invergordon.

*102nd Brigade (later 14th Reserve Infantry Brigade)*
14th Bn The Royal Scots (Lothian Regt). Formed at Weymouth.
9th Bn The King's Own Scottish Borderers. Formed at Portland.

*11th Bn, Welsh Regt, Eastbourne, 30 Sept 1914.*
Welch Regt Museum

*Six Lancashire Fusiliers, 16 Nov 1914, wearing the emergency blue uniform.*   D. Barnes

*15th Bn, Royal Warwickshire Regt (2nd Birmingham) marching to a church parade, 1914. The men are still in their civilian clothes but wear a small round lapel badge consisting of a crown between the letters 'GR' and BIRMINGHAM BATTALION below.*

7th Bn The Dorsetshire Regt. Formed at Weymouth.
8th Bn The Duke of Edinburgh's (Wiltshire Regt). Formed at Weymouth.

*103rd Brigade (later 15th Reserve Infantry Brigade)*
16th Bn The Royal Fusiliers (City of London Regt). Formed at Falmouth.
14th Bn The Prince of Wales's Own (West Yorkshire Regt). Formed at Falmouth.
9th Bn The Duke of Cornwall's Light Infantry. Formed at Falmouth.
8th Bn The Northamptonshire Regt. Formed at Weymouth.

No artillery was formed for the Division and the two engineer field companies (105th and 106th) went to the 25th Division. The three field ambulances (102nd, 103rd and 104th) became part of the new 34th Division.

## 35th Division (Original)

*104th Brigade (later 16th Reserve Infantry Brigade)*
12th Bn The Royal Welsh Fusiliers. Formed at Wrexham.
9th Bn The South Wales Borderers. Formed at Pembroke Dock.
12th Bn The Welsh Regt. Formed at Cardiff.
9th Bn The King's (Shropshire Light Infantry). Formed at Pembroke Dock.

*7th Bn, King's (Shropshire Light Infantry) Sept 1914. A mixture of scarlet tunics and khaki service dress is being worn.* Shropshire Regimental Museum

*10th or 11th Bn, Cheshire Regt, Bournemouth 1914. Worn with the emergency blue uniform is a brown leather belt, the 'Queen's' crown displayed on its fastener indicating that the item is of pre-1901 vintage. A 'Drummer's' badge is worn on the right sleeve.* D. Barnes

*105th Brigade (later 17th Reserve Infantry Brigade)*
15th Bn The King's (Liverpool Regt). Formed at Formby.
16th Bn The King's (Liverpool Regt). Formed at Hoylake.
14th Bn The Cheshire Regt. Formed at Birkenhead.
10th Bn The Prince of Wales's Volunteers (South Lancashire Regt). Formed at Crosby.

*106th Brigade (later 18th Reserve Infantry Brigade)*
10th Bn The Bedfordshire Regt. Formed at Dover-court.
11th Bn The Gloucestershire Regt. Formed at Abbey Wood, Woolwich.
12th Bn The Essex Regt. Formed at Harwich.
13th Bn Princess Louise's (Argyll and Sutherland Highlanders). Formed at Blackheath.

No artillery was formed for the Division and the 107th and 108th Field Companies went to the 26th Division. The three field ambulances (105th, 106th and 107th) joined the new 35th Division.

*above left*
*Three men of the 9th Bn, Worcestershire Regt wearing blue uniforms with khaki caps.*   D. Barnes

*above right*
*Member of the Royal Sussex Regt in the emergency blue uniform.*   D. Barnes

*below*
*York and Lancaster Regt. A mixture of civilian clothes, with both blue and khaki uniform is being worn. Note the strips of cloth being worn around the left arm for unit identification.*   D. Barnes

*opposite right above*
*Members of a King's Royal Rifle Corps service battalion. Some men are wearing brass general service buttons in lieu of cap badges.*   B. Nevison

*opposite right below*
*Members of 'B Coy, 9th Bn, Suffolk Regt wearing brass shoulder titles on the collars of their blue emergency uniforms. Note that with the exception of the NCO on the right, the jackets have no shoulder straps. The man standing with pipe (second left front) wears the ribbons for the Queen's and King's South Africa Medals, 1899-1902.*

While the divisions of the first three New Armies were under formation during August and September 1914, another type of Kitchener's Army unit came into being. These were the locally raised battalions, which later fought bravely on the Western Front, and whose massive casualties left hardly a home without a loss in the cities, towns and villages from which they were formed.

Known unofficially as 'Pals' or 'Chums' battalions these units provided the greater part of the infantry for the Fourth and Fifth New Armies, and were raised by committees set up by cities, towns, organisations, businesses and individuals. Although authorised by the Government, at first each battalion was clothed, quartered and fed by their sponsoring committee. However, in 1915 the War Office took over responsibility for the battalions and all expenses so far incurred were refunded.

Although the concept of local battalions was almost entirely confined to the Fourth and Fifth New Armies, the idea was not new, a number of battalions of the first three New Armies having been formed along the same lines.

*South Wales Borderers recruit (10th or 11th Bn) early 1915.*  C. Lewis

*The Northamptonshire Regt. A mixture of blue emergency and khaki service dress uniform and headdress can be seen in this illustration, some men wearing a combination of both. On the blue jackets, brass shoulder titles are being worn on the collars and an additional curved identification has been placed at the top of the sleeve.*  D. Barnes

*No 3 Section, 25th Div Signal Coy, Boscombe, early 1915. Brass 'RE' shoulder titles are being worn on the collars.*

*In a number of battalions, where uniform but not badges had been issued, a brass button was worn in the caps.*
B. Nevison

In the Cheshire Regiment, the 13th Battalion had been raised at Port Sunlight as the result of an appeal by Lord Leverhulme to his employees. Over 1,000 men at once came forward – a staff of clerks were even loaned from the factory to carry out the administration and paperwork involved.

The men from Lord Leverhulme's works were later joined by another 200 from Wallasey who had been recruited by Mr Gershom Stewart, Member of Parliament for the Wirral. In its early days this group was known as the Wirral Battalion.

There was also in Cardiff the 11th Battalion, Welsh Regiment, known both as the 'Commercial Battalion' or 'Cardiff Pals'. There were no doubt many more, but these locally raised battalions differed from those formed later in that they did not include any previous unofficial title in that eventually granted by the War Office.

The reasons behind the formation of local units were several. In some areas it was felt that the War Office was unable to deal with the large numbers of men coming forward for service. Existing Army Recruiting Offices and their staffs, it seemed, were far from adequate, and were simply unable to cope efficiently. It was also felt that a potential recruit could possibly be put off in some cases by the thought of being placed into a unit from some other part of the country and service among strangers. With the formation of local battalions, the opportunity was given for men from the same area, work-place, school, club, etc to fight alongside their mates. 'Those that enrol together – serve together,' it was guaranteed.

At first the battalions raised in the early months of the war received no numbers and were known until November 1914, when numbers were issued, by their local names. These names were subsequently permitted to be used as part of the battalion's full title, and gave good indication as to the origin of each unit.

In the senior infantry regiment of the British Army – the Royal Scots, there was the 1st Edinburgh Battalion (later 13th) raised and sponsored by the Lord Provost of the City. The Northumberland Fusiliers had in their ranks a large number of locally raised battalions including two complete brigades – the Tyneside Scottish (20th to 23rd) and Tyneside Irish (24th to 27th). Raised at Epsom and known as the 'Public Schools and University Men's Force', were the 18th to 21st Battalions of the Royal Fusiliers. The West Yorkshire Regiment had the 'Wool Textile Pioneers' (21st Battalion), and the Middlesex Regiment its 'Football' and 'Public Works' Battalions (17th, 18th, 19th, 23rd, 26th).

Formation of the Fifth New Army was authorised on 10 December 1914, its divisions bearing the numbers – 37th to 42nd and the battalions being found from locally raised units. As previously mentioned, the original Fourth New Army was broken up in April 1915. At the same time, the Fifth New Army was redesignated as the new Fourth, and its six divisions assumed the numbers previously held by those with the original Fourth, *viz* 30th to 35th.

*Party from a Royal Welsh Fusiliers service battalion, Llandudno, Jan 1915. Each man wears the blue emergency uniform.*   D. Barnes

*K Battery, 96th Bde, RFA at Berkhamsted, Hertfordshire, training with improvised gun and limber.*   P. Scott

The last of the New Armies to be formed, the Fifth, was authorised in March 1915 and was to be designated as Sixth but for the dispersal of the original Fourth and the subsequent renumbering of the original Fifth New Armies in the following April.

Included in the Fifth New Army were the 36th (Ulster) Division, formed out of the Ulster Defence Force; the 37th Division which was originally numbered as 44th and later replaced the 16th (Irish) Division in the Second New Army; the 38th (Welsh), at first numbered 43rd; the 39th, the 40th consisting almost entirely of Bantam battalions, and the 41st Divisions.

*One of the Liverpool Pals Bns at a review held by Earl Kitchener in Liverpool, April 1915.*

*15th Bn, Kings Royal Rifle Corps, Belhus Park Camp near Purfleet, 1915.*   D. Barnes

# 2
# THE EARLY MONTHS

### Recruiting – Training

It was probably the tremendous response to Earl Kitchener's appeal, and the speed in which the volunteers came forward, that caused many of the problems experienced by the New Armies during the early months of their existence. Recruiting, housing, clothing, training, were just some of the numerous difficulties that the Army incurred in its attempt to put into the field a force many times larger than it had ever maintained.

The machinery of a peacetime recruiting centre was not designed to pass into the Army within a twenty-four hour period a similar number of men that it would normally expect to enrol during a full year. Long queues, some as much as one mile in length, formed outside every office in the country, and their staffs, although working day and night, were quite unable to cope.

Realising that the number of existing recruiting centres was far from sufficient, and that the system could not be accelerated above a certain speed, the Government was soon to establish additional offices throughout the country. These new centres, which occupied premises of all types – police stations, church halls, theatres, factories etc, were not only to be in the larger cities and towns, but in villages and outlying rural areas. Consequently, men from every part of the British Isles were eventually given the opportunity to enlist into the Army with the minimum of delay.

There can be no doubt that the staffs of the Army Recruiting Centres were under tremendous pressure throughout the early months of the war. However, their duty, it would seem, was generally carried out in an efficient and cheerful manner, and their service to the country at such an important time must be held in the highest esteem.

Having been accepted into the Army, a recruit was

*Party from one of the Gloucestershire Regt's service battalions. Both emergency blue and khaki uniforms are worn together with a mixture of white buff and brown leather equipment.*

*Recruiting staff, Devonshire Regt, Ilfracombe, June 1915.* D. Barnes

*Ex-soldier serving with one of the New Army battalions of the Welsh Regt. He wears both the Queen's and King's Medals for the Boer War.* C. Lewis

then sent to his regimental depot, where he would be kitted out and gradually introduced to army discipline and training. Consequently, as a trained soldier he would eventually join his battalion.

Once again the sheer volume of recruits that were coming into the Army during the first weeks of the war marred what, in peacetime anyway, was hitherto an efficient and satisfactory system. Just as the recruiting procedure had been overwhelmed by sheer volume, so too were the regimental depots. With an intake of more men in two days than a regiment might deal with in several years, the problems were legion.

Within hours, all stocks of uniform and kit were used up and consequently the vast majority of men joining the New Army remained in their own clothing for many weeks. As almost every man possessed only the clothes that he stood up in, problems soon arose concerning their upkeep. Gradually, due to the training programme, garments were being torn and generally wearing out. Boots also suffered and in at least one division, the 18th (Eastern), men whose

*C/Sgt J. F. Bettles, an old soldier serving as an instructor with the 8th Bn, Northamptonshire Regt. Colchester, May 1915.*   J. Lowe

*Some senior NCOs of the 11th Border Regt (Lonsdale) Prees Heath, May 1915. Both the usual Border Regt badge and the special pattern showing the Crest of the Earl of Lonsdale are being worn. The sergeant sitting on the right is a member of the Army Physical Training Staff.*   C. Lewis

*Members of 155th Bde, Royal Field Artillery in billets, 1915. Some men are wearing overalls, often referred to as 'Canvas'.* S. Barr

*16th Bn, West Yorkshire Regt (1st Bradford) at Buckingham Palace (probably Skipton) 1915.* P. Howling

*Royal Army Medical Corps recruits in training.* B. Nevison.

footwear was in need of repair were given permission to do slow marching only, and on grass. There was also the added discomfort of having no dry change of clothing.

*Huts belonging to the 23rd Bn, Royal Fusiliers (1st Sportsmen's) at Hornchurch early in 1915.* B. Nevison

*Lt-Col F. C. Maitland (CO) and Capt H. J. H. Inglis (Adj) 23rd Bn, Royal Fusiliers (1st Sportsmen's), Clipstone Camp, June 1915.* B. Nevison.

To overcome these particular problems, and to get the men out of 'civvies' and into some kind of uniform, a number of measures were taken. In some instances old and obsolete clothing and equipment were taken from stores and issued to recruits. This was to include scarlet jackets of Boer War vintage, old buff leather equipment originally issued in 1871 (the 23rd Division received 400 sets per battalion in November 1914), canvas fatigue overalls and a number of full-dress tunics, normally only worn on ceremonial parades. A large amount of non-military uniforms, such as postmen's suits, were also made available.

There can be no doubt that the wearing of a smart uniform was good for morale and helped with the men's training. With this in mind, the War Office gave its permission for the private purchase of uniform and boots, and any unit wishing to do so could clothe its men until government kit arrived. This concession was to be at no expense to the Army and consequently many battalions acquired their first uniforms only through the aid of public collections and donations. Being privately made, the uniforms obtained were not always of regulation cut and shade. One battalion of the 22nd Division is on record as wearing a colour of a slightly browner tint than the usual khaki, while others were seen in various shades of grey and blue.

The uniform most widely adopted by the New Army while waiting for khaki to arrive consisted of a blue smock and trousers, worn with blue field service caps. This dress, which was issued by the Government, is referred to in unit histories and records in a number of ways, 'Kitchener' or 'Emergency' blue being the more frequent terms used.

As the issue of even temporary uniforms was erratic and the clothing sent to individual formations often varied in colour and type, it was not unusual to see men on parade in strange mixtures of dress. In one division

*11th Bn, Welsh Regt. A special badge, worn prior to the issue of regimental badges, is being worn in the cap. The disc has the wording CARDIFF COMMERCIAL BATTALION around the edge and THE WELSH REGIMENT in the centre.* D. Ashwin.

*11th Bn, Welsh Regt outside billet in Hastings, 1915. Three of the men are still wearing the disc badge issued in lieu of a regimental pattern.* D. Ashwin

there is an account of a parade that took place in October 1914 where the men were seen in red jackets, khaki trousers and putties, civilian overcoats and an assortment of military and civilian headgear. In fact it is not in the least unusual, while inspecting photographs of the period, to see civilian dress, old uniforms of numerous periods, khaki, emergency blue, all being worn in a variety of combinations.

Until uniforms were available, and even then where no badges had been received, various methods were employed to distinguish the recruits of different units. A frequently used practice was to attach a piece of coloured cord or cloth to the arm, as in the 26th Division who had patches of buff, blue, white or green, according to brigade. The NCOs of some battalions, where no chevrons were available, were also identified by the use of coloured cord around the arm.

The desire to recognise one unit from another in a training camp filled with several thousand men was obviously of great importance to the Army and would have been of great assistance in the training programme. However, it was often the soldier himself who felt the need to show who he was and to what formation he belonged. A soldier's pride in the wearing of his regimental badge had existed in the British Army for centuries, and the men of the New Army were going to be no exception.

*11th Bn, Welsh Regt, Hastings 1915. A special battalion badge is being worn in both civilian and uniform jackets. One man (centre front) also has the initials 'CCB' (Cardiff Commercial Bn) worn below the badge.*   P. Blagojevic

*16th Bn, Welsh Regt training at Colwyn Bay in 1915.*
Welch Regt Museum

In researching the many unit histories and examining photographs taken in the early months of the First World War, numerous instances appear illustrating just how important it must have been to a soldier to have some kind of badge.

In a number of battalions special badges were ordered and paid for by the men, solely for wear in the lapels and buttonholes of their civilian jackets. These were also given to members of a soldier's family and can often be seen in photographs being worn by wives and sweethearts. In some cases these badges, although strictly unofficial and against regulation, were worn in uniform in lieu of regimental patterns.

The private purchase of badges was often the case after uniform, but no insignia, had been issued. In their impatience to put up their regimental badge, soldiers would often buy badges from local shops which, if in a garrison town, could generally provide quite a generous supply. Occasionally, old soldiers rejoining their former regiment would produce the badge that they had worn during their previous service. Examples of this have been noted in photographs where a man can be seen proudly wearing a pattern of cap badge discontinued several years prior to 1914.

A number of temporary measures were introduced in order to give the men some form of insignia in uniform. In many cases, after khaki had been issued, General Service buttons bearing the Royal Arms were worn in the caps in lieu of a badge. Likewise, assuming they were available, both collar badges and shoulder titles found their way up onto the headdress. In a number of cases where shoulder titles had been issued, and the only uniform available was the emergency blue which had no shoulder straps, these badges were worn on the collars as a form of unit identification.

*No 4 Platoon, 19th Bn, King's Liverpol Regt (3rd City). Knowsley Park, early 1915.* D. Barnes

*Service battalion of the Royal Welsh Fusiliers, 1915.* C. Lewis

Although the men of the New Army soon gained pride of regiment and were proud to wear its badges and honours, a number of battalions in the Fourth and Fifth New Armies adopted their own distinct patterns. In the Northumberland Fusiliers there was the Tyneside Scottish, who incorporated the Cross of St Andrew and Scottish Lion into no less than four patterns of cap badge; and the Tyneside Irish who wore a harp on their shoulder straps. The ceremonial seven-branched candlestick, the Menorah, with the Hebrew

motto *Kadimah*, was worn as a cap badge by the Jewish Battalions of the Royal Fusiliers, while in the same regiment the 25th Battalion (Frontiersmen) had three types of badge, all incorporating the grenade of the Royal Fusiliers. The Arms of the cities in which they were raised were worn in the caps by the Leeds Pals and on the collars by the 16th Welsh Regiment of Cardiff. Wandsworth was the home of the 13th East Surrey Regiment and its Arms replaced the usual central device of the regimental badge. Family crests also featured as badges, both the Lords Derby and Lonsdale giving permission for their devices to be adopted as cap badges by some of the units that they had helped form. The 14th Bn, Royal Irish Rifles were allowed to retain the shamrock badge bearing the Red Hand of Ulster that had been worn prior to the war by the Young Citizens Volunteers of the Ulster Volunteer Force. In some battalions a scroll bearing its title was added to the normal cap badge, and in others distinctive metal shoulder titles were used to identify the wearer as a member of Kitchener's Army. Very few of these special badges and shoulder titles survived and those specimens that did are now highly prized by collectors.

With such large numbers coming into the Army, and so many new units being formed, there was in August 1914 a serious shortage of experienced officers. To overcome this problem the Army at once recalled officers on the Reserve List, while at the same time the War Office ordered all officers of the Indian Army then on leave to remain. These men were shortly afterwards posted to units of the First New Army.

After the higher posts had been filled by existing officers (in the 24th Division no battalion had more than two retired or regular officers) there soon became a shortage of subalterns. There was, however, no lack of volunteers for these positions but the process of dealing with them was slow, and no applicant for a commission could possibly have been accepted and trained in time.

In September 1914 commanding officers were given the power to put forward candidates for temporary second-lieutenants. These recommendations were subject to approval, but many young officers with previous military experience in the Officers Training Corps were accepted and did much to bring their units through the early weeks of training. A large number of the new officers, however, were completely ignorant of military matters and these had to learn with their battalions.

There was also a shortage of experienced non-commissioned officers, the backbone of the British Army that would make the greatest contribution to the training and moulding of a soldier. A large number of New Army recruits had previously served in the Army, and these men were quick to establish themselves in their units and take up positions of command.

Pensioners, however, were also recalled and their vast experience must have been of the greatest value, both to the recruit and junior officer. In the South Staffordshire Regiment, four former NCOs, with a

*Local people watching the 11th Bn, Welsh Regt building a pontoon bridge at Eastbourne, 1915.* Welsh Regt Museum

total service of 142 years dating from 1876, rejoined their regiment in 1914 and subsequently made a great contribution to the training of its 10th (Reserve) Battalion.

When the regimental depots and training centres became full, various types of emergency accommodation had to be provided. Churches, schools, cinemas, halls were all used and in some divisions the men even remained in their own homes and carried out their training locally until space could be found. Parks, racecourses and other open spaces were also taken over and organised into makeshift camps.

The existing accommodation at the several army training centres was far from adequate for the number of men that were received in the early weeks of the war. Huts designed for twenty men, it was noted in the 20th Division, had to house fifty, and the lack of washing and toilet facilities made life almost unbearable.

Until more huts could be built, the men had to live in tents, an uncomfortable experience at the best of times, but in 1914 this was made worse due to inclement weather conditions. Heavy rain throughout October and November had made conditions in the camps insufferable – 'the tents had no floor boards and the sixteen occupants had to lie on a floor of mud' (31st Division).

The arrival of trainloads of men at their assembly areas was often chaotic and has been described as looking like 'a football excursion crowd'. When units of one division arrived at Colchester in September 1914, most of its battalions knew no word of command and were accompanied by not a single officer or NCO.

The lance corporal sent to meet the men, it is recorded, could issue no other instruction but 'follow me'.

If clothing and accommodation were in short supply during late 1914 and early 1915, it must come as no great surprise that rifles, guns and ammunition were also at a premium. In many cases, whole divisions did not see a rifle, let alone fire one, until well into 1915 and important musketry training was often non-existent or, at best, well behind schedule. The artillery in particular suffered greatly in its training programme; with every available gun being sent to France, there was simply nothing left for the New Army gunners to learn their trade.

There are a number of recorded examples that illustrate the degree of shortages within the New Army divisions, and what measures were undertaken in order to overcome the problem. The British soldier, both before the First World War and since, has always been expert in making do with what was available at the time, and the men of Kitchener's Army were no exception.

In the 12th Division there were no rifles available for many months so improvised wooden weapons were soon constructed and these were used for drill. Other formations received varying numbers of old and obsolete weapons but these were not intended for

*Royal Welsh Fusiliers. Only one man (front left) wears the regiment's cap badge; the remainder have some other device which is probably a small grenade collar badge in the centre of a disc. Each man wears the '1908 Pattern' Web equipment.* B. Nevison

*Corporal, 25th Bn, Royal Fusiliers (Frontiersmen). He wears the 'Wolseley' pattern foreign service helmet with special battalion badge.* M. Ingrey

*Guard, 23rd Bn, Royal Fusiliers (1st Sportsmen's).* B. Nevison

firing and could only be used for drill purposes. When one battalion of the 31st Division was ordered to assist in the manning of the Humber Defences in December 1914, its commanding officer was asked to report as to the serviceability of his rifles. In his reply the officer said that the weapons would most certainly go off, but he was doubtful as to what end.

When the King inspected the 15th Division at Aldershot in September 1914, only enough rifles were available to arm the front ranks of each battalion, and these were obsolete patterns suitable for drill only. At the same time the artillery of the Division was training with an improvised gun made up from a log of wood mounted on the Borden Camp funeral gun-carriage. Later, however, things improved when a nine-pounder brass muzzle-loading gun was acquired from the Ordnance Officers' Mess and after that some early French breech-loaders, some twenty years out of date, were received. When this division eventually received modern guns they came with no sights, this most necessary item of equipment being unavailable until mid-June 1915.

Initially, the several units within a division were scattered throughout a general assembly area. In the case of the 11th Division, whose headquarters were first at Grantham in Lincolnshire, the infantry were at Grantham, the engineers at Newark, the train at Lichfield, the field ambulances at Sheffield, while the artillery was located at Leeds, Sheffield, Norwich and Weedon.

As training progressed and exercises at brigade level had been completed, units were then concentrated in areas where divisional manoeuvres and final war training took place. By spring 1915 five out of the six divisions of the First New Army were located at Aldershot. The rest were to follow, and eventually all divisions of the New Army were trained and ready for the field.

# 3

# WAR SERVICE

Despite the shortages of weapons and equipment, the training of the New Army divisions progressed at a steady rate. By April 1915 most of the first three New Armies were concentrated around Aldershot and divisional training was in an advanced state. Gradually each division was issued orders instructing it to make ready for war.

On 7 May 1915 the first of the New Army divisions, the 9th (Scottish), received its orders to prepare for overseas service. Advance parties began to move on 8 May and by midday on 15 May the Division was concentrated south-west of St Omer in France. In the same month both the 12th and 14th Divisions received their embarkation orders and also proceeded to France.

The 10th (Irish) Division crossed to England in May 1915 and in the following month, along with the 11th and 13th Divisions, was ordered to Gallipoli. July saw five more divisions leave for the Western Front and by the end of the year some nineteen New Army divisions were in France, two were in Macedonia and one was on its way to Egypt. The remaining five New Army divisions were all sent to France and left England between January and June 1916.

The arrival of a division in France was often spread over a number of days, each unit leaving England independently and making for a collecting point after disembarkation. Having completed its concentration, which was usually around the St Omer area, a division would then move towards the front line and into one or other of the several Corps sectors. In these early weeks in France the heat was intense and the men experienced much discomfort, either on the march or in French railway waggons bearing the now famous marking '8 horses or 40 men'.

Training in trench warfare under actual battle conditions could now begin, and for this purpose individual units were attached for instruction to divisions already at the front. While much of this could be covered in England, there was nothing quite like the real thing for gaining an insight into life in the forward trenches.

Each unit was generally occupied for about a month in its front-line training. Tuition included practical instruction in the use of trench-mortars, bombing and sniping, combined with the skills of the construction and maintenance of trenches. Throughout this period the men of the New Armies were to receive their baptism of fire and, although not yet involved in any major engagement, casualties were heavy.

Towards the end of July 1915 the Germans began a series of attacks at Hooge, a village on the Ypres-Menin Road. At the time, this part of the front line was in VI Corps area and included in that formation was the 14th (Light) Division. On 30 July, 41st Brigade from the division was taking its turn in the trenches when very early in the morning the enemy began to project burning liquid into their positions. This dreadful weapon was being used for the first time and immediately cleared its target of men, enabling the Germans to advance into the British trenches.

Later in the day, 41st Brigade launched a counter-attack which only managed to take back from the enemy a small portion of the lost ground. During this

*5th Bn, Royal Irish Fusiliers, in trenches at Gallipoli, 1915.*
Imperial War Museum

*An artist's impression of L/Cpl W. Dolby, 9th Leicestershire Regt, winning the DCM in France, 27 Nov 1915.*

operation the New Army gained its first Victoria Cross when 2/Lt Sidney Woodroff of the 8th Battalion, Rifle Brigade lost his life while attempting to cut the wire obstacles holding up his party's advance. This gallant officer was aged just nineteen and had been commissioned in December 1914.

Throughout the summer of 1915 the Allies had been preparing for a large-scale assault in Artois. This was to involve both British and French troops and accompany a co-ordinated attack by the French in Champagne. The British attack, under General Sir Douglas Haig and using poison gas for the first time, covered a front line from La Bassée Canal to Lens and concentrated on the village of Loos.

The Battle of Loos, the first in which the New Army was used in an attack, commenced after a preliminary bombardment on 25 September. During the initial stages of the battle some ground was gained and part of one division even managed to reach the suburbs of Lens. However, the assault was soon checked by a series of German counter-attacks and the fighting eventually ended on 8 October. During the Battle of Loos, eight New Army divisions fought with great courage and determination, and without exception performed their duty with the same spirit as the most experienced of veterans.

On 25 April 1915 three separate amphibious landings were made on the Gallipoli Peninsula, two taking place on the southern tip, while the third, Sir William Birchwood's ANZAC Corps, attacked up the west coast. This attempt by the Allies, who hoped to capture Istanbul and, with Russia, launch an offensive on Germany from the east, followed an abortive naval attack on the Dardanelles in the previous March.

The first of the three New Army divisions to arrive at Gallipoli was the 13th, which reached Alexandria on 28 June and later set up headquarters on the Island of Lemnos, some 40 miles off the peninsula. By the end of July the 10th Division had also joined the 13th at Lemnos, and the 11th Division had concentrated on the neighbouring island of Imbros.

In an attempt to end the stalemate on the peninsula, where the Allied force had not been able to push far enough inland to move the enemy from the high ground overlooking the beaches, the three New Army divisions were used in an assault at Suvla on 6 August. Throughout the rest of August a number of engagements involving the three divisions took place – Sari Blair, Russell's Top, Chocolate Hill, Karakol Dagh, Scimitar Hill and Hill 60, but after much hard fighting a new stalemate set in and the 10th, 11th and 13th were later evacuated from Suvla.

The general evacuation of Suvla took place during the night of 19-20 December, the 11th Division returning to Imbros while the 13th headed for its base

*Pte Allan Carmichael, 16th Bn, Highland Light Infantry. Allan Carmichael was posted missing after the Battle of the Ancre, Nov 1916.*

*2/Lt John Neilson Carpenter – 17th Bn, Highland Light Infantry. John Neilson Carpenter was awarded the MC in France and was killed in action on 1 July 1916.*

at Mudros. Prior to this, however, the 10th Division had left the peninsula on 30 September, having been instructed to return to Lemnos where it was to prepare for service in Macedonia.

The 13th Division was involved in the final evacuation of the Gallipoli Peninsula at Helles during the night of 8-9 January 1916. The Division had returned there during the last few days of 1915 to take over part of VIII Corps front line and had been present at the last Turkish attacks of the campaign.

After a skilful withdrawal from Helles, in which not a single life was lost, the Allies finally gave up their attempts to open up the precious Dardanelles waterway, the cost of this mismanaged affair having been tremendous. As on the Western Front, the New Army divisions at Gallipoli had proved its worth, with casualties figuring high among the 250,000 incurred by the Allies throughout the whole campaign.

During October 1915 two New Army divisions, the 22nd and 26th, learned that they were to be transferred from France to the Macedonian theatre of war. The Bulgarian Army had been mobilised in September 1915 and, together with Austria-Hungary and Germany, were to attack Serbia.

Already on its way to the area from Gallipoli was the

10th (Irish) Division, its 29th Brigade being the first to arrive at Salonika in Greece on 5 October. By the end of October the bulk of the 10th had also arrived and they were joined by the 22nd and 26th Division in the following month.

The Allied advance northward to aid Serbia came too late. The Bulgarians pushing rapidly to the west soon cut the railroad from Salonika and in doing so kept the mainly French force at bay and were able to move deep into Serbia. After a general withdrawal, first to Lake Doiran on the Greek border, and then to the coast, the Allies dug themselves in at Salonika.

To summarise the position regarding the thirty divisions of the New Army after the first full year of war, there was at the end of 1915, nineteen in France, three in Macedonia, two in Gallipoli, one in Egypt and five still training in England.

The first engagement of any significance to involve a division of the New Army in 1916 took place at The Bluff, a narrow ridge on the northern banks of the Ypres-Comines Canal held by the 17th Division. On 14 February, and after blowing a mine below The Bluff, the enemy stormed the British trenches and was able to capture part of the line. This surprise attack, and the subsequent fighting, was at great cost to the 17th

Division, its casualties amounting to 67 officers and 1,227 other ranks over a three-day period. Later, on 2 March, a successful counter-attack was launched and the lost ground was restored, together with a sizeable section of the German line.

When the Battle of Loos closed on 8 October 1915, only the western half of the Hohenzollern Redoubt remained in British hands. The Germans later took part of the line known as The Chord and after blowing a number of mines, soon commanded valuable observation posts from which they were able to inflict high casualties.

Having returned to the area in February 1916, the 12th Division was made responsible for the line opposite Cité St Eli to opposite the dump at Fosse 8. On 2 March, and in front of these positions, a great attack had been planned in which the objective was to take back The Chord. Three deep mines had been planned by the tunnellers of the Royal Engineers, and the lips of huge craters that these would leave after detonation would give the attackers great advantage over the enemy.

The fighting around the Hohenzollern craters lasted for just over two weeks and throughout that time all attempts to recover The Chord had failed. The attacking brigade on the 2 March (the 36th) was relieved after three days by the 37th whose casualties for the remainder of the battle amounted to over 1,000 killed, wounded or missing.

It came as no surprise to the 15th and 16th Divisions when on 27 April, on the Hulluch front, the enemy released chlorine gas towards their lines. Some days previously a German prisoner had warned of an attack of this nature and this confirmed prior suspicions aroused after huge numbers of rats were observed leaving the enemy's trenches due, it was thought, to a leaking cylinder.

Although gas helmets were worn, and these were in use as far back as Brigade Headquarters some three miles behind the front, a large number of casualties were incurred on 27 April and in a subsequent attack on the 29th. The total number of men affected by gas within the two divisions amounted to 1,260 of which 338 died.

There was also prior warning of another gas attack that was launched on 30 April on the Wulverghem front. This time it was the 24th Division holding the line and, like their colleagues in the 15th and 16th, the men of that division were subjected to much discomfort and suffering. Casualties on this occasion were over 300 officers and men.

During the evening of 11 May the whole of the 15th Divisional front was subjected to a huge bombardment of high explosive and gas shells. At about 4.30pm the enemy began to concentrate on the part of the Division's line known as The Kink. This sector, which was situated just south-east of the Hohezollern Redoubt, was considered to be one of the worst on the British front and at the time was manned by the 13th Royal Scots.

*16th (Irish) Div ambulance in difficulty, Somme 1916.*
*The shamrock sign can be seen to the bottom right of the red cross.*   Imperial War Museum

By 5.45pm the enemy's shelling, which is on record as being one of the heaviest concentrations of artillery on a small area during the war, had accounted for more than half of the Royal Scots. A little later the German infantry attacked and, in view of the small resistance that was put up, were able to overrun the British line with ease. Of the 935 total casualties, more than half were incurred during the enemy's preliminary bombardment of the area. Most of the 258 missing are believed to have been buried by shell fire.

The 25th Division had moved into the Vimy Ridge sector at the end of April and, during the four weeks leading up to its first major battle on 21 May, incurred over 1,200 casualties. Ten days later, in the Ypres sector, the 20th Division gave good account of itself at the Battle of Mount Sorrel, 1,200yds north-east of Hill 60.

Throughout the early months of 1916 a steady flow of troops had been moving into France. The last of the New Army divisions had left England for the Western Front and both the 11th and 31st Divisions had arrived from Egypt. With this gradual concentration of men in the area it was soon obvious that a large-scale attack had been planned in the region of the Somme. In fact the French had asked for an offensive to be launched early in 1916 with the purpose of relieving the pressure they had been suffering since February at Verdun. This move would also assist the Italians and Russians by preventing the transfer of German divisions from the Western Front.

With the intention of completing the training of a number of its divisions, the British delayed the Somme

*10th Worcestershire Regt with German prisoners taken after La Boisselle, July 1916.*

*16th (Irish) Div returning from Guillemont, 3 Sept 1916. Note shamrock sign on vehicle doors.*   Imperial War Museum

*An artist's impression (F. Wright) of Pte Herbert William Lewis, 11th Welsh Regt, winning the VC in Salonika, 22-23 Oct 1916.*

offensive for some time. The French, however, eventually made it clear that they could not possibly hold out at Verdun after the first half of 1916 had passed and that the attack should start by the beginning of July.

The Battle of the Somme commenced on 1 July 1916 and was to last through the summer and into the winter, when it eventually came to a halt on 18 November. Throughout this period all of the twenty-six New Army divisions in France were heavily involved and the men of Kitchener's Army were to figure high among the 420,000 British casualties.

On the first day of the battle, when some 60,000 casualties alone were incurred, the Fourth Army under General Sir Henry Rawlinson was holding the battle front. The line which extended some fifteen miles had the French Sixth Army to its right, while the British Third Army was on the left and northern boundary.

The divisions comprising the Fourth Army, and those to head the initial attack, included Regulars, Territorials and New Army, the latter being represented by the 18th, 21st, 30th, 31st, 32nd, 34th and 36th with 9th, 17th and 19th in reserve. Of the seven New Army divisions to go over the top on 1 July, only one, the 21st which had been at Loos in September 1915, had been involved in any major battle. For the remainder, mostly the Pals battalions of the Fourth New Army, this day was to be their first fight.

The first two weeks of the 1916 Somme offensive (1-13 July) is now known as the Battle of Albert and was, for the New Army, to include some of the hardest and most costly engagements of the war. Within this period the casualty rate was such that some New Army divisions had to be taken out of the line and subsequently had to spend many weeks resting and taking in drafts from England.

After its hard fight at Montauban, the 30th Division was eventually relieved and did not take part in any major action until almost the middle of October. Likewise, after Bazentin Ridge, the 32nd Division was out of the line until the Ancre operations in late October.

In the 31st Division the casualties were so great, due to its attack at Serre on 1 July, that after just one day's fighting the division was not used again until the closing stages of the Somme offensive in November. The 33rd Division had to spend almost three months away from the battle after leaving High Wood on 21 July, while as a result of the July and August fighting the 35th Division was not seen on the field until March 1917.

Two other divisions which were to be greatly affected during the early weeks of fighting on the Somme in July 1916 were the 36th and 38th. Hardly a

*Capt Hutchinson, MC (CO), Lt Tanner (2i/c), WO and NCOs, 100th Machine Gun Coy, 33rd Div, Arras, March 1917.*

*Member of 9th (Scottish) Div (see Thistle sign on helmet) using two salvaged sewing machines as a writing desk, Frampoux, 21 July 1917.* Imperial War Museum

home in Ulster was not touched when the casualties were made known after the 36th Division's gallantry and supreme sacrifice at the Schwaben Redoubt on 1 and 2 July. A week after the Ulstermen's fight the Welsh of the 38th attacked Mametz Wood and in five days of fighting the casualties were in their thousands.

Both of these heroic divisions took a great deal of time to reorganise and get back to fighting strength; the 36th joined its first major battle after the Somme at Messines on 7 June 1917, while the 38th were able to fight again at Pilckem Ridge on 31 July – over a year since it left Mametz.

The Battle of Albert included the following New Army divisions – 9th, 12th, 17th, 18th, 19th, 21st, 23rd, 25th, 30th, 31st, 32nd, 33rd, 34th, 36th and 38th. Throughout the two weeks, a number of tactical gains were made and those that involved the divisions of the New Army included: Montauban (30th), Fricourt (17th), Contalmaison (23rd) and La Boisselle (19th).

The next stage of the Somme offensive was the Battle of Bazentin, 14-17 July. New Army divisions involved in these operations were 9th, 18th, 21st, 25th, 32nd, 33rd, 34th and the success included the captures of Longueval by the 9th Division, and Trônes Wood by the 18th and 30th.

*Capt H. M. Salmon, Adj, 16th Bn Welsh Regt (Cardiff City), Boesinghe, June 1917.* Welch Regt Museum

On 15 July the Battle of Delville Wood opened and was to involve the 9th, 14th, 17th, 18th, 20th and 24th New Army Divisions at various stages until its conclusion in September. At High Wood, which was finally captured on 15 September, both the 19th and 23rd Divisions made a contribution during attacks in the area between 20-25 July. Likewise, the 35th Division was to play an important role at Arrow Head Copse between 19-30 July.

In the Battle of Pozières (23 July-3 September) the 12th, 15th, 19th, 23rd, 25th, 34th Divisions fought alongside the 1st, 2nd and 4th Australian Divisions. These operations included the savage fighting for Mouquet Farm which involved both the 12th and 25th Divisions.

Between 3-6 September, the 16th, 20th and 24th Divisions fought at Guillemont and then on 9 September it was the turn of the 16th at Ginchy. On 15 September, the Battle of Flers-Courcelette commenced and was to involve the 11th, 14th, 15th, 20th, 21st, 23rd, 34th and 41st Divisions through to 22 September.

On the first day of these operations the 14th and 41st Divisions, together with New Zealand troops being used for the first time on the Western Front since their arrival from Gallipoli, bore the main thrust of the attack. They were, however, and for the first time in war, supported by tanks which offered the advancing infantry hitherto undreamed-of cover. 15 September also saw the heroic capture by the 15th Division of Martinpuich.

25 September was to be the start of a general attack by the British Fourth Army towards Morval. The village was a maze of fortifications, both above and below ground, and posed a serious obstacle in the way of any further Allied advance. Included in this successful operation, which lasted until 28 September, were three New Army divisions – 20th, 21st and 23rd.

Running simultaneously with the Battle of Morval was the attack by the 11th and 18th Divisions, with three Canadian divisions, on Thiepval Ridge. This vast and seemingly impregnable enemy fortress which had accounted for thousands of lives since July, including in one day the almost total loss of the 36th (Ulster) Division, featured a number of deadly strongholds; among them the Schwaben, Zollern and Stuff Redoubts.

After a massive bombardment the infantry left their trenches just after noon on 26 September, the 11th Division, and in particular the 12th Middlesex Regiment, bearing the brunt of the attack. Over a front of 5,000yds the fighting was intense, with severe hand-to-hand combat and bayonet charges accounting for many of the enemy's dead.

By the evening of 26 September the village of Thiepval, with its maze of fortifications and trenches, had fallen to the 18th Division. During the following day the Zollern Redoubt was taken but at the end of four days' fighting only parts of Schwaben and Stuff Redoubts had been occupied by the Allies. Both the Schwaben and Stuff Redoubts were to remain with the enemy until October, when both positions were eventually cleared by the 39th Division.

In front of the line running from Sailly-Saillisel, through Le Transloy on to Beaulencourt, lay a strong system of trenches known as the Le Transloy Ridges. The speedy capture of this high ground was considered to be of utmost importance as the enemy had yet to construct any formidable defences behind this position. Much hard fighting took place in the area throughout the best part of October. The New Army divisions involved in the Le Transloy operations were the 9th, 12th, 15th, 20th, 21st, 23rd, 30th and 41st. Of these the 23rd was to distinguish itself at the capture of Le Sars on 7 October, and later with the 9th and 15th Divisions it put up a hard fight during the attacks on Bute de Warlencourt.

Also commencing at the beginning of October was the Battle of the Ancre Heights which was to run through to 11 November and involve the 18th, 19th, 25th and 39th Divisions. Two days later the last of the 1916 Somme operations commenced along the banks and north of the River Ancre. Throughout the summer and autumn the enemy had managed to make great improvements to his defences in this area. The ruined villages of St Pierre Divion, Beaucourt and Beaumont Hamel were now veritable fortresses and it was clear

*Officers of 16th (Irish) Div with souvenirs after the capture of Wytschaete, June 1917.* Imperial War Museum

*Officers of 17th Div in wrecked house in Arras, 30 April 1917.* Imperial War Museum

that the Germans were intent on holding this part of its line at all costs.

After a two-day bombardment the assaulting infantry went into the attack at zero hour – 5.45am. By 7.20 all objectives east of St Pierre Divion, including the village, had been achieved, and by 9am the number of prisoners taken had exceeded that of the attacking force. Great gains were also made north of the river. The New Army divisions involved in the last battles of 1916 were 18th, 19th, 25th, 31st, 32nd, 37th, 39th and 40th.

The battles of the Somme were over. Every unit had been engaged and each had fought splendidly and at all times upheld the honour of the regiments of which they formed part. In the fighting on the Somme it was always the Allies who made the attacks, the Germans being content to hold their positions and defend them at all costs.

As the hot summer ended and the cold wet autumn and early winter turned the battlefields into a sea of mud, the men of the New Army had to fight under the most terrible of conditions. Casualties were always high, but so too was the courage and devotion to duty

*CSM Glanfrwyd Buse, MM and a C/Sgt, 14th Bn Welsh Regt, 'Somewhere in France', 1917.*   C. Lewis

displayed by all ranks. Of the fifty-two Victoria Crosses awarded for gallantry on the Somme in 1916 almost half were won by men of the New Army.

Turning now to the four New Army divisions that were not on the Western Front in 1916 we find the 10th, 22nd and 26th in Macedonia and the 13th in Mesopotamia.

It was not until August 1916 that any large-scale operation was carried out in Macedonia. The Bulgarians had set up positions covering Doiran on a series of steep ridges running mostly from north-west to south-east of the town. Between 10-18 August a series of successful attacks were made by the 22nd and 26th Divisions. Among the gains were a number of small heights – Kidney Hill, Castle Hill; but the most important victory was that at Horseshoe Hill. Throughout these operations the highest praise was given to the artillery, the gunners doing tremendous work in hauling their guns over the mountainous country.

The next engagement took place at Machukovo between 13-14 September and involved the 22nd Division in some fierce hand-to-hand fighting during their attack on these positions. Later, on the night of

22-23 October, a member of that Division, Pte H. W. Lewis of the 11th Welsh Regiment received the first of only two Victoria Crosses to be won on the Macedonian Front.

Two brigades of the 10th Division were involved in actions in Macedonia during September and October. The 29th Brigade fought at Karajaköis between 30 September and 2 October and then, from 3-4 October, 30th Brigade captured Yenikoi.

After the evacuation of Helles on the night of 8-9 January 1916 the 13th Division had moved to Egypt by the end of the month. From there, in February, the Division sailed for Mesopotamia where it was to serve for the remainder of the war, the only British Division in that theatre.

During the early months of 1917, on the Western Front, the 11th, 18th, 31st and 32nd Divisions were active in a number of operations around the Ancre. However, in what was generally an inactive period, both the Allied and German Staffs were busy planning for their spring campaigns. As a result of the Somme battles a large salient had been driven into the enemy's lines. Their normally superior defences had been smashed and the German Army had throughout the winter of 1916-17 laboured intensively, but with little success, to improvise some kind of resistance to attack.

Having decided that their next large-scale push was to be on the Eastern Front and launched towards the Russians, the German commanders gave orders in February 1917 to shorten their line in France. This would subsequently have the effect of releasing a large number of men while at the same time a new and more secure line could be occupied.

These new German positions, running south from Arras to Soissons, had been constructed during the winter. With its maze of trenches, elaborate field works and row upon row of barbed wire, the new line rendered deep-rooted defences stronger than any that had yet been seen in the war. Its existence known to the Allies, the enemy's new position became known as the Hindenburg Line, after the German Commander-in-Chief, General von Hindenburg.

The official dates given for the German retreat eastwards to the Hindenburg Line are 23 February to 5 April. Throughout this period the Allies were always in strong pursuit of the enemy and the New Army divisions involved in these operations were 14th, 18th, 20th, 21st, 30th, 32nd, 35th and 40th.

While the advance to the Hindenburg Line was in progress the initial plans for an Allied attack further north in Artois were issued. This great offensive was to be in the form of a dual operation: the French in Champagne, while the British advanced on a front of thirteen miles, extending from north of Croiselles, south-east of Arras, to south of Givenchy-en-Gohelle at the northern foot of the Vimy Ridge.

Commencing on 9 April, and after a five-day bombardment from 2,800 guns, the Arras offensive featured on its left an assault by the 24th and four Canadian Divisions on Vimy Ridge. At the same time, and to the south, General Sir Edmund Allenby's Third Army, which included ten New Army Divisions: 9th,

12th, 14th, 15th, 17th, 21st, 30th, 33rd, 34th and 37th, made an advance of over three miles during the First Battle of the Scarpe.

After the first week's fighting at Arras the enemy had been driven back over four miles, more than 13,000 prisoners had been taken together with some 200 guns, and the new British line now commanded the high ground east of Arras. The city itself was cleared by 19 April and a new attack all along the line was fixed to take place within the next few days.

In the Second Battle of the Scarpe (23 and 24 April) the 15th, 17th, 30th, 33rd, 34th and 37th New Army Divisions were involved in two days' hard fighting which included the gallant capture by the 15th Division of Guémappe. After this a two-day battle (28 and 29 April) saw the 12th, 34th and 37th Divisions engaged at Arleux.

On 3 May, the last of the great 1917 Arras battles, the Third Battle of the Scarpe, opened over a front of sixteen miles, Sir Douglas Haig having extended the fighting area in order to assist French operations further south. Throughout the three-day battle the enemy contested fiercely every inch of ground and bitter fighting accounted for high casualties among the 9th, 12th, 14th, 18th, 21st and 31st New Army Divisions. At two important points, Roeux and Oppy Wood the fighting was intense, both positions representing highly protected trench systems. After great loss and courage of the highest order, Roeux was finally captured on 14 May by the 12th and 17th Divisions, while Oppy Wood fell to the 31st Division on 28 June.

*Maj Judson, Capt Wilson, MC, Capt Cross, MC and Pte Kane, MM, 33rd Bn, Machine Gun Corps, Tyne Cotts Pillbox, 1918.*

*Sighting machine-gun positions, 33rd Bn, Machine Gun Corps, Passchendaele, 1918.*

*11th Bn, Welsh Regt, Salonika, 1917.*   Welch Regt Museum

During April to August a number of flanking engagements to the Arras offensive took place which have been divided into two operations. In the first, around Bullecourt (11 April-16 June), the 20th, 21st and 33rd Divisions were active in a number of attacks on the Hindenburg Line. The second, which did not involve any New Army divisions, was towards Lens 3 June-26 August.

Turning to the Flanders Front in 1917, preparations for a large-scale attack on the Messines Ridge were well under way by the middle of May. The capture of this commanding position was considered an essential preliminary to an offensive planned later, east and north of Ypres.

To clear the enemy from the Messines Ridge, Sir Douglas Haig had ordered his engineers to set nineteen mines, containing almost a million pounds of high explosives, deep under the German line. The capture of the ridge was the task of General Sir Herbert Plumer's Second Army; its three Corps comprising eight New Army Divisions: 11th, 16th, 19th, 23rd, 24th, 25th, 36th and 41st, along with the Territorial 47th Division and the Australians and New Zealanders of the Anzac II Corps.

Just after 3am on 7 June the mines were exploded and nine divisions rushed forward to seize the ridge. After a week's fighting all objectives had been taken, and the whole of the ridge had been captured by 14 June. Of the many successes of the Messines operation, the capture of Wytschaete by the two Irish Divisions, 16th and 36th, ranks high. All of the eight Irish infantry regiments of the British Army were represented, including no less than ten battalions from the Royal Irish Rifles.

With the capture of the Messines Ridge the way was now clear for the planned Allied offensive at Ypres. The battle opened on 31 July with an attack by the British Fifth Army on the whole of the enemy's positions from just north of the Ypres Comines Canal to west of Pilckem. The Second Army was on the right and the French on the left.

There were eight major battles during the 1917 offensive in the Ypres Salient. The first of these was at Pilckem 31 July-2 August and the New Army divisions involved were 15th, 16th, 18th, 24th, 25th, 30th, 37th, 38th, 39th and 41st. At 4.45am on 16 August the second battle of the campaign opened five miles north of Ypres at Langemarck. Here the 11th, 14th, 15th, 16th, 18th, 20th, 24th, 36th, 38th and 39th Divisions fought with distinction until the close of the battle on 18 August.

Moving into September and the five-day period from the 20th to 25th, the following divisions took part in the Battle of the Menin Road: 9th, 11th, 19th, 20th, 23rd, 33rd, 37th, 39th and 41st. The next day an attack was launched on Polygon Wood which saw the 11th, 19th, 20th, 21st, 23rd, 33rd, 37th and 39th Divisions engaged through till 3 October.

After their successes at Polygon Wood the 11th, 19th, 21st and 37th Divisions fought the Battle of Broodseinde on 4 October and then, on 9 October these same formations, less the 21st Division, were engaged at the Battle of Poelcappelle.

On 12 October the Second Army took part in the first of two battles at Passchendaele. This operation lasted just for the one day, persistent bad weather and deterioration of the ground calling to a halt any further activity. After a few minor operations in the area, including on 22 October the capture of some important ground east of Poelcappelle by the 18th, 34th and 35th Divisions, a much larger force, Second and Fifth Armies, once again attacked at Passchendaele. This, the last of the 1917 Ypres battles, commenced on 26 October and eventually came to a halt on 10 November. The fighting at Passchendaele included some of the bloodiest of the war, the New Army divisions involved during the two battles being 9th, 14th, 17th, 18th, 19th, 21st, 23rd, 35th, 37th, and 39th.

Not mentioned in the official list of battles on the Ypres Salient in 1917 but included in Sir Douglas Haig's despatch of 25 December were a number of actions fought in the neighbourhood of St Julien on 19, 22 and 27 August. In these engagements the 11th, 14th,

*Rifle inspection, members of 8th/10th Gordons, France, March 1918.*  Imperial War Museum

*Officers of the 38th Infantry Bde, 13th Div talking to arabs at Kirkuk, Mesopotamia in May 1918.* Imperial War Museum

15th and 38th Divisions made gains of 800yds, over a front of two miles, together with the capture of many hundreds of prisoners.

Ending officially on 10 November, the battles of Ypres had accounted for some 240,000 British casualties. Large gains in territory had been made and many thousands of German prisoners, together with large quantities of guns and equipment, had been taken. In his comments regarding the battle, Sir Douglas Haig said of his troops: 'They advanced every time with absolute confidence in their power to overcome the enemy, even though they had sometimes to struggle through mud up to their waists to reach him. So long as they could reach him they did overcome him, but physical exhaustion placed narrow limits on the depths to which each advance could be pushed and compelled long pauses between the advances.'

The British offensive on the Ypres Salient had caused the German command to transfer large numbers of troops from other parts of the front to the area. As a result, the enemy were now in possession of certain sectors that were undermanned and in a general weakened condition. It was against one such position that Sir Douglas Haig decided to launch one more offensive in northern France.

On 20 November the British Third Army, under General Sir Julian Byng, attacked south-west of Cambrai. In this highly successful assault the usual preliminary artillery bombardment was dispensed with and consequently the initial assault came as a complete surprise to the enemy. Spearheaded by over 300 tanks, the first massed armoured assault in history, the advance carved a massive salient into the German lines of over ten miles wide and six miles deep.

By the evening of 20 November mechanical failures among the tanks and a heavy German resistance had halted the attack. Following the tank advance, the troops of IV Corps captured Bourlon Wood 23-28 November. However, after severe fighting all along the front, the British could make no further penetration.

On 30 November the Germans commenced a strong counter-attack down both flanks of the salient. British casualties were high and on the first day of this reverse over 6,000 prisoners were taken by the enemy. As a result a general British withdrawal was ordered by Haig on 4 December, the cost of the battle after just over two weeks amounting to over 43,000 killed, wounded or missing. In the Cambrai operations the following New Army divisions were engaged: 12th, 20th, 21st, 36th and 40th.

At the end of October 1917 Germany sent troops to assist the Austrians, then weary after two years' fighting against the Italians. Subsequently an attack

*Nos 14 and 15 Platoon 'D' Coy, 9th Bn Northumberland Fusiliers' lines in France after transfer to the 61st Div, May 1918. The platoon boards show the battalion sign over that of the 61st Div.* G. Stewart

was launched which resulted in the Italian armies being driven back to Italy. To assist the Italians, five British divisions under the command of General Sir Herbert Plumer were sent to Italy from the Western Front. Of the five, two, the 23rd and 41st were New Army formations and both these were occupying positions behind the River Piave by the end of November 1917. The 23rd Division was to remain in Italy until after the Armistice with Austria brought hostilities to a close on 4 November 1918. However, after just over three months, the 41st Division was returned to France to take part in the Battle of St Quentin.

On the Macedonian Front in 1917 both the 22nd and 26th Divisions took part in the Battle of Doiran 24-25 April and 8-9 May. In the same theatre, the 10th Division was not involved and on 18 August had received orders to make ready for service in Palestine. The 10th left Salonika on 1 September. The Division reached Ismailia on the 5th and during November and December took part in the Third Battle of Gaza and the fighting in and around Jerusalem.

The British Army had been left weak after the exhausting battles of 1917. Reinforcements from England had fallen off and a number of divisions were at almost cadre strength. To overcome this problem Sir

*L/Cpl H. Weale, VC, 14th Bn Royal Welsh Fusiliers. L/Cpl Weale won his VC on 26 Aug 1918 at Bazentine-Le-Grand.*

*6th Bn, King's Own Scottish Borderers marching past HM The King, Aug 1918.* Imperial War Museum

Douglas Haig, in February 1918, ordered the disbandment in each brigade of one battalion, thus reducing the number in each division from twelve to nine. Although this necessary move had the effect of building up the weak divisions, many heroic battalions were lost and their passing noted with sadness among their ranks.

The situation on the German side, although their losses in 1917 were also tremendous, was not as grave as that of the British. The collapse of Russia had released large numbers of troops from the Eastern Front and these were, throughout the winter of 1917-18, concentrating in France and Flanders.

The German offensive in Picardy began on 21 March 1918. In the weeks prior to this, one of the largest artillery bombardments of the war had been aimed at British positions in the area. At the same time, gas shells were employed and in one division alone over 2,000 casualties occurred due to gas poisoning.

On the morning of the attack the British line lay roughly between La Fère, northward to Croisilles, just south-east of Arras, a front of some 54 miles. The responsibility for the area lay with the Fifth Army (on the right) and the Third Army (on the left), a total of 33 divisions. On the German side some 76 divisions were

on hand and of these 63 were used in the first three waves of the attack.

The two-week German attack was divided into six major battles. From 21 to 23 March the Battle of St Quentin took place and involved the 17th, 19th, 25th, 31st, 34th, 40th and 41st New Army Divisions in the Third Army, with 9th, 14th, 16th, 18th, 20th, 21st, 24th, 30th, 36th and 39th in the Fifth. In their first attack the enemy assaulted the British line with such force that it was unable to hold. Consequently, on 22 March a withdrawal to behind the Somme River was ordered.

During the following two days the battle turned towards Bapaume where the 12th, 15th, 17th, 19th, 25th, 31st, 40th and 41st Divisions were heavily engaged. The Battle of Rosières followed on 26-27 March (16th, 20th, 24th, 30th, 36th and 39th Divisions) and then on 28 March, a one-day affair, officially designated as the First Battle of Arras (12th, 15th, 31st, 32nd and 41st Divisions). This last attack in March by a now weakening German Army was successfully repulsed by the Third Army.

After a brief period where little action took place the fifth of the six battles opened on 4 April. This was the Battle of the Avre but only three New Army divisions – 14th, 18th and 24th took part in what was generally an Australian operation. In the last battle, the Battle of the Ancre, 5 April, only the 12th, 32nd and 37th Divisions took the field while once again Anzac troops were heavily engaged.

*Some of 'D' Coy, 16th Bn, Lancashire Fusiliers in Bonn, Germany, 28 July 1919. Each man wears the ribbon of the British War Medal.* D. Barnes

On 9 April the enemy, turning his attention to Flanders, opened a series of battles in the Lys Valley. Many of the divisions that had fought on the Somme during March were now in the area and their battle-torn ranks were weak and exhausted.

The German offensive in Flanders lasted until 29 April and, like the Somme operations of March and April, was divided into several battles. In the first battle, Estaires 9-11 April, only the 31st, 34th and 40th New Army Divisions were engaged. The Battle of Messines followed on 10-11 April and on this occasion the 9th, 19th, 21st, 25th, 33rd, 34th and 36th Divisions fought at vastly reduced strength, often as little as one brigade taking the field.

At the Battle of Hazebrouck, 12-15 April, which included the defence of Nieppe Forest, the 31st and 40th Divisions fought alongside the Australians and a composite force of pioneers, among them two companies of the 18th Middlesex Regiment. Operations at Bailleul followed on 13-15 April, and two days later the First Battle of Kemmel opened and lasted until 19 April.

These bloody engagements caused great casualties among the British divisions, those of the New Army being represented by the 9th, 19th, 21st, 25th, 30th, 33rd, 34th, 36th and 39th. Also included in these operations was a composite unit known as Wyatt's Force. Brigadier-General L. J. Wyatt was commander of 116th Infantry Brigade, 39th Division, and had organised a mixed contingent, mostly New Army personnel, out of IX Corps units.

No New Army divisions were directly involved on 19 April at the Battle of Bethune. However, a week later a two-day action at Kemmel began and the following New Army divisions were heavily engaged: 9th, 21st, 25th, 30th and 39th. The same divisions, along with the South Africans of the 9th, fought at Scherpenberg on 29 April.

At the end of April and early in May, five British divisions, three of which, the 19th, 21st and 25th, being of the New Army, were transferred to the French Sixth Army sector and what was considered a quiet part of the front on the Aisne. At 1am on 27 May the

German's third offensive of 1918 began with a bombardment of the British and French line north of the river. Three hours later, through dense mist, the first wave of men and tanks were seen advancing towards the Allied trenches. In the ensuing battle, which ended on 6 June, the enemy made considerable gains, taking many prisoners, guns and equipment. However, his advance was checked and the Allies soon began to consolidate their position and refit.

After the spring 1918 German offensives had come to a standstill, both sides were in great need of a period of rest and reorganisation. The losses within the New Armies had been enormous, the casualties among the 16th Division alone amounting to over 7,000, and as a result a number of divisions had to be reduced to training cadres only.

Out of the line, five New Army divisions were involved for a while in the instruction of American troops. Later three divisions were returned to England where they were reconstituted and later sent back to France.

The Allied advance to victory began with the Marne Battles of 20 July-2 August. Of the two major engagements of this period both the 15th and 34th Divisions fought under XX French Corps. The Battle of Amiens followed on 8-11 August and in this operation the 12th and 18th Divisions formed part of III Corps with American regiments, while the 32nd Division fought side by side with four Canadian Divisions, and the 17th with the Australians.

On 21 August twenty-six divisions (12th, 17th, 18th, 21st, 32nd, 37th and 38th New Army) were engaged in the Somme region; two major battles taking place around Albert and Bapaume and lasting until 3 September. Meanwhile, in Flanders a general advance had begun on 18 August which saw the 9th, 19th, 30th, 31st, 34th, 36th, 40th and 41st Divisions heavily engaged.

The final breaking of the Hindenburg Line commenced on 26 August and with the Battle of the Scarpe. This action, which involved the 11th Division, lasted until 30 August and then, on 2-3 September the 11th were again in action, this time at Drocourt-Queant.

Eleven New Army divisions (11th, 12th, 17th, 18th, 21st, 24th, 25th, 32nd, 33rd, 37th and 38th) were engaged during the Battles of the Hindenburg Line 12 September-9 October. Under this heading the following battles took place: Havrincourt (12 September), Epéhy (18 September), Canal Du Nord (27 September-1 October), St Quentin Canal (29 September-2 October), Beaurevoir (3-5 October) and Cambrai (8-9 October).

The operations between 9-12 October have been officially designated as 'The Pursuit to the Selle' and included the 11th, 17th, 24th, 25th, 33rd and 37th Divisions.

For the remaining weeks of the war, operations in Flanders, commencing on 28 September and lasting until the Armistice, included the following battles: Ypres (28 September-2 October), Courtrai (14-19 October), Ooteghem (25 October) and Tieghem (31 October). The New Army divisions engaged were 9th, 14th, 30th, 31st, 34th, 35th, 36th, 40th and 41st.

In Artois the last battles were fought by the 12th, 15th and 16th Divisions. The final advance in Picardy, which commenced on 17 October, saw the 17th, 18th, 19th, 21st, 25th, 33rd, 37th and 38th Divisions engaged at the Battle of the Selle (17-25 October), the 19th and 24th at Valenciennes (1-2 November) and the 11th, 17th, 18th, 19th, 24th, 25th, 32nd, 37th and 38th at the Battle of the Sambre on 4 November.

In Palestine, on 8-12 March 1918, the 10th Division fought at Tell 'Asur. Then between April and June, all personnel, with the exception of some divisional staff, were transferred to France and the battalions were allocated to other divisions. Meanwhile, the 10th Division was Indianised and after the Armistice with Turkey returned to Egypt for demobilisation.

Hostilities were brought to a close on the Macedonian Front on 30 September 1918. During the year both the 22nd and 26th Divisions had not been active until 18 September and the second battle of Doiran.

*NCOs 14th Bn, Royal Warwickshire Regt (1st Birmingham) Italy, Feb 1918.*

# 9th
## (SCOTTISH)
# DIVISION

**9th (Scottish) Division**
Divisional sign: A thistle

The 9th (Scottish) Division was the senior division of the First New Army. It was formed during late August 1914 under the command of Maj-Gen C. J. Mackenzie and recruited throughout both the Highlands and Lowlands of Scotland. The 9th Division comprised 26th, 27th and 28th Infantry Brigades, the latter being replaced in 1916 by units from South Africa.

*26th Brigade*
8th Bn The Black Watch (Royal Highlanders). Formed at Perth.
7th Bn Seaforth Highlanders (Ross-shire Buffs, The Duke of Albany's). Formed at Fort George.
8th Bn The Gordon Highlanders. Formed at Aberdeen. Transferred to the 15th Division and amalgamated with 10th Gordons in May 1916.
5th Bn The Queen's Own Cameron Highlanders. Formed at Inverness.
10th Bn Princess Louise's (Argyll and Sutherland Highlanders). Joined from 27th Brigade as a replacement for 8th Gordons in May 1916. Transferred to 32nd Division in February 1918.

*27th Brigade*
11th and 12th Bns The Royal Scots (Lothian Regt). Formed in Edinburgh.
6th Bn The Royal Scots Fusiliers. Formed at Ayr. Transferred to the 15th Division and amalgamated with 7th Royal Scots Fusiliers in May 1916.
10th Bn Princess Louise's (Argyll and Sutherland Highlanders). Formed at Stirling. Transferred to 26th Brigade in May 1916.
6th Bn The King's Own Scottish Borderers. Joined from 28th Brigade as a replacement for 6th Royal Scots Fusiliers in May 1916.
9th Bn The Cameronians (Scottish Rifles). Joined from 28th Brigade as a replacement for 10th Argylls in May 1916. Became part of 14th Division in February 1918, but rejoined 9th Division in the following April when it was posted to the South African Brigade.

*28th Brigade*
6th Bn The King's Own Scottish Borderers. Formed at Berwick-on-Tweed. Transferred to 27th Brigade in May 1916.

*Pte Alex Morrison, 7th Seaforths, killed in the attack on Longueval, 14 July 1916.*

*8th Black Watch Pipe Band playing in Carnoy Valley after the capture of Longueval, 14 July 1916.* Imperial War Museum

9th Bn The Cameronians (Scottish Rifles). Formed at Hamilton. Transferred to 27th Brigade in May 1916. 10th and 11th Bns The Highland Light Infantry. Formed at Hamilton. The battalions were amalgamated in May 1916, having transferred to the 15th Division.

The 28th Infantry Brigade was broken up and replaced by the South African Brigade in May 1916. In September 1918 the South Africans transferred to the 66th Division and in their place a new 28th Brigade was formed comprising 2nd Royal Scots Fusiliers (a Regular Army battalion), 9th Cameronians (formerly of 27th and 28th Brigades), and 1st Royal Newfoundland Regiment.

### South African Brigade
The Brigade consisted of the 1st to 4th South African Infantry and had left South Africa in September 1915, arriving in Egypt via England during the following January. Having moved to France in April 1916, the Brigade joined the 9th Division as a replacement for the 28th Brigade in May.

Sometimes known as 28th (South African) Brigade, the Brigade contained Scotsmen from South African regiments such as The Duke of Edinburgh's Own Volunteer Rifles, The Transvaal Scottish and The Cape Town Highlanders. The Brigade transferred to the 66th Division in September 1918.

### Pioneers
9th Bn Seaforth Highlanders (Ross-Shire Buffs, The Duke of Albany's). Formed at Fort George.

Other units forming the 9th (Scottish) Division included 'B' Squadron, 1/1st Queen's Own Royal Glasgow Yeomanry, which joined from Cupar in Fifeshire in May 1915 and served with the Division for a year; 50th-53rd Brigades, Royal Field Artillery; 63rd, 64th and 90th Field Companies, Royal Engineers; 104th-107th Companies, Army Service Corps and 27th, 28th, 29th Field Ambulances.

After initial training at the Salisbury Training Centre, the Division assembled around Borden. It suffered the usual scarcity of arms and equipment but nevertheless soon reached a high standard of proficiency.

On 5 May 1915 the Division was inspected by Lord

*Wounded of 6th King's Own Scottish Borderers at*
*Regimental Aid Post, 18 Aug 1918.*   Imperial War Museum

Kitchener and within days embarkation orders were received. The following message from HM King George V was received by the Division on 10 May:

'Officers, Non-Commissioned Officers, and Men of the Ninth (Scottish) Division
'You are about to join your comrades at the Front in bringing to a successful end this relentless war of more than nine months' duration. Your prompt patriotic answer to the Nation's call to arms will never be forgotten. The keen exertions of all ranks during the period of training have brought you to a state of efficiency not unworthy of my Regular Army. I am confident that in the field you will nobly uphold the traditions of the fine regiments whose name you bear. Ever since your enrolment I have closely watched the growth and steady progress of all units. In bidding you farewell I pray God may bless you in all your undertakings.'

Under the command of Maj-Gen H. J. S. Landon the 9th (Scottish) Division commenced its crossing to France on 8 May 1915, when advanced parties of artillery left Borden. Within the next few days the remainder of the Division followed, and by 15 May the 9th was concentrated in billets to the south-west of St Omer. The 9th (Scottish) Division was in France and

was the first of the New Army divisions to cross the channel.

It was not long before arrangements were made to train the Division in trench warfare. This was done by attaching units to the 6th Division with whom a series of duties in the line were performed near Armentières.

On 1 July the Division was for the first time made responsible for a section of the front line, when it relieved the 7th Division near Festubert. It remained on these duties until 18 August when a move was made to Busnes for further training.

When the Division took over trenches east of Vermelles on 2 September it was instructed to make final preparations for what was to be its first major battle of the war. The attack at Loos began on 25 September and was to be the first occasion that the British used poison gas. Having attacked the German position on the Hohenzollern Redoubt, the 5th Camerons became cut off and unsupported. The Battalion held off a number of counter-attacks by the enemy and on 27 September one of its members – Cpl J. D. Pollock – gained the Victoria Cross for his gallantry while defending the part of the redoubt known as Little Willie trench. When the Camerons were eventually relieved, only two officers and seventy men remained out of the 820 who had started the attack.

With its first battle over, the 9th (Scottish) Division concentrated near Bethune and later received a message from General Gough, the Commander of I Corps, expressing his regard for their gallantry and self-sacrifice. Casualties during the battle had been heavy; the divisional commander had been killed and 190 officers and 5,867 other ranks were either killed, wounded or missing.

After Loos, the Division was moved to the Ypres Salient where it took over trenches near Hill 60, and then later in the Ploegsteert Wood area. In May 1916 the Division received orders that took it to the Somme. It was soon obvious, after arrival in the area, that a great battle was being planned.

The Battle of the Somme began on 1 July 1916, and on the second day 27th Brigade was ordered to relieve part of the 30th Division then holding Montauban. On 3 July, and still under the orders of the 30th Division, 27th Brigade attacked at Bernafay Wood and was successful in taking all of its objectives.

On 14 and 15 July the Division was sent in to attack at Longueval and Delville Wood. At Delville Wood, on 18 July, Pte William Faulds of the 1st South African Infantry gained the Victoria Cross for his bravery while retrieving a wounded officer from no-man's land. The following October the Division took an active part in the Somme battles at the Transloy Ridges and Butte de Warlencourt.

The Division moved to Arras in December 1916, and in April and May of the following year took part in the engagements around the Scarpe River. During the latter months of 1917 the Division fought in the Ypres Sector, being involved at the Battle of the Menin Road Ridge and the action on 12 October now known as the First Battle of Passchendaele. Two Victoria Crosses were gained during this period – Capt Henry Reynolds, MC of the 12th Royal Scots, for his gallantry near Frezenberg on 20 September, and L/Cpl W. H. Hewitt, 2nd South African Infantry, east of Ypres on the same day. The last action of 1917 took place on 30 December when the 10th Argylls took Welch Ridge.

When the Germans began their major offensive on the Somme in March 1918, the 9th (Scottish) Division was positioned by St Quentin. It fought in that area and around Bapaume during March, and gained a special mention from Sir Douglas Haig regarding its 'great gallantry' during the defence and withdrawal.

After being relieved on 1 April, the 9th (Scottish) Division moved north, where two days later it took over positions from the Australians. The Division spent a week in its new line which ran from Hollebeke across the Ypres-Comines Canal to the south end of Bulgar Wood. Here the conditions were generally quiet until 9 April when the enemy opened his second offensive of 1918 in the Valley of the Lys.

Throughout April the Division was heavily engaged, taking part in the Battles of Messines, Bailleul, Kemmel Ridge, the Scherpenberg and a stubborn struggle for the ridge at Wytschaete.

The 9th (Scottish) Division had once again distinguished itself. Its performance during both German offensives had been second to none and in a flattering message received from Sir Douglas Haig the highest praise was again bestowed.

On 19 July, while serving under XV Corps, the South Africans, along with 26th Brigade, captured the village of Meteren. Four weeks later Hoegenacker Ridge, just beyond Meteren, was taken by the Lowlanders of 27th Brigade. The capture of this position, which provided superb observation, was of great importance and undoubtedly played a big part in the enemy's decision, later, to abandon the whole of the Lys salient.

The Division then played a major part in the final advance through Flanders, fighting at the battles of Ypres (28 September-2 October), Courtrai (14-19 October) and Ooteghem on 25 October. During this period another three Victoria Crosses were added to those that had already been gained by the Division.

The Division was relieved on 26 October when it moved back to billets near Harlebeke. On 4 December Germany was entered and positions responsible for the left divisional sector of the Cologne bridgehead were allotted. The total casualties suffered by the 9th (Scottish) Division throughout the war amounted to 52,055 killed, wounded and missing.

*L/Cpl, 1st South African Infantry. The chevrons worn on the lower right arm (one red and four blue) denote overseas service from 1914-18.*

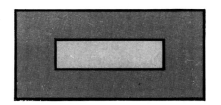

# 10th
## (IRISH)
# DIVISION

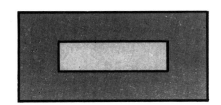

**10th (Irish) Division**
Divisional sign: A narrow green stripe

The 10th (Irish) Division was formed in Ireland and began to assemble under the command of Lt-Gen Sir Bryan Mahon during late August 1914. As part of the First New Army the Division comprised the following infantry brigades:

*29th Brigade*
5th Bn The Royal Irish Regt. Formed at Clonmel and served as part of 29th Brigade until becoming the divisional pioneer battalion by June 1915.
6th Bn The Royal Irish Rifles. Formed at Dublin and disbanded in May 1918.
5th Bn The Connaught Rangers. Formed at Dublin. Left the Division in April 1918 and later served in France with the 66th Division.
6th Bn The Prince of Wales's Leinster Regt (Royal Canadians). Formed at Dublin. Left the Division in May 1918 and later served in France as part of the 66th Division.
10th Bn The Hampshire Regt. Formed at Winchester and attached to the 10th Division in Ireland as Army Troops. Became part of 29th Brigade just prior to going overseas, and as a replacement for 5th Royal Irish Regiment which had been converted to pioneers. The Battalion transferred to the 27th Division in November 1916.
1st Bn The Prince of Wales's Leinster Regt (Royal Canadians). A Regular Army battalion which joined the Brigade from 27th Division in November 1916 as a replacement for the 10th Hampshires.

*Lt-Gen Sir Bryan Mahon, KCVO, CB, DSO. CO 10th (Irish) Div. Aug 1914-Aug 1915.*

By May 1918 all of the Brigade's original New Army battalions had either been disbanded or transferred. Subsequently three Indian battalions, 1/54th Sikhs, 1/101st Grenadiers and 2/151st Infantry, were added which together with the 1st Leinsters comprised the Brigade until the end of the war.

*30th Brigade*
6th and 7th Bns The Royal Munster Fusiliers. Both formed at Tralee, and in November 1916 were amalgamated as 6th. The battalion left the Division in April 1918 and was later absorbed into the 2nd Munsters in France.
6th and 7th Bns The Royal Dublin Fusiliers. Both

formed at Nass. The 6th Battalion left the Division in May 1918, and on 3 July went to France where it served for the remainder of the war as part of the 66th Division. The 7th also transferred and was later absorbed into the 11th Royal Irish Fusiliers and 2nd Royal Dublin Fusiliers. In August 1914 an appeal had been made to the young professional men of Dublin. Subsequently 'D' Company, 7th Royal Dublins was formed and this was known unofficially as the 'Pals' Company.
1st Bn The Royal Irish Regt. A Regular Army battalion that joined the Brigade from the 27th Division as as replacement for the 7th Royal Munsters in November 1916.

None of the original New Army battalions remained after May 1918. The Brigade was then made up from Indian battalions and until the end of the war comprised 1st Royal Irish Regiment, 38th Dogras, 46th Punjabis and 1st Kashmir Rifles.

*31st Brigade*
5th and 6th Bns The Royal Inniskilling Fusiliers. Both formed at Omagh. The battalions left the Division in May 1918 and later served in France as part of the 50th (6th Bn) and 66th (5th Bn) Divisions.
5th and 6th Bns Princess Victoria's (Royal Irish Fusiliers). Both formed at Armagh and amalgamated as 5th in November 1916. The battalion left the 10th Division for France in May 1918, where it later served with the 16th and 66th Divisions.
2nd Bn Princess Victoria's (Royal Irish Fusiliers). A Regular Army battalion which joined the Brigade in November 1916 as a replacement for 6th Royal Irish Fusiliers.

From May 1918, after the New Army battalions had left for France, the Brigade comprised 2nd Royal Irish Fusiliers, 2/42nd Deoli, 74th Punjabis and 2/101st Grenadiers.

*Pioneers*
5th Bn The Royal Irish Regt. The battalion originally formed part of 29th Brigade and assumed its pioneer role by June 1915. After moving to France in April 1918, the battalion later served as part of the 50th and 52nd Divisions.

Other units which formed part of the 10th (Irish) Division included 54th, 55th, 56th, 57th, 67th and 68th Brigades, Royal Field Artillery; 65th, 66th and 85th Field Companies, Royal Engineers; and 30th, 31st and 32nd Field Ambulances. The 10th Divisional Train did not go overseas with the Division and later served as part of 22nd Division. Transport and Supply was provided by companies formed from the 52nd (Lowland) Division.

The three brigades of the 10th (Irish) Division were made up of troops from all over Ireland; the 29th consisting of units from the four provinces, the 30th which had its depots in the south, and the 31st from Ulster.

In May 1915 the Division crossed to England where it soon concentrated around the Basingstoke area for its final war training. The King saw the Division on 28 and 29 May, then on 1 June an inspection was carried out by Field-Marshal Lord Kitchener at Hackwood Park.

On 27 June news was received that the Division was soon to go overseas. This was confirmed on 1 July when orders were issued instructing the 10th to prepare for service in Gallipoli. Very soon helmets and khaki drill clothing was issued, while at the same time regulation belts and accoutrements replaced the supply of American equipment that had been given out in March.

According to the history of the Division in Gallipoli

by Major Bryan Cooper, the fitting of the new kit posed a certain amount of problems. In particular the adjusting of pagris around the helmets occupied much attention, but the assistance of several men in the Division who had served in India proved of great use.

In leaving England there had been little time to obtain the coloured cloth to sew to the side of the helmets in order to distinguish the different units. However, some battalions had managed to improvise their badges – the Royal Irish Rifles had a green and black patch and the Hampshires had claret and yellow. In the Leinsters, a large black 'L' was painted on the side of each helmet, while the 7th Munsters went into action with a green shamrock on each arm.

Embarkation for the peninsula began on 9 July when advance parties left from Liverpool. The

*C/Sgt Billie Clancy, 7th Bn, Royal Dublin Fusiliers.*
D. Barnes

remainder of the Division soon followed, most of the 10th being situated on the Island of Lemnos by the end of July. This was to make the 10th the first Irish Division ever to take the field of war.

On 6 August the 29th Brigade was selected to accompany Australian and New Zealand units in a landing at Anzac Cove and the subsequent battle of Sari Bair. The Brigade was to see a great deal of fighting throughout its first weeks in action, the Hampshires and Connaughts playing an important role during the hand-to-hand fighting that took place at the end of August around Hill 60. So, too, did the remaining brigades of the Division that landed at Suvla on 6 and 7 August, launching an immediate assault on the Turkish positions. On the night of 7-8 August 31st Brigade, with the 7th Royal Dublin Fusiliers from 30th Brigade, attacked and subsequently captured a heavily defended system of trenches later known as Chocolate Hill.

At the end of September 1915, orders were received instructing the 10th to withdraw from Gallipoli and prepare for service in Macedonia. On 30 September the Division left Suvla for Mudros, where it was to make up deficiencies, some units being as much as 75% below establishment. By 24 October the bulk of the 10th had landed at Salonika.

The Division spent just under two years in Macedonia, taking part in the operations at Kosturino, north of Lake Doiran, on 7 and 8 December 1915, the

*6th Bn, Royal Irish Fusiliers, Basingstoke, 1915.*

engagement at Karajaköis 30 September-2 October 1916, and the capture of Yeniköi by the 30th Brigade on 3 and 4 October. In this period the Division suffered high casualties, and subsequently each brigade had to lose one battalion either by transfer or disbandment. Three Regular Army battalions later made up the strength in November 1916.

Having left Salonika during September 1917, the 10th (Irish) Division moved to Egypt where it was to prepare for the invasion of Palestine. It completed its assembly on 16 October and between 1-7 November took part in the Third Battle of Gaza. The 31st Brigade played an important role in the attack and subsequent capture of the enemy's position at Sheria on 6 November. Jerusalem was taken on 9 December and throughout the rest of the month the Division played an active part in its defence.

After the action at Tell 'Asur between 8-12 March 1918, the 10th (Irish) Division underwent a major reorganisation when one of its New Army battalions was disbanded and the remainder transferred to other divisions in France. Their places were taken up within the Division by Indian Army units.

With this reconstruction, all that remained of the original division that went overseas in 1915 was a small number of divisional personnel. The Division went on to fight at the Battle of Nablus on 19-21 September and, after its conclusion of active service in Palestine, was placed on salvage work. During the First World War the 10th (Irish) Division lost over 9,000 killed, wounded and missing.

# 11th
## (NORTHERN)
# DIVISION

**11th (Northern) Division**

Divisional sign: The origins of the badge of the Division are unknown. It is supposed to represent the *Ankus* or 'Key of Life'.

The 11th (Northern) Division was formed in late August 1914 and assembled around Grantham under the command of Maj-Gen F. Hammersley. The three infantry brigades, 32nd, 33rd, 34th, at first consisted entirely of North Country battalions; however, the 5th Dorsetshire Regiment later joined from Wessex.

*32nd Brigade*
9th Bn The Prince of Wales's Own (West Yorkshire Regt). Formed at York. In late 1917 the battalion absorbed some 400 men of the 1/1st Yorkshire Hussars and from that point was known as 9th (Yorkshire Hussars Yeomanry) Battalion.
6th Bn The East Yorkshire Regt. Formed at Beverley and became the divisional pioneer battalion in January 1915.
6th Bn Alexandra, Princess of Wales's Own (Yorkshire Regt). Formed at Richmond. Reduced to a training cadre in May 1918 and later transferred to the 25th Division.
6th Bn The York and Lancaster Regt. Formed at Pontefract.
8th Bn The Duke of Wellington's (West Riding Regt). Joined from 34th Brigade in January 1915 as a replacement for 6th East Yorks. Disbanded in February 1918.
2nd Bn Alexandra, Princess of Wales's Own (Yorkshire Regt). A Regular Army battalion which joined the Brigade in May 1918 as a replacement for 6th Yorkshire Regiment.

*33rd Brigade*
6th Bn The Lincolnshire Regt. Formed at Lincoln.
6th Bn the Border Regt. Formed at Carlisle and disbanded in February 1918.
7th Bn The South Staffordshire Regt. Formed at Lichfield.
9th Bn The Sherwood Foresters (Nottinghamshire and Derbyshire Regt). Formed at Derby.

*34th Brigade*
8th Bn The Northumberland Fusiliers. Formed at Newcastle-on-Tyne.

*Christmas and New Year greetings card (1918-19) from the 11th Div. The card shows the divisional sign with the towers and slag-heaps of Lens in the background.* P. Blagojevic

9th Bn The Lancashire Fusiliers. Formed at Bury and disbanded in February 1918.

8th Bn The Duke of Wellington's (West Riding Regt). Formed at Halifax and transferred to 32nd Brigade in January 1915.

11th Bn The Manchester Regt. Formed at Ashton-under-Lyne.

5th Bn The Dorsetshire Regt. Formed at Dorchester and attached to the 11th Division as Army Troops. Became part of 34th Brigade in January 1915 as a replacement for 8th Duke of Wellington's Regiment.

*Pioneers*
6th Bn The East Yorkshire Regt. Part of 32nd Brigade until assuming its pioneer role in January 1915.

Other components of the Division included 58th, 59th, 60th, 61st Brigades, Royal Field Artillery; 67th, 68th, 86th Field Companies, Royal Engineers and 33rd, 34th, 35th Field Ambulances. 'B' Squadron of the 1st Hertfordshire Yeomanry was attached for a period during 1916. The divisional train originally comprised 112th, 113th, 114th, 115th Companies, Army Service Corps, but these remained in England and later joined the 26th Division at Salonika. New companies joined in Egypt and were numbered 479th, 480th, 481st and 482nd.

On 18 October 1914 Lord Kitchener inspected the infantry at Grantham. For the next few months the Division was scattered and was located at Grantham, Leeds, Sheffield, Norwich, Newark, Weedon and

*No 11 (Irish) Platoon, 8th Bn, The Northumberland Fusiliers, France, 20 June 1918.* G. Stewart

*Cloth identification (black numerals on a yellow ground) for 9th Bn, Lancashire Fusiliers. Yellow was the colour of the 34th Infantry Bde, the numerals indicating that the battalion was the second senior unit in that formation.*

Lichfield. At the beginning of April 1915 the Division began to concentrate for training at Witley and Frensham. HM The King inspected the 11th on 31 May, and on 12 June orders were received instructing the Division to make ready for service in the Dardanelles.

Embarkation began on 30 June when the bulk of the Division left Liverpool aboard the *Empress of Britain* and the *Aquitania*. Shortly after leaving England, the latter vessel was the victim of an unsuccessful submarine attack off the Scilly Isles. The 11th Division was finally complete at Imbros on 28 July 1915.

On 6 August the Division boarded motor lighters and at night took part in the assault landings at Suvla Bay. For the next ten days a number of actions were fought from the beaches, including the 34th Brigade's capture of Karakol Dagh on 7 August, and a gallant engagement by 33rd Brigade at Yilghin Burnu on 9 August. It was at Yilghin Burnu, later known as Chocolate Hill, that Capt Percy Hansen, Adjutant of the 6th Lincolns, won the Victoria Cross for his heroic action in rescuing a number of wounded from burning scrub.

After the August fighting the Division settled down in holding positions within the Suvla Bay defences. The 11th could now take toll of its casualties; even though some 75% had been lost in battle, sickness had claimed many more.

After almost four months on the Peninsula, where a stalemate situation now existed, it was decided to evacuate the area around Suvla. This was carried out on the night of 19-20 December, the 11th Division embarking on lighters for Imbros. At the end of January 1916, the Division moved to Egypt where it took over 'A' Section of the Suez Canal Defences. The 11th remained on these duties until the following June when orders were received to proceed to France.

Concentration of the 11th Division was complete around the village of Flers on 15 July, the Somme offensive having started two weeks earlier on 1 July. For the next few weeks a period of training was undertaken in which the troops accustomed themselves to war conditions on the Western Front.

It was not until September that the Division became involved in any major engagement, fighting on 14 September at the Wundt Werk ('Wonder Work'), south-east of Thiepval and later in the Battles of Flers-Courcelette and Thiepval Ridge. At the end of September the Division took the Stuff Redoubt and for four days fought gallantly in its defence. During this period, Capt Archie Cecil Thomas White of the 6th Yorkshire Regiment, who had previously been wounded at Gallipoli, won the Victoria Cross.

Between 11-19 January 1917, the Division was involved in the operations on the River Ancre. It later fought at the Battle of Messines between 9-14 June. Further engagements during 1917 were in the XVIII Corps area of the Ypres Sector and included Langemarck, St Julien, Polygon Wood, Broodseinde and Poelcappelle. A further five Victoria Crosses were earned by members of the Division for their gallantry during these actions.

On 29 August 1918 the 11th Division took over positions in the line south of the River Scarpe and was involved in fierce fighting throughout that and the next day. During the following months the Division advanced on the Hindenberg Line, fighting alongside Canadian troops at the Canal du Nord, Cambrai and during the pursuit to the Selle. The Division then took part in the final advance in Picardy, where it fought in the Battle of the Sambre on 4 November.

On 9 November the 11th Division halted beyond the Mons-Maubeuge road and two days later, when the Armistice was signed, occupied positions to the east of Havay. For the remainder of the year the troops were provided with educational training, until demobilisation began in January 1919. Throughout the war the 11th (Northern) Division suffered over 32,000 killed, wounded and missing.

# 12th
## (EASTERN)
# DIVISION

## 12th (Eastern) Division
Divisional sign: The Ace of Spades.

Formed in late August 1914, the 12th (Eastern) Division was part of the First New Army and was mainly recruited from the Eastern and Home Counties. It comprised the following infantry brigades:

*35th Brigade*
7th Bn The Norfolk Regt. Formed at Norwich.
7th Bn The Suffolk Regt. Formed at Bury St Edmunds. The battalion was broken up in May 1918 with over 400 men going to the 1/1st Cambridgeshire Regiment. Some personnel were formed into a training cadre and later served with the 39th and 66th Divisions.
9th Bn The Essex Regt. Formed at Warley.

5th Bn Princess Charlotte of Wales's (Royal Berkshire Regt). Formed at Reading and transferred to 36th Brigade in February 1918.
1/1st Bn The Cambridgeshire Regt. A Territorial Force unit which joined the Brigade in May 1918 as a replacement for 7th Suffolk.

*36th Brigade*
8th and 9th Bns The Royal Fusiliers (City of London Regt). Formed at Hounslow. The 8th Battalion was disbanded in February 1918.
7th Bn The Royal Sussex Regt. Formed at Chichester.
11th Bn The Duke of Cambridge's Own (Middlesex Regt). Formed at Mill Hill and disbanded in Feb 1918.
5th Bn Princess Charlotte of Wales's (Royal Berkshire Regt). Joined from 35th Brigade in February 1918.

*Royal Artillery officer observing fire with Royal Engineers
telephonists at Cuthbert Crater, 2½ miles north-east of
Arras, April 1917.*   Imperial War Museum

### 37th Brigade
6th Bn The Queen's (Royal West Surrey Regt).
Formed at Guildford.
6th Bn The Buffs (East Kent Regt). Formed at
Canterbury.
7th Bn The East Surrey Regt. Formed at Kingston-on-
Thames and disbanded in February 1918.
6th Bn The Queen's Own (Royal West Kent Regt).
Formed at Maidstone.

### Pioneers
5th Bn The Northamptonshire Regt. Formed at
Northampton. The battalion was at first attached to the
12th Division as Army Troops and assumed its pioneer
role in January 1915.

Other units that made up the Division included 62nd,
63rd, 64th, 65th Brigades, Royal Field Artillery; 69th,
70th, 87th Field Companies Royal Engineers; 116th,
117th, 118th, 119th Companies Army Service Corps;
36th, 37th, 38th Field Ambulances, Royal Army
Medical Corps and 23rd Mobile Veterinary Section.
'A' Squadron of 1st King Edward's Horse formed part
of the Division between May 1915 and May 1916.

By November 1914 the three infantry brigades were

in the Hythe area and in the following February the
whole Division had concentrated at Aldershot where it
commenced its final war training. On 24 May 1915
orders were received to move to France. Advance
parties left the following day and by 4 June all units had
reached an area south of St Omer.

After a period of training in trench warfare, the
Division took its place in a section of the front line
north-west of Armentières and reaching through
Ploegsteert Wood.

During the following months the Division carried
out the usual patrols and generally had a quiet time.
The enemy, it is recorded, were even inclined to
fraternise on occasion and, according to the divisional
history, the 7th East Surreys were complimented at
one time when a board appeared in the German trench
saying: 'Don't Fire, East Surrey; you shoot too well.'

The Battle of Loos began in late September 1915
and news of the successes gained in the opening days by
the 9th and 15th New Army Divisions soon reached the
12th Eastern.

The Division eventually entered the battle on 30
September, after relieving the Guards at the line east
and north-east of Loos. On 2 October the Division
suffered a heavy loss when its commander, Maj-Gen F.
D. V. Wing, was killed by a shell while inspecting gun
positions. It later played a major role, however, in the
capture of the quarries at Hulluch.

The Division left the area in November, but in the
following February returned to take over positions

holding the Quarries and Hohenzollern Sectors. Subsequently, between 2-19 March, the Division was involved in the heavy fighting around the craters in the area. L/Cpl William Richard Cotter of the 6th East Kents later received the Victoria Cross for the conspicuous bravery and devotion to duty that he showed on 6 March.

On 1 July 1916, the first day of the Somme offensive, the Division was in reserve at Henencourt and Millencourt. On the 2nd, orders were received to attack the village of Ovillers, but this action was not a success and resulted in over 2,300 casualties. Further Somme engagements during 1916 include the battle at Pozières Ridge 28 July-13 August and le Transloy Ridges on 1-18 October.

January 1917 saw the Division in headquarters at Le Cauroy with its men taking their first rest since the beginning of the Battle of the Somme. Soon, preparations for the next battle, Arras, commenced. The Division took over positions by the River Scarpe and during the next few months were to see a great deal of action in that area. On 9 April Sgt Harry Cator of the East Surreys was awarded the Victoria Cross. The following month Cpl George Jarratt, Royal Fusiliers,

was also awarded the VC after he lost his life by placing both feet over a grenade that had just landed in his dugout. The position was also occupied by a number of wounded men who, thanks to Cpl Jarratt's bravery, were later moved to safety.

Before the end of 1917 the Division was to take part in the tank attack at Cambrai. This was followed by the capture of Bourlon Wood 23-28 November, and in the German counter-attack that followed both Capt Neville Bowes Elliott-Cooper, DSO, MC of the Royal Fusiliers and Temp. Lt Samuel Thomas Dickson Wallace, Royal Field Artillery won Victoria Crosses.

The Division returned to the Somme in 1918 and fought at Bapaume, Arras and on the River Ancre during March and April. The 'Advance to Victory' commenced in August, and on the 9th the Division gained its sixth Victoria Cross when Sgt T. J. Harris of the 6th Royal West Kents was killed while attempting to take enemy machine guns near Morlancourt.

The final battles fought by the 12th (Eastern) Division included those at Albert, Epéhy and the St Quentin Canal. By the end of the war the Division was located at Sameon, having suffered over 41,000 casualties since arriving on the Western Front in 1915.

# 13th
## (WESTERN)
# DIVISION

**13th (Western) Division**
Divisional sign: A black horseshoe

The 13th (Western) Division began to assemble in late August 1914 and by the end of February 1915 had concentrated at Blackdown near Farnborough. The Division included battalions from Lancashire, Warwickshire, Gloucestershire, Worcestershire, Staffordshire, Cheshire, Wiltshire and Wales. The three infantry brigades were made up as follows:

*38th Brigade*
6th Bn The King's Own (Royal Lancaster Regt). Formed at Lancaster.
6th Bn The East Lancashire Regt. Formed at Preston.
6th Bn The Prince of Wales's Volunteers (South Lancashire Regt). Formed at Warrington.
6th Bn The Loyal North Lancashire Regt. Formed at Preston.

*39th Brigade*
9th Bn The Royal Warwickshire Regt. Formed at Warwick.

7th Bn The Gloucestershire Regt. Formed at Bristol.
9th Bn The Worcestershire Regt. Formed at Worcester.
7th Bn The Prince of Wales's (North Staffordshire Regt). Formed at Lichfield.

*40th Brigade*
8th Bn The Cheshire Regt. Formed at Chester.
8th Bn The Royal Welsh Fusiliers. Formed at Wrexham.
4th Bn The South Wales Borderers. Formed at Brecon.
8th Bn The Welsh Regt. Formed at Cardiff. Became divisional pioneer battalion in December 1914.
5th Bn The Duke of Edinburgh's (Wiltshire Regt). Formed at Devizes and attached to the Division as Army Troops. Joined the Brigade as a replacement for 8th Welsh Regiment in December 1914.

*Pioneers*
8th Bn The Welsh Regt. Became the Division's pioneer battalion in December 1914. Originally part of 40th Brigade.

*Members of the 13th (Western) Div Cyclist Coy, Hampshire, 1915.*

*CSM J. Robinson, 8th Bn, Cheshire Regt. Mr Robinson wears foreign service uniform and has his battalion identification – a red and buff diamond – at the side of his helmet.*

*Turks surrendering to 38th Bde in May 1918.*
Imperial War Museum.

Other units included in the Division were 66th, 67th, 68th, 69th Brigades, RFA (55 Brigade joined later); 71st, 72nd, 88th Field Companies, Royal Engineers; 120th 121st, 122nd, 123rd Companies, Army Service Corps (these companies did not go overseas with the Division and later served abroad with the 28th Division); 39th, 40th, 41st Field Ambulances, Royal Army Medical Corps and 24th Mobile Veterinary Section.

On 7 June 1915 the Division was informed that it was to make ready for service in the Mediterranean. The first units left England on 13 June and by 4 July Divisional Headquarters had been set up at Mudros on the Island of Lemnos.

Between 6-16 July the infantry moved to Gallipoli, relieving the 29th Division at Helles. The three brigades returned to Mudros at the end of July, but on 3 August again landed on the peninsula, this time via Anzac Cove.

While in this area the Division, between 6-10 August, fought at Sari Bair and at Russell's Top where the 8th Cheshires and 8th Royal Welsh Fusiliers distinguished themselves. Also, and before the end of August, the other battalion of 40th Brigade, the 4th South Wales Borderers, played an important role during the assault on Hill 60.

The Division later moved to the front at Suvla where, during the night of 19-20 December, it assisted with the evacuation back to Mudros. 39th Brigade did good work that night acting as rearguard throughout the operations.

The Division (less 38th Brigade) returned to Gallipoli in the New Year, landing at Helles to join the left section of VIII Corps at the front line. After a series of attacks by the Turks on 7 January a general evacuation of the Gallipoli Peninsula, this time via Helles, commenced. This was completed during the night of the 8-9 January without casualties, and the 13th Division again returned to Mudros.

Within a few weeks the Division left Lemnos for Egypt and was concentrated by the end of January at Port Said. After a period of duty on the Suez Defences, the 13th then moved to Mesopotamia, joining the Tigris Corps at Shaikh Saad.

*13th (Western) Div Christmas card from Mesopotamia, 1916-17.*

'Ave you read a'bart the perils
Of this 'ere salubrious spot.
Where the flies are big as spare'rs
And the 'ens lay eggs red 'ot.
Or a'bart the creepy crawly things
Which bite us day and night,
'Ow spite of all we're going strong
And eager for the fight?
But Xmas-tide is 'ere once more
And though so far away,
We wish you all the best of Cheer
And a HAPPY XMAS DAY.

WE'RE SLICING "HIM" UP
AND HOPE YOU ARE DOING THE SAME

GREETINGS 1916-17

At the beginning of April 1916 a third attempt by the British to relieve Kut Al Imara was made. The Division took part in four major engagements during these operations, which lasted until the third attack at Sanniyat on 22 April. It was in the first of these actions – the capture of the Fallahiya Lines on 5 April – that the 13th Division gained its first Victoria Cross. Capt Angus Buchanan, 4th South Wales Borderers, who had already won the Military Cross at Gallipoli, courageously brought two wounded men to cover while under heavy machine-gun fire. Four days later another South Wales Borderer – Pte James Finn – and 2/Lt Edgar Myles of the Welsh Regiment (attached to the Worcesters), also won VCs.

After the failed attempt to relieve the garrison at Kut, which eventually surrendered on 29 April, the Division did little of any importance during the summer and autumn of 1916. The heat was intense throughout these months and would not permit much in the way of activity by either side.

On 13 December 1916 British operations for the capture of Kut began, all objectives being taken by 25 February 1917. Next came the advance to Baghdad, which was taken early in March after severe hand-to-hand fighting had been incurred during the pursuit of the enemy. During the Battle of Kut Al Imara, and the engagements leading to the occupation of Baghdad, a further three Victoria Crosses were earned by members of the Division.

The Division was to take part in the remaining battles of the Mesopotamia Campaign which, between March and December 1917, consolidated the British position at Baghdad. On 29 April 1918 the last major action was fought at Tuz Khurmati. Divisional Headquarters were later opened at Dawalib, and here the Division remained until after the Armistice.

While in Mesopotamia orders were received sending 39th Brigade, along with 72nd Field Company, Royal Engineers and 40th Field Amublance, Royal Army Medical Corps, to join a force in North-Western Persia. The enemy had opened operations around Merv and Baku, posing a threat to the British flank in Mesopotamia or even to Central Asia and the Indian Frontier.

Advance units of the Brigade reached the area in early August 1918 and between 26 August-15 September the small force took part in the severe and courageous fighting around Baku.

The 13th (Western) Division was the only British Division to serve in Mesopotamia and lost almost 8,000 of its 12,656 casualties in that theatre.

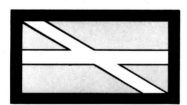

# 14th
## (LIGHT)
# DIVISION

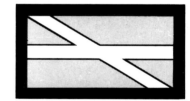

**14th (Light) Division**
Divisional sign: Two crossing white lines on a green oblong.

When formed in September 1914 , the Division was at first numbered as 8th and its brigades 23rd, 24th, 25th. As such, it represented the senior New Army Division. However, certain Regular Army battalions which had been released from overseas garrisons were grouped as a division and with effect from 11 September 1914 assumed the designation 8th Division. On the same day the New Army Division became the 14th (Light) Division with 41st, 42nd and 43rd Brigades. The original composition of the Division was of battalions provided by light infantry and rifle regiments.

*41st Brigade*
7th Bn The King's Royal Rifle Corps. Formed at Winchester and transferred to 43rd Brigade in February 1918.
8th Bn The King's Royal Rifle Corps. Formed at Winchester. Reduced to a training cadre in April 1918 and later attached to the 39th Division.
7th Bn The Rifle Brigade (The Prince Consort's Own). Formed at Winchester. Reduced to a cadre in April 1918 and in the following June absorbed into the 33rd Battalion, London Regiment.
8th Bn The Rifle Brigade (The Prince Consort's Own). Formed at Winchester. Reduced to a cadre in June 1918 and later disbanded.
18th Bn The York and Lancaster Regt. Formed at Margate in June 1918.
29th Bn The Durham Light Infantry. Formed at Margate in June 1918.
33rd (City of London) Bn The London Regt (Rifle Brigade). Formed at Clacton-on-Sea in June 1918 and absorbed the remainder of 7th Rifle Brigade.

*42nd Brigade*
5th Bn The Oxfordshire and Buckinghamshire Light Infantry. Formed at Oxford. Reduced to a cadre in April 1918 and later transferred to the 16th Division

where it was absorbed into the 18th Gloucestershire Regiment.

5th Bn The King's (Shropshire Light Infantry). Formed at Shrewsbury and disbanded in February 1918.

9th Bn The King's Royal Rifle Corps. Formed at Winchester. Reduced to a cadre in April 1918 and later disbanded.

9th Bn The Rifle Brigade (The Prince Consort's Own). Formed at Winchester. Reduced to a cadre in April 1918 and later disbanded.

6th (Royal Wiltshire Yeomanry) Bn The Duke of Edinburgh's (Wiltshire Regt). Joined the Brigade from the 19th Division in June 1918. Absorbed the 9th Dorset Regiment in the following July.

16th Bn The Manchester Regt (1st City). Joined the Brigade from the 30th Division in June 1918 and absorbed the 29th Battalion Manchester Regiment formed that month.

14th Bn Princess Louise's (Argyll and Sutherland Highlanders). Joined from the 30th Division in June 1918 and amalgamated with the 17th Argylls formed that month.

### 43rd Brigade

6th Bn Prince Albert's (Somerset Light Infantry). Formed at Taunton. Reduced to a cadre in April 1918 and later transferred to the 16th Division.

6th Bn The Duke of Cornwall's Light Infantry. Formed at Bodmin and disbanded in February 1918.

6th Bn The King's Own (Yorkshire Light Infantry). Formed at Pontefract and disbanded in February 1918.

10th Bn The Durham Light Infantry. Formed at Newcastle and disbanded in February 1918.

9th Bn The Cameronians (Scottish Rifles). Joined from the 9th Division in February 1918. Returned to the 9th in the following April.

7th Bn The King's Royal Rifle Corps. Joined from 41st Brigade in February 1918. Transferred to the 16th Division in June and absorbed into the 34th London Regiment.

12th Bn The Suffolk Regt (East Anglia). Joined from the 40th Division in June 1918 and absorbed the 16th Battalion Suffolk Regiment formed in the same month.

20th Bn The Duke of Cambridge's Own (Middlesex Regt) (Shoreditch). Joined from the 40th Division in June 1918 and absorbed the 34th Battalion Middlesex Regiment formed that month.

10th Bn The Highland Light Infantry. Joined from the 40th Division in June 1918 and absorbed the 22nd Battalion HLI formed that month.

### Pioneers

11th Bn The King's (Liverpool Regt). Formed at Seaforth, Liverpool. Reduced to a cadre in April 1918 and later merged with the 15th Battalion, Loyal North Lancashire Regiment.

*Two men of the 10th Bn, Durham Light Infantry. They wear the blue 'emergency' uniform with brown leather equipment and canvas haversack.*   A. Gavaghan

15th Bn The Loyal North Lancashire Regt. Formed at Cromer in June 1918 and absorbed the cadre of 11th King's (Liverpool Regiment).

Other units that served as part of the Division included 46th, 47th, 48th, 49th Brigades, Royal Field Artillery; 61st, 62nd, 89th Field Companies, Royal Engineers; 100th, 101st, 102nd, 103rd Companies, Army Service Corps; 42nd, 43rd, 44th Field Ambulances, Royal Army Medical Corps and 26th Mobile Veterinary Section. 'D' Squadron, 1/1st Duke of Lancaster's Own Yeomanry formed part of the Division for a period during 1915-16.

The Division concentrated around the Guildford area late in November 1914. It was inspected by Lord Kitchener on 22 January 1915 and in mid-February moved to Aldershot for divisional field manoeuvres and final war training.

Orders to move overseas were received by the Division in May. It left from Southampton, and by 25 May was formed up around Watten, north-west of St Omer under the command of Maj-Gen V. A. Couper.

During 30-31 July 1915 the Division suffered heavy losses at Hooge, where the Germans attacked using liquid fire for the first time. 2/Lt S. C. Woodroffe of the 8th Rifle Brigade was posthumously awarded the Victoria Cross for his part in that action.

The Division took part in the attack on the Bellewaard Farm position on 25 September, and in November a second Victoria Cross was gained by the

8th Rifle Brigade when Cpl A. G. Drake was killed while attending a wounded officer near La Brique.

In 1916 the 14th (Light) Division became part of XV Corps, Fourth Army. It took part in the severe fighting at Delville Wood 13-20 August and on 15-16 September saw action at Flers and Courcelette.

In the early part of 1917 the Division was involved in the German retreat and subsequent British advance towards the Hindenburg Line. The Battle of Arras commenced on 9 April 1917 and the Division, as part of VII Corps, Third Army, fought at the First and Third Battles of the Scarpe. For the last months of 1917 the Division served in the Ypres Sector and saw action at Langemarck. It was also involved in fighting on the Menin Road in which a gallant attack on Inverness Copse took place, and at Passchendaele.

Having moved back to the Somme in 1918, the 14th (Light) Division was engaged 21 March-4 April at the Battles of St Quentin and Avre. During this period the Division suffered almost 6,000 casualties and as a result was withdrawn from the line by 6 April. Before the end of April the Division's battalions, which had almost ceased to exist, were either disbanded or reduced to cadre strength.

In June 1918 the 14th (Light) Division was sent back to England where it would be brought up to strength, mostly from newly raised battalions. When eventually it returned to France in July, none of the original battalions was included.

The reconstituted 14th Division took over a section of the line north-west of Ypres on 29 August. It later took part in the final advance in Flanders and fought its last major battle at Courtrai on 14-19 October. On 11 November 1918 the 14th (Light) Division occupied positions astride the Schelde River from Helchin to Herseaux. After the Armistice it was employed on road repairs and other maintenance work. Demobilisation began in December and by March the Division had ceased to exist. Throughout the war the Division lost over 37,000 killed, wounded or missing.

# 15th
## (SCOTTISH)
# DIVISION

## 15th (Scottish) Division

Divisional sign: A red triangle within a black circle. The circle, or 'O', is the fifteenth letter of the alphabet, and the triangle represents a scotch, (a block for jamming wheels).

The 15th (Scottish) Division was the senior of the Second New Army. It began to assemble at Aldershot during September 1914 and contained battalions from both the Highlands and Lowlands of Scotland.

*44th Brigade*
9th Bn The Black Watch (Royal Highlanders). Formed at Perth and transferred to 46th Brigade in February 1918.
8th Bn Seaforth Highlanders (Ross-shire Buffs, The Duke of Albany's). Formed at Fort George.
9th Bn The Gordon Highlanders. Formed at Aberdeen and became divisional pioneer battalion in January 1915.
10th Bn The Gordon Highlanders. Formed at Aberdeen. Amalgamated with 8th Gordons (transferred from the 9th Division) as 8th/10th

*L/Cpl John Jones, 7th Bn, Cameron Highlanders. Killed in action, 14 Sept 1915.*

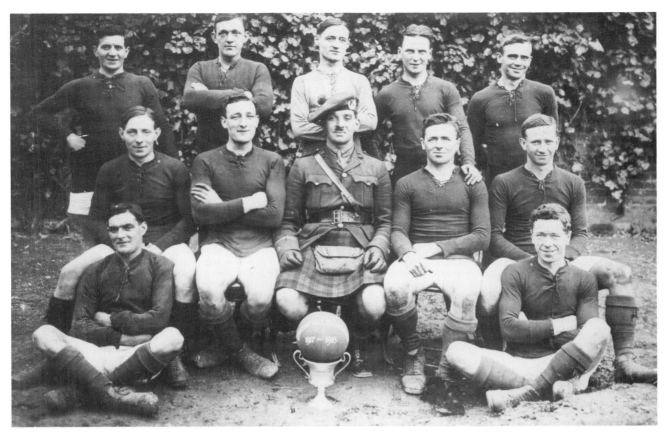

*9th Bn, Gordon Highlanders (Pioneers) football team
Divisional Champions 1917-18.*   D. Barnes

*15th (Scottish) Division Christmas Card, 1918.*   P. Blagojevic

Battalion in May 1916. Reduced to cadre in June 1918
and later disbanded.
7th Bn The Queen's Own Cameron Highlanders.
Formed at Inverness. Joined the Brigade as a
replacement for 9th Gordons in January 1915.
Reduced to a cadre in June 1918 and later disbanded.
4th/5th Bn The Black Watch (Royal Highlanders). A
Territorial Force battalion which joined from 46th
Brigade in June 1918.
1/5th Bn The Gordon Highlanders. A Territorial Force
battalion which joined from the 61st Division in June
1918.

*45th Brigade*
13th Bn The Royal Scots (Lothian Regt). Formed at
Edinburgh.
7th Bn The Royal Scots Fusiliers. Formed at Ayr.
Amalgamated as 6th/7th Battalion with 6th Royal
Scots Fusiliers (transferred from 9th Division) in May
1916. Transferred to 59th Division, as pioneers, in
February 1918.
6th Bn The Queen's Own Cameron Highlanders.
Formed at Inverness and included a complete company
of Glasgow University students and many men from
the Glasgow Stock Exchange.
11th Bn Princess Louise's (Argyll and Sutherland

"Here the noble THISTLE of SCOTLAND will flourish
for ever amidst the ROSES of FRANCE."

*Senior Pipers and Drummers of the 15th (Scottish) Div, France, May 1917.*   Imperial War Museum

Highlanders). Formed at Stirling. Reduced to a cadre in June 1918 and later disbanded.

1/8th (The Argyllshire) Bn Princess Louise's (Argyll and Sutherland Highlanders). A Territorial Force battalion which joined in June 1918 as a replacement for the 11th Argylls.

### 46th Brigade

7th and 8th Bns The King's Own Scottish Borderers. Both formed at Berwick-on-Tweed and amalgamatd as 7th/8th Battalion in May 1916.

10th Bn The Cameronians (Scottish Rifles). Formed at Hamilton.

12th Bn The Highland Light Infantry. Formed at Hamilton and transferred to the 35th Division in February 1918.

10th/11th Bns The Highland Light Infantry. Amalgamated and transferred from the 9th Division in May 1916 as a replacement for 8th King's Own Scottish Borderers. Moved to the 40th Division in February 1918.

9th Bn The Black Watch (Royal Highlanders). Joined from 44th Brigade in February 1918. Reduced to a cadre in May 1918 and later joined the 16th Division.

1/9th (Highlanders) Bn The Royal Scots (Lothian Regt). A Territorial Force battalion which joined from the 61st Division in June 1918.

### Pioneers

9th Bn The Gordon Highlanders. Became the pioneer battalion in January 1915, having been part of 44th Brigade.

Other components of the Division included 70th, 71st, 72nd, 73rd Brigades, Royal Field Artillery; 73rd, 74th, 91st Field Companies, Royal Engineers; 138th, 139th 140th, 141st Companies, Army Service Corps; 45th, 46th, 47th Field Ambulances, Royal Army Medical Corps and 27th Mobile Veterinary Section. 'B' Squadron, 1/1st Westmorland and Cumberland Yeomanry served with the Division between June 1915 and May 1916.

The Division moved from Aldershot to Salisbury Plain in November 1914, having been inspected by HM The King on 26 September. On that day, all but the divisional staff paraded in civilian clothes. On 22 January 1915 it was the turn of Lord Kitchener, accompanied by the French Minister of War, Monsieur Millerand, to view the 15th (Scottish) Division. This time, uniforms had been issued, but only a small number of drill rifles, enough for the front ranks, had been received in time for the parade.

Orders to move to France were received at the beginning of July 1915. The first units left on 7 July and by the 13th concentration was complete around Tilques, near St Omer.

Under the command of Maj-Gen F. W. N. McCracken the Division entered its first major battle on 25 September 1915 when, after many days'

*2/Lt Thomas Hutcheon, 7th Royal Scots Fusiliers. Died of wounds received at Pozières Ridge on 12 August 1916.*

*7th Bn, King's Own Scottish Borderers. A cover for the Balmoral bonnet is being worn and khaki slip-on shoulder titles bearing the white letters 'KOSB'.* A. Gavaghan

bombardment, the British attacked at Loos. That same day, two men – Piper Daniel Laidlaw of the 7th King's Own Scottish Borderers, and Pte Robert Dunsire – 13th Royal Scots, gained Victoria Crosses during an action around Hill 70. In leaving its positions, the 7th KOSB experienced difficulties in making any headway due to slippery trenches and the heavy state of the ground mud. Piper Laidlaw got up on the parapet under heavy fire, and gave the men great encouragement by playing them over the top until he fell wounded.

On 26 September the 6th Camerons played an important role in the capture of Hill 70. They were commanded on this occasion by Lt-Col Angus Douglas-Hamilton, who was later awarded a posthumous Victoria Cross for his gallantry and leadership on that day. The Division spent the winter of 1915-16 at Loos holding the line at Hohenzollern and Hulluch.

The 15th (Scottish) Division joined the Battle of the Somme on 8 August 1916. It fought at Pozières Ridge until 3 September and then accompanied British tanks when they went into action for the first time at Flers on 15 August. Tanks were also in support when Martinpuich was captured on the same day.

The Division commenced an assault on the German positions at Arras on 9 April 1917. It took part in the First and Second Battles of the Scarpe during that month, and on 23 April took over 2,000 prisoners at the Capture of Guemappe.

Having moved to the Ypres sector, the Division took part in the attack on Passchendaele Ridge on 31 July, the enemy being pushed back over 2,000 yards by 2 August. On 17-18 August 46th Brigade were engaged at Langemarck, and on the 22nd the Division took part in the fighting for Zevenkote.

During the March 1918 German offensive on the Somme a great deal of action was seen around Arras. Heavy casualties were incurred and in May-June a number of battalions had to be replaced by Territorial Force units.

The Division moved south to support the French Army in July 1918, and for a number of weeks operated in the Épernay section on the River Marne. When the Division commenced its final advance in October 1918, it was situated in the vicinity of Loos and Hulluch, where it had first gone into action in 1915. On 8 November the Division crossed the Schelde; it then moved eastwards and by 11 November had reached the line of the Dendre to the south of Ath. Demobilisation commenced on 10 December. Throughout the war, the 15th (Scottish) Division lost 45,542 killed, wounded and missing.

# 16th
## (IRISH)
# DIVISION

## 16th (Irish) Division

Divisional sign: The 16th (Irish) Division had two signs. One was the monogram 'LP' which was shown on transport and HQ boards, etc. These letters were adopted as a compliment to Lt-Gen Sir L. W. Parsons, the Division's first commander. The sign worn on the men's uniforms was a shamrock.

As part of the Second New Army, the 16th (Irish) Division began to assemble in Ireland during September 1914. The Division, which had its headquarters in Dublin, comprised 47th, 48th and 49th Infantry Brigades.

### 47th Brigade

6th Bn The Royal Irish Regt. Formed at Clonmel. In March 1915 volunteers from the Guernsey Militia joined the Battalion and formed one company. The Battalion was disbanded in February 1918.

6th Bn The Connaught Rangers. Formed at Kilworth. Reduced to a training cadre in April 1918 and later disbanded.

7th Bn The Prince of Wales's Leinster Regt (Royal Canadians). Formed at Fermoy and disbanded in February 1918.

8th Bn The Royal Munster Fusiliers. Formed in Ireland and disbanded November 1916.

1st Bn The Royal Munster Fusiliers. A Regular Army battalion which joined from 48th Brigade in November 1916. Transferred to the 57th Division in April 1918.

2nd Bn The Prince of Wales's Leinster Regt (Royal Canadians). A Regular Army battalion which joined from the 24th Division as a replacement for 7th Leinsters in February 1918. Transferred to the 29th Division in April 1918.

14th Bn The Leicestershire Regt. Formed at Aldeburgh in June 1918.

18th Bn The Welsh Regt (2nd Glamorgan). Joined from the 40th Division in June 1918 and in the same month absorbed the 25th Welsh Regiment which had been formed at North Walsham on 1 June 1918.

9th Bn The Black Watch (Royal Highlanders). Joined from the 15th Division in June 1918 and that same month absorbed the 15th Black Watch which had been formed at Deal on 1 June 1918.

### 48th Brigade

7th Bn The Royal Irish Rifles. Formed at Belfast. In

*L/Cpl, 11th Bn, Hampshire Regt. The battalion's role as pioneers is shown by the crossed pick and rifle collar badges, while the letters 'LG' above the chevron indicate that the wearer is a Lewis Gunner.* M. Ingrey

March 1915 volunteers from the Jersey Militia joined the battalion and formed 'D' Company. Battalion transferred to 49th Brigade in August 1917.

9th Bn The Royal Munster Fusiliers. Formed in Ireland and disbanded in May 1916.

8th and 9th Bns The Royal Dublin Fusiliers. Formed in Ireland and in October 1917 were amalgamated to form 8th/9th Battalion. Disbanded in February 1918.

1st Bn The Royal Munster Fusiliers. A Regular Army battalion which joined in May 1916 as a replacement

*Royal Dublin Fusiliers with souvenirs taken after the capture of Wytschaete, 7 June 1917.* Imperial War Museum

for 9th Royal Munsters. Transferred to 47th Brigade in November 1916.

2nd Bn The Royal Dublin Fusiliers. A Regular Army battalion which joined from the 4th Division as a replacement for 1st Royal Munsters in November 1916. Reduced to a cadre in April 1918 and later attached to the 31st Division.

10th Bn The Royal Dublin Fusiliers. Joined from the 63rd Division in June 1917 and disbanded in Feb 1918.

1st Bn The Royal Dublin Fusiliers. Joined in October 1917 as a replacement for 9th Royal Dublin Fusiliers. Transferred to the 29th Division in April 1918.

2nd Bn The Royal Munster Fusiliers. A Regular Army battalion which joined in February 1918. Reduced to a cadre in the following April and later attached to the 31st Division.

22nd Bn The Northumberland Fusiliers (3rd Tyneside Scottish). Joined from the 34th Division in June 1918, and that same month absorbed the 38th Battalion Northumberland Fusiliers formed at Margate on 1 June.

18th Bn The Cameronians (Scottish Rifles). Formed at Aldershot in June 1918.

5th Bn Princess Victoria's (Royal Irish Fusiliers). Joined from the 66th Division in August 1918, absorbing the 11th Royal Irish Fusiliers formed in June 1918 at Greatham near West Hartlepool.

*49th Brigade*
7th and 8th Bns The Royal Inniskilling Fusiliers. Formed at Omagh and amalgamated in August 1917 as 7th/8th Battalion. Reduced to a cadre in April 1918, later attached to the 34th Division.

7th and 8th Bns Princess Victoria's (Royal Irish Fusiliers). Formed at Armagh and amalgamated in October 1916 as 7th/8th Battalion. Disbanded in February 1918.

2nd Bn The Royal Irish Regt. A Regular Army battalion which joined the Brigade as a replacement for 8th Royal Irish Fusiliers in October 1916. Transferred to the 63rd Division in April 1918.

7th Bn The Royal Irish Rifles. Joined from 48th Brigade in August 1917 as a replacement for 8th Royal Inniskilling Fusiliers. Transferred to the 36th Division and amalgamated with the 2nd Royal Irish Rifles in the following October.

7th (South Irish Horse) Bn The Royal Irish Regt. The 1st and 2nd South Irish Horse were part of the Special Reserve and in September 1917, after being dismounted, formed the 7th Royal Irish Regiment. The battalion joined 49th Brigade in October 1917, and in July of the following year transferred to the 30th Division.

6th Bn Prince Albert's (Somerset Light Infantry). Joined from the 14th Division in June 1918 and that same month absorbed the 13th Duke of Cornwall's LI formed at Aldeburgh on 1 June 1918.

18th Bn The Gloucestershire Regt. Formed at Clacton in June 1918 and that same month absorbed the 5th Oxfordshire and Buckinghamshire LI.

34th (County of London) Bn The London Regt. Formed at Clacton in June 1918, and that same month absorbed the 7th King's Royal Rifle Corps.

*Pioneers*
11th Bn The Hampshire Regt. Formed at Winchester. Having been reduced to a cadre in May 1918, the battalion returned to England where it was made up to strength by absorbing the 13th Border Regiment (formed at Lowestoft in June 1918).

The divisional artillery originally included the 74th, 75th, 76th, 77th Brigades, Royal Field Artillery. Later, after reorganisations, the 177th, 180th and 182nd Brigades joined. The three engineer field companies were at first 75th, 76th and 95th, but these were later replaced by 155th, 156th and 157th. The divisional train included 142nd, 143rd, 144th, 145th Companies, Army Service Corps. The field ambulances were at first 48th, 49th and 50th, but these were replaced in September 1915 by 111th, 112th and 113th. The 47th Mobile Veterinary Section also formed part of the Division. 'C' Squadron, South Irish Horse went to France with the Division but left in May 1916.

Training progressed at a slow rate, there never being enough arms and equipment to go round, which in consequence put the Division far behind schedule. By August 1915 much of the Division, including all the infantry, were still behind and subsequently a number of artillery, engineer and medical units which had made some advancement were removed and transferred to other divisions in France.

The remainder of the 16th Division eventually left Ireland for England in September 1915, concentrating for final divisional training at Aldershot. Embarkation orders for France were received on 10 December, and by the 22nd most of the Division was positioned south of Bethune. At this time, however, the 16th Division was far from complete. New artillery did not join until 22 February 1916 and then, two days later, 49th Infantry Brigade arrived.

The Division went into action at Hulluch on 27 and 29 April 1916, suffering greatly during the German gas attacks in this area. After a period of rest and in reserve positions, the 16th Division fought its first battle of the 1916 Somme offensive at Guillemont. Here, on 3 September, two members of the Division – Lt J. V. Holland and Pte T. Hughes – gained the Victoria Cross. Ginchy followed on 9 September.

Between 7-9 June 1917 heavy losses were incurred at Messines. On the first day of these operations, two Irish divisions – 16th and 36th – fought side-by-side during the battle and subsequent capture of Wytschaete.

After moving to the Ypres sector and XIX Corps area at the end of July, the 16th Division was in reserve throughout the Battle of Pilckem Ridge (31 July-2 August). Then, between 16-18 August, it fought at Langemarck. On 20 November 1917 an attack planned mainly as a diversion to assist the operations at Cambrai was made north of Bullecourt by the 16th Division. Coming as a complete surprise to the Germans, the assault was a great success, with over 1,800yds of front and two important pill-boxes being quickly taken.

During the March 1918 German offensive on the Somme the Division suffered over 7,000 casualties throughout the operations around St Quentin, Rosières and in front of Amiens. These engagements were to be the last in which the 16th Division fought as an Irish formation. It was relieved by 3 April, the artillery and machine-guns, however, remaining in the line to cover the 14th Division.

After concentrating in the Hallencourt area for reorganisation and rest, what remained of the infantry was formed into a composite brigade. This was employed in the training of American troops until 18 June, when the Division returned to England where it was to be reconstituted.

When the Division returned to France on 27 July 1918 it bore little resemblance to that formed in Ireland at the beginning of the war. Only the pioneers (11th Hampshires) remained, and the rest of the infantry included only one Irish battalion. After a period in reserve, the new 16th joined in the final advance in Artois and Flanders. The Schelde was crossed on 9 November and on the 11th engineers were at work repairing and strengthening bridges on the river. The Division was eventually broken up in France in May 1919. Throughout the war the 16th (Irish) Division lost over 28,000 killed, wounded and missing.

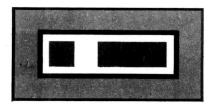

# 17th
## (NORTHERN)
# DIVISION

**17th (Northern) Division**
Divisional sign: A Dot and Dash. Said to represent the top of a one and seven.

The 17th (Northern) Division began its formation around Wareham, Dorsetshire in September 1914. It comprised units from the Midlands, the North of England and Dorsetshire, and included the following infantry brigades:

*50th Brigade*
10th Bn The Prince of Wales's Own (West Yorkshire Regt). Formed at York.
7th Bn The East Yorkshire Regt. Formed at Beverley.
7th Bn Alexandra, Princess of Wales's Own (Yorkshire Regt). Formed at Richmond and disbanded in February 1918.
7th Bn The York and Lancaster Regt. Formed at Pontefract and became divisional pioneer battalion in March 1915.
6th Bn The Dorsetshire Regt. Formed at Dorchester and attached to the Division as Army Troops. Replaced 7th York and Lancs in March 1915.

*51st Brigade*
7th Bn The Lincolnshire Regt. Formed at Lincoln.
7th Bn The Border Regt. Formed at Carlisle.

*Pte T Frankland, 9th Bn, Duke of Wellington's Regt. Died of wounds in France, 21 Oct 1918.*   D. Barnes

*Three members of the 9th Bn, Northumberland Fusiliers prior to the issue of uniforms. Bovington Camp, Dorset, Oct 1914.*   G. Stewart

*Officers and men of the 10th Sherwood Foresters with souvenirs taken on the Somme, July 1916.* Imperial War Museum

Absorbed the Westmorland and Cumberland Yeomanry in September 1917 and from then on was known as 7th (Westmorland and Cumberland Yeomanry) Battalion.
8th Bn The South Staffordshire Regt. Formed at Lichfield and disbanded in February 1918.
10th Bn The Sherwood Foresters (Nottinghamshire and Derbyshire Regt). Formed at Derby.

*52nd Brigade*
9th Bn The Northumberland Fusiliers. Formed at Newcastle. Transferred to the 34th Division in August 1917.
10th Bn The Lancashire Fusiliers. Formed at Bury.
9th Bn The Duke of Wellington's (West Riding Regt). Formed at Halifax.
12th Bn The Manchester Regt. Formed at Ashton-under-Lyne. Absorbed part of the Duke of Lancaster's Own Yeomanry in September 1917 and from then on was known as 12th (Duke of Lancaster's Own Yeomanry) Battalion.

*Pioneers*
7th Bn The York and Lancaster Regt. Served as part of 50th Brigade until taking on a pioneer role in March 1915.

Other units which served as part of the Division included 78th, 79th, 80th, 81st Brigades, Royal Field Artillery; and 77th, 78th, 93rd Field Companies, Royal

*Capt J. A. Benjamin, 9th Bn, Duke of Wellington's Regt. Killed on the Somme, 5 July 1916.*

Engineers. The divisional train was made up of 146th, 147th, 148th, 149th Companies, Army Service Corps; and medical units were 51st, 52nd and 53rd Field Ambulance and 29th Mobile Veterinary Section. Also, 'A' Squadron, Yorkshire Dragoons formed part of the Division between June 1915 and May 1916.

Having received orders to move overseas, advance parties left for Southampton on 6 July 1915, the whole Division beginning its embarkation for France six days later. Concentration south of St Omer was complete by 17 July, and on the 19th a move into V Corps, Second Army area, south-west of Ypres, took place.

Instruction in trench warfare soon began, the several battalions being attached to divisions already occupying sections of the front line. On 9 August 1915, after several days artillery bombardment, the British attacked the village of Hooge on the Ypres-Menin Road. The 17th Division took part in this operation by putting up a series of fire attacks and bombardments.

Prior to the commencement of the Somme offensive on 1 July 1916, the 17th Division were involved in both the loss, and recapture of The Bluff, a narrow ridge on the northern banks of the Ypres-Comines Canal, on 14 February and 2 March respectively. On 2 July Fricourt was captured, and between 1-12 August the Division was engaged during the battle for Delville Wood.

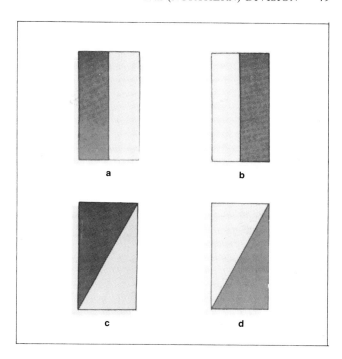

*Dark red and yellow identification patches worn by 'A', 'B', 'C' and 'D' Coys of the 10th Bn, Lancashire Fusiliers.*

*Sgt, Royal Field Artillery, 17th Div. Note the 'Dot-Dash' divisional sign worn at the top of the arm and the gold stripe on the cuff indicating that the Sgt had been wounded.*
C. Lewis

*Sgt Harold Jackson, 7th Bn, East Yorkshire Regt. Sgt Jackson was awarded the VC for most conspicuous bravery and devotion to duty at Hermies, 22 March 1918.*

An advance on the area east of Arras began on 9 April 1917, when two attacks were made on a parallel – north from Vimy Ridge and south along the River Scarpe. The 17th Division fought in both the First and Second Battles of the Scarpe, and in May was involved in the capture and, later, defence of Roeux. Just prior to involvement in this area, Pte Tom Dresser of the 7th Yorkshire Regiment won the Victoria Cross for his bravery and devotion to duty while delivering an important message to the front line, although twice wounded and under heavy fire throughout.

During the October-November 1917 operations on the Ypres Salient, the 17th Division was engaged in both the First and Second Battles of Passchendaele. It came under XIV Corps area on 12 October, and then between 8-10 November, XIX Corps.

During the German Somme offensive of 21 March-5 April 1918, the 17th Division saw action at St Quentin and Bapaume, Sgt H. Jackson of the 7th East Yorks winning the Victoria Cross at Hermies on the second day of the fighting. On 25 August it was the turn of the Lancashire Fusiliers to add another VC to its long list, Acting Sgt Colley showing great bravery and devotion to duty while holding an important position at Martinpuich.

The Division was again on the front at Bapaume between 31 August-3 September and saw its final battles of the war at Epéhy, Cambrai and on the Selle and Sambre Rivers. On 8 November advance parties crossed the Avesnes-Maubeuge road and on the following day occupied Beaufort. The Division later moved back to the Hallencourt area where demobilisation began at the beginning of 1919. During the war the 17th (Northern) Division lost over 40,000 killed, wounded and missing.

 # 18th
(EASTERN)
## DIVISION

### 18th (Eastern) Division
Divisional sign: The letters 'ATN' within a circle. The letters sound like 'Eighteen' when pronounced rapidly.

As part of the Second New Army, the 18th (Eastern) Division began to assemble around Colchester, Essex in September 1914. The Division was, in the main, recruited throughout East Anglia and the Home Counties, and comprised the following infantry brigades:

*53rd Brigade*
8th Bn The Norfolk Regt. Formed at Norwich and disbanded in February 1918.
8th Bn The Suffolk Regt. Formed at Bury St Edmunds and disbanded in February 1918.
10th Bn The Essex Regt. Formed at Warley.
6th Bn Princess Charlotte of Wales's (Royal Berkshire Regt). Formed at Reading and disbanded in February 1918.
8th Bn Princess Charlotte of Wales's (Royal Berkshire Regt). Joined from the 1st Division in February 1918.
7th Bn The Queen's Own (Royal West Kent Regt). Joined from 55th Brigade in February 1918.

*54th Brigade*
11th Bn The Royal Fusiliers (City of London Regt). Formed at Hounslow.
8th Bn The Royal Sussex Regt. Formed at Chichester and became divisional pioneer battalion in February 1915.
6th Bn The Northamptonshire Regt. Formed at Northampton.
12th Bn The Duke of Cambridge's Own (Middlesex Regt). Formed at Mill Hill and disbanded in February 1918.
7th Bn The Bedfordshire Regt. Formed at Bedford and attached to the 15th Division as Army Troops. Joined the 18th Division as a replacement for 8th Royal Sussex in February 1915. Reduced to a training cadre in May 1918 and was later absorbed into the 2nd Battalion.
2nd Bn The Bedfordshire Regt. A Regular Army battalion which joined from the 30th Division as a replacement for 7th Bedfords in May 1918.

*55th Brigade*
7th Bn The Queen's (Royal West Surrey Regt). Formed at Guildford.
7th Bn The Buffs (East Kent Regt). Formed at Canterbury.
8th Bn The East Surrey Regt. Formed at Kingston-on-Thames.
7th Bn The Queen's Own (Royal West Kent Regt). Formed at Maidstone and transferred to the 53rd Brigade in February 1918.

*Pioneers*
8th Bn The Royal Sussex Regt. Became the Division's

*An artist's impression (J. F. Campbell) of Pte Robert Ryder, 12th Middlesex Regt, winning the VC at Thiepval, 26 Sept 1916.*

pioneers in February 1915, having been part of the 54th Brigade since formation.

The field artillery brigades were numbered 82nd, 83rd, 84th, 85th and the engineer companies 79th, 80th and 92nd. The 150th-153rd Companies, Army Service Corps, provided the divisional train and the field ambulances were numbered 54th, 55th and 56th. Other units included in the Division were 30th Mobile Veterinary Section and 'C' Squadron, Westmorland and Cumberland Yeomanry which served between June 1915 and May 1916.

The Division moved to Salisbury Plain between 4-12 May 1915. Headquarters were set up at Codford under the command of Maj-Gen F. I. Maxse, and on 24 June the troops were inspected by HM The King.

News that the Division was to move to the Western Front was received in July. Embarkation soon began, and by 30 July concentration was complete in Third Army area, near Flesselles, south of Doullens.

It was almost a year before the Division took part in any major action, spending its time in war training and on tours of duty in the trenches. On 1 July 1916, the first day of the Somme offensive, the Division attacked south and west of the village of Montauban and made

good all of its objectives that day. The remaining Somme battles of 1916 in which the 18th Division took part included Bazentin Ridge, Trônes Wood (54th Brigade), Delville Wood (53rd Brigade), Thiepval Ridge, Ancre Heights and the Schwaben Redoubt.

During the 1916 Somme campaign, four members of the Division won Victoria Crosses, these were: Sgt W. E. Boulter (6th Northampton) at Trônes Wood; Pte F. J. Edwards and R. Ryder, both of the 12th Middlesex at Thiepval; and 2/Lt T. E. Adlam (7th Bedfords), also at Thiepval.

Throughout the early months of 1917, the 18th Division was engaged in operations along the Ancre River. It fought at Miraumont on 17-18 February and on 10 March the 53rd Brigade helped take Irles. This was followed by the German retreat to the Hindenburg Line between 14-20 March in which the 18th were engaged on a number of occasions.

Before moving to the Ypres Sector the Division played a part in the Arras offensive and fought in the Third Battle of the Scarpe on 3-4 May. On 31 July and 10 August 1917 respectively, the Division was engaged in the actions at Pilckem Ridge and Westhoek. 53rd Brigade was at Langemarck on 16-17 August, and during October-November the Division fought in both the battles for Passchendaele.

Returning to the Somme in 1918, the Division was in action during March and April at the battles of St Quentin, Avre and Villers Bretonneux. In August the

Battle of Amiens took place on the 8th and 9th, which was followed at the end of the month by operations at Albert, Usna and Tara Hills, Trônes Wood and Bapaume.

In September the Division was involved in two major actions around the Hindenburg Line, Epéhy on the 18th and the St Quentin Canal between 29 September and 1 October.

The final advance in Picardy began in October 1918, the 18th Division being engaged at the Battle of the Selle between the 20th and 26th, and in the last month of the war at the Sambre River. When the Armistice brought hostilities to an end on 11 November, billets had been occupied around Le Cateau. For the next weeks all ranks were given educational training and a number were employed on salvage work. Demobilisation commenced during the second week in December and the Division had ceased to exist by the middle of March 1919. During the war the 18th (Eastern) Division gained eleven Victoria Crosses and its losses amounted to 46,503 killed, wounded and missing.

# 19th
### (WESTERN)
## DIVISION

## 19th (Western) Division
Divisional sign: A butterfly.

The 19th (Western) Division formed part of the Second New Army and included units recruited from Lancashire, Warwickshire, Gloucestershire, Staffordshire, Cheshire, Wiltshire and Wales. The Division comprised the 56th, 57th and 58th Infantry Brigades and in September 1914 began its assembly near Bulford.

*56th Brigade*
7th Bn The King's Own (Royal Lancaster Regt). Formed at Lancaster and disbanded in February 1918.
7th Bn The East Lancashire Regt. Formed at Preston and disbanded in February 1918.
7th Bn The Prince of Wales's Volunteers (South Lancashire Regt). Formed at Warrington and disbanded in February 1918.
7th Bn The Loyal North Lancashire Regt. Formed at Preston and disbanded in February 1918.
9th Bn the Cheshire Regt. Joined from 58th Brigade in February 1918.
1/4th Bn The King's (Shropshire Light Infantry). A Territorial Force battalion which joined from the 63rd Division in February 1918.
8th Bn The Prince of Wales's (North Staffordshire Regt). Joined from the 57th Brigade in February 1918.

*57th Brigade*
10th Bn The Royal Warwickshire Regt. Formed at Warwick.
8th Bn The Gloucestershire Regt. Formed at Bristol.

*Pte John Kelsall, 7th Bn, Loyal North Lancashire Regt. Pte Kelsall was a Battalion Scout (see arm-badge) and was killed at Pozières Ridge on 23 July 1916.*

10th Bn The Worcestershire Regt. Formed at Worcester. Reduced to a training cadre in June 1918 and later merged with the 17th Worcesters, then pioneer battalion with the 40th Division.

8th Bn The Prince of Wales's (North Staffordshire Regt). Formed at Lichfield and transferred to the 56th Brigade in February 1918.

3rd Bn The Worcestershire Regt. A Regular Army battalion which joined from the 25th Division in June 1918.

### 58th Brigade

9th Bn The Cheshire Regt. Formed at Chester and transferred to 56th Brigade in February 1918.

9th Bn The Royal Welsh Fusiliers. Formed at Wrexham.

5th Bn The South Wales Borderers. Formed at Brecon and in January 1915 became the divisional pioneer battalion.

9th Bn The Welsh Regt. Formed at Cardiff.

6th Bn The Duke of Edinburgh's (Wiltshire Regt). Formed at Devizes and attached to the Division as Army Troops. Became part of 58th Brigade in January 1915 as a replacement for the 5th South Wales

Borderers. Amalgamated with the Royal Wiltshire Yeomanry in September 1917 and from then on was known as 6th (Royal Wiltshire Yeomanry) Battalion. Reduced to a training cadre in May 1918 and later became part of the 14th Division.

2nd Bn The Duke of Edinburgh's (Wiltshire Regt). A Regular Army battalion which joined from the 30th Division in May 1918.

### Pioneers

5th Bn The South Wales Borderers. Became pioneer battalion in January 1915, having been with 58th Brigade since formation.

The divisional field artillery brigades were numbered 86th, 87th, 88th and 89th, while the three engineer field companies were 81st, 82nd and 94th. The 154th-157th Companies, Army Service Corps made up the divisional train and 57th, 58th and 59th Field Ambulances were included in the medical units.

*HM The King talking to Capt E. Jordan of the 10th Worcestershire Regt, France 1918.*  Imperial War Museum

The mobile veterinary section attached was the 31st. 'C' Squadron, 1/1st Yorkshire Dragoons formed part of the Division between June 1915 and April 1916.

On 23 June 1915 the Division was inspected by HM The King, who commented that it was as good as any of the New Army that he had seen. Orders to move to the Western Front were later received and on 11 July an advance party left for France.

Having reached France and concentrated around St Omer, the Division, like others of the New Armies during their first weeks on the Western Front, spent its time in training and gaining experience in trench

*An artist's impression (M. Dovaston) of Temporary Lt T. O. L. Wilkinson, 7th Loyal North Lancashire Regt, winning the VC at La Boisselle, 5 July 1916.*

warfare. On 25 September New Army divisions were used for the first time in a major attack. This took place at Loos and until 2 October the 19th Division, together with the Indian Corps, fought its first battle.

During 1916 the 19th Division was involved in a number of the major actions of the Somme Offensive. It helped with the capture of La Boisselle, where three Victoria Crosses were won, between 2-5 July, and later that month suffered heavy casualties at High Wood and Pozières Ridge. The year ended with the severe fighting that took place around the Ancre River.

The three La Boisselle VCs were Pte T. G. Turrall (10th Worcesters); Lt T. O. L. Wilkinson (7th Loyal North Lancs); and Temp/Lt-Col Adrian Carton de Wiart. The latter was a remarkable man, a regular soldier who had been twice wounded in South Africa. While serving with the Somaliland Camel Force between July 1914 and March 1915, he lost an eye and was awarded the DSO. Then, after going to the Western Front, he was wounded several times in Flanders and eventually lost his left hand at Zonnebeke. As Commanding Officer of the 8th Glosters he showed great gallantry and leadership at La Boisselle.

After spending the best part of the first half of 1917 resting and training, the Division again saw action, between 7-14 June, at Messines. Later, in September, the Third Battle of Ypres had already begun, and on 20 September the Division went into action at the Menin Road Ridge. Subsequent engagements in the area included Polygon Wood (26 September-3 October), Broodseinde (4 October), Poelcappelle (9 October) and the two battles of Passchendaele (12 October-10 November).

Due to the heavy casualties suffered during the last months of the previous year, the commencement of 1918 saw the reorganisation of the Division on a nine-battalion basis. All of 56th Brigade's four Lancashire battalions were disbanded and their places taken by units from 57th and 58th Brigades and a Territorial Force battalion of the King's Shropshire Light Infantry.

The Germans began their 1918 offensive in Picardy and the Somme in March. The 19th Division at this time were in position by St Quentin and were to take the main force of the attack between 21-23 March. With the onslaught curbed in Picardy, the Germans turned their objectives to Flanders and the Lys. Throughout the month of April the Division was engaged at Messines, Bailleul and Kemmel Ridge and from 29 May-6 June fought at the battle of the Aisne.

The Division was moved out of the line and sent back for rest and reinforcements until October. On the 18 October it commenced its advance to victory and saw its last battles at the Selle, Sambre River and Grande Honnelle. The advance continued through Malplaquet, but on 9 November a halt was called and the troops passed into Corps Reserve, west of Bavai. Demobilisation began at the end of December and the last units had returned to England by the middle of March 1919. Casualties throughout the war amounted to 39,381 killed, wounded and missing.

# 20th
## (LIGHT)
# DIVISION

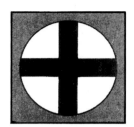

### 20th (Light) Division
Divisional sign: A white disk bearing a red cross with a black bull's-eye in the centre.

The 20th (Light) Division was the last division to be formed for the Second New Army. With battalions from light infantry and rifle regiments, it began to assemble during September 1914 in the Aldershot area.

### 59th Brigade
10th and 11th Bns The King's Royal Rifle Corps. Formed at Winchester. The 10th was disbanded in February 1918.
10th and 11th Bns The Rifle Brigade (The Prince Consort's Own). Formed at Winchester. The 10th was disbanded in February 1918.
2nd Bn The Cameronians (Scottish Rifles). A Regular Army battalion which joined the Brigade from the 8th Division in February 1918.

*Signal Section, 6th Bn, King's (Shropshire Light Infantry).*
D. Barnes

### 60th Brigade
6th Bn The Oxfordshire and Buckinghamshire Light Infantry. Formed at Oxford and disbanded in February 1918.
6th Bn The King's (Shropshire Light Infantry). Formed at Shrewsbury.
12th Bn The King's Royal Rifle Corps. Formed at Winchester.
12th Bn The Rifle Brigade (The Prince Consort's Own). Formed at Winchester.

### 61st Brigade
7th Bn Prince Albert's (Somerset Light Infantry). Formed at Taunton.
7th Bn The Duke of Cornwall's Light Infantry. Formed at Bodmin.
7th Bn The King's Own (Yorkshire Light Infantry). Formed at Pontefract and disbanded in February 1918.
11th Bn The Durham Light Infantry. Formed at Newcastle and became the divisional pioneer battalion in January 1915.
12th Bn The King's (Liverpool Regt). Formed at

*11th Bn, Durham Light Infantry. This was the divisional pioneer battalion and the subject of this photograph wears the pioneers' collar badge – a crossed pick-axe and rifle.*
A. Gavaghan

Seaforth, Liverpool and allotted to the 20th Division as Army Troops. Joined the Brigade as a replacement for the 11th DLI in January 1915.

*Pioneers*
11th Bn The Durham Light Infantry. Became the pioneer battalion in January 1915 having been part of 61st Brigade since formation.

The four field artillery brigades were numbered as 90th, 91st, 92nd, 93rd. Engineers were 83rd, 84th and 96th Field Companies and the divisional train consisted of the 158th-161st Companies, Army Service Corps. The 60th, 61st and 62nd Field Ambulances were the Division's medical units and the veterinary services were provided by the 32nd Mobile Section. Part of the 1/1st Westmorland and Cumberland Yeomanry were attached to the Division between June 1915 and April 1916.

By June 1915 the Division's war training was almost complete. The King made an inspection at Knighton Down on 24 June and within four weeks advance parties were on their way to France.

The Division completed its concentration in an area to the west of St Omer on 26 July 1915. It underwent the usual training in trench warfare and took a share of duty in the line near Fleurbaix.

The Battle of Loos began on 25 September 1915 after a period of heavy bombardment by the British.

*An officer of the Rifle Brigade giving refreshment to German prisoners after the battle of St Quentin, 22-23 March 1918.*
Imperial War Museum

The Division was one of the first of the New Armies to take part in a major offensive on the Western Front and was occupied in the attack towards Fromelles.

In January 1916 the Division was moved to Second Army area and the Ypres Salient. For the following month it took its turn in the front line and was subject to numerous attacks from the enemy. On 2 June the Germans attacked and took Mount Sorrel, just north-east of Hill 60. During the following ten days the Division fought alongside Canadian troops, and on 13 June was successful in recapturing that area.

The 1916 offensive on the Somme began on 1 July and on the following 21 August the Division entered the battle at Delville Wood. This lasted until 3 September when the next two days were spent fighting around Guillemont. It was at Guillemont that Sgt David Jones of the 12th King's Liverpools gained the Victoria Cross. His officer having been killed, Sgt Jones took command of his platoon and subsequently held a forward position for two days and nights. He was under heavy fire the whole time and on the second day held off three counter-attacks by the enemy.

On 16 September the men of the Division went into action at Flers and were among the first infantry to serve with tanks in battle. The remaining Somme battles of 1916 in which the 20th (Light) Division took part were at Morval (27 September) and the action at the Transloy Ridges in front of Bapaume between 1-8 October.

In the early months of 1917 the Division was involved in the British advance (11 January-13 March) and subsequent German retreat (14 March-5 April) to the Hindenburg Line. Later it took part in the numerous actions on the Line between 26 May-16 June.

During August and September 1917 the Division saw a great deal of action in the Ypres Sector. The Battle of Langemarck, where two Victoria Crosses were won, took place between 16-18 August, followed by engagements at the Menin Road Ridge and Polygon Wood, 20-28 September.

Another Victoria Cross was won by a member of the Division on 20 November 1917, the first day of the Battle of Cambrai. This was a successful surprise attack and was the first major action in which tanks took part. The 20th Division advanced with the tanks and between 23-28 November attacked and captured Bourlon Wood. The Germans began a counter-attack on 30 November and until 3 December the 20th Division inflicted heavy casualties on the enemy while defending its positions.

The Division spent the remainder of 1917, and the first months of 1918, out of the line and on 21 March, when the Germans launched their offensive in Picardy, were in reserve around Nesle. On 22 March the Division fought at the Battle of St Quentin. The actions at the Somme Crossings followed on 24-25 March, and then on the 26th a major engagement was fought at Rosières.

The Division was again withdrawn from action on 20 April, moving into an area ten miles south-west of Amiens. During the following months reinforcements were received and by October the Division was ready to take its part in the final advance to victory. By the time of the Armistice, Headquarters had reached Feignies and on 2 December a general withdrawal through Cambrai had been effected. Demobilisation began in January 1919 and the last units left for England in the following May. During the war the Division lost 35,470 killed, wounded and missing.

# 21st
## DIVISION

**21st Division**
Divisional sign: Three sevens (total twenty-one) joined at the base.

The formation of the Third New Army was authorised by Army Order 388 of 13 September 1914. This sanctioned the raising of six more divisions which received the numbers 21st to 26th. The senior division, the 21st, was commanded by Lt-Gen Sir E. T. H. Hutton and its original infantry brigades numbered 62nd, 63rd and 64th. In July 1916, after the fighting on the Somme, the 63rd Brigade was transferred complete

in exchange for 110th Brigade of the 37th Division.

*62nd Brigade*
12th and 13th Bns The Northumberland Fusiliers. Formed at Newcastle and amalgamated as 12th/13th in August 1917.
8th Bn The East Yorkshire Regt. Formed at Beverley and transferred to the 3rd Division in November 1915.
10th Bn Alexandra, Princess of Wales's Own (Yorkshire Regt). Formed at Richmond and disbanded in February 1918.
1st Bn The Lincolnshire Regt. A Regular Army

battalion which joined from the 3rd Division in exchange for 8th East Yorks in November 1915. This battalion contained a contingent from the Burmuda Rifle Volunteer Corps.

3/4th Bn The Queen's (Royal West Surrey Regt). A Territorial Force battalion which joined as a replacement for 13th Northumberland Fusiliers in August 1917. Disbanded in February 1918.

2nd Bn The Lincolnshire Regt. A Regular Army battalion which joined from the 8th Division as a replacement for 3/4th Queen's in February 1918.

### 63rd Brigade

8th Bn The Lincolnshire Regt. Formed at Lincoln.

8th Bn Prince Albert's (Somerset Light Infantry). Formed at Taunton.

12th Bn The Prince of Wales's Own (West Yorkshire Regt). Formed at York and transferred to the 3rd Division in November 1915.

10th Bn The York and Lancaster Regt. Formed at Pontefract.

4th Bn The Duke of Cambridge's Own (Middlesex Regt). A Regular Army battalion which joined from the 3rd Division in exchange for 12th West Yorks in November 1915.

### 64th Brigade

9th and 10th Battalion The King's Own (Yorkshire Light Infantry). Formed at Pontefract. The 10th was disbanded in February 1918.

14th and 15th Bns The Durham Light Infantry. Formed at Newcastle. The 14th Battalion was transferred to the 6th Division in November 1915.

1st Bn The East Yorkshire Regt. A Regular Army battalion which joined from the 6th Division in

*8th Bn, Lincolnshire Regt, 1914.*

exchange for 14th Durham Light Infantry in November 1915.

### 110th Brigade

6th, 7th, 8th, 9th Bns The Leicestershire Regt. All battalions were formed at Leicester in September 1914. The 8th was reduced to a cadre in June 1918 and later transferred to the 25th Division. The 9th was absorbed into the other battalions in February 1918.

1st Bn The Duke of Edinburgh's (Wiltshire Regt). A Regular Army battalion which joined from the 25th Division as a replacement for 8th Leicesters in June 1918.

### Pioneers

14th Bn The Northumberland Fusiliers. Formed at Newcastle.

The four field artillery brigades were numbered 94th, 95th, 96th and 97th and the engineer field companies were 97th, 98th and 126th. The original two field companies were the 85th and 86th, but these were transferred to the 10th and 11th Divisions respectively in February 1915. The 182nd-185th Companies, Army Service Corps made up the divisional train and medical units were 63rd, 64th and 65th Field Ambulances. 'A' Squadron, South Irish Horse was attached to the Division between September 1915 and May 1916.

Having moved from its original assembly area in Hertfordshire to Aldershot in July 1915, the Division began its move to France on 2 September 1915 and by the 13th was concentrated west of St Omer. After additional training in trench warfare, the Division soon took part in its first major battle, when on 25th September it went into action at Loos.

After Loos the Division was withdrawn from the front and sent for training at Armentières. In

November, in accordance with a new scheme in which New Army units were to be interchanged with Regular Army battalions, one battalion from each brigade was transferred to the 3rd Division.

From July to October 1916 the 21st Division played its part in the Somme Offensive of that year. On 1 July it attacked by Fricourt and after three days of heavy fighting throughout the Battle of Albert, it was relieved. At this time the 63rd Brigade, owing to severe casualties, was transferred to the 37th Division in exchange for 110th Brigade.

With its replacement for the 63rd Brigade, the Division returned to the battle on 11 July. It then went on to fight at Bazentine Ridge, Flers-Courcelette, Morval, Gueudecourt and the Transloy Ridges.

Between 29 March-5 April 1917 the Division took part in a number of engagements during the German retreat to the Hindenburg Line. The Arras battles followed, including the great Scarpe actions where two Victoria Crosses were won and then in September-November, the Division fought at Polygon Wood, Broodseinde and Passchendaele on the Ypres Salient.

Before the end of 1917 the 21st Division was involved in the German counter-attacks at Cambrai. On 3 December Capt Arthur Lascelles of the 3rd Durham Light Infantry and now attached to the 15th Battalion, was severely wounded while defending an important position at Masnières. Capt Lascelles, who had previously won the Military Cross on the Somme in 1916, was later awarded the Victoria Cross for his gallantry and leadership.

The Germans commenced their great attack in Picardy on 21 March 1918. The Division engaged the enemy around St Quentin until the 23rd and then on

*An artist's impression (A. Pearse) of Temporary Maj Stewart Walter Loudoun-Shand, 10th Yorkshire Regt, winning the VC near Fricourt, 1 July 1916.*

*12th Bn, West Yorkshire Regt. Note '12 W.Y.' arm band.*
A. Gavaghan

the following day fought at Bapaume. During the March offensive a number of composite forces from the 21st Division served with the 35th and 3rd Australian Divisions.

Having been contained in Picardy, the Germans then began a new offensive in Flanders. This lasted from 9-29 April and during this period the Division fought at Messines, Bailleul, Kemmel Ridge and Scherpenberg.

The Division was next engaged at the Battle of the Aisne, between 27-30 May, and then, during the advance to victory, again at Albert and Bapaume. Actions on the Hindenberg Line followed in September-October and on 23-25 October the Division fought its last major action at Selle where it added another Victoria Cross to its list, that of Lt-Col Harry Greenwood, DSO, MC, 9th King's Own Yorkshire Light Infantry.

On 5 November Berlaimont was captured and after a further two days' advance the Division was relieved in the front line at Eclaibes. During December a move back to south of the Somme took place. Here a training programme was introduced, combined with a period of rest and education. Demobilisation commenced in January 1919 and week by week a steady flow of men returned home. During the war the 21st Division lost 55,581 killed, wounded and missing.

# 22nd
## DIVISION

**22nd Division**
Divisional sign: A black strip.

The 22nd Division was formed in September 1914 and included battalions from Lancashire, Cheshire, Shropshire and Wales. The three infantry brigades were numbered 65th, 66th and 67th and were organised as follows:

*65th Brigade*
9th Bn The King's Own (Royal Lancaster Regt). Formed at Lancaster.
14th Bn The King's (Liverpool Regt). Formed at Seaforth, Liverpool. Left the Division in June 1918 and joined the 66th Division in France.
12th Bn The Lancashire Fusiliers. Formed at Bury. Transferred to France and the 66th Division in July 1918.

9th Bn The East Lancashire Regt. Formed at Preston.
8th Bn The South Wales Borderers. Joined from 67th Brigade in June 1918 as a replacement for 14th King's.

*66th Brigade*
9th Bn The Border Regt. Formed at Carlisle and became the divisional pioneer battalion in February 1915.
9th Bn The Prince of Wales's Volunteers (South Lancashire Regt). Formed at Warrington.
8th Bn The King's (Shropshire Light Infantry). Formed at Shrewsbury.
13th Bn The Manchester Regt. Formed at Ashton-under-Lyne and transferred to the 66th Division in France in June 1918.

*Recruits, 11th Bn, Welsh Regt, Cardiff 1914. Note mouth-organ player at the head of the column.* Welch Regt Museum

12th Bn Cheshire Regt. Formed at Chester and attached to the Division as Army Troops. Joined the Brigade in February 1915 as replacement for 9th Border.

*67th Brigade*
11th Bn The Royal Welsh Fusiliers. Formed at Wrexham.
7th and 8th Bns The South Wales Borderers. Formed at Brecon. The 8th Battalion was transferred to the 65th Brigade in June 1918.
11th Bn Welsh Regt. Formed at Cardiff.

*Pioneers*
9th Bn The Border Regt. Became the pioneer battalion in February 1915, having been part of 66th Brigade.

Artillery brigades were numbered 98th, 99th, 100th and 101st and the three engineer field companies were 99th, 100th and 127th. Originally the engineers were 87th and 88th, but these were transferred to the 12th and 13th Divisions respectively at the beginning of 1915. The 186th to 189th Companies, Army Service Corps made up the divisional train while the 66th, 67th and 68th Field Ambulances provided medical services. The 34th Mobile Veterinary Section also formed part of the Division as did 'D' Squadron, 1/1st Lothians and Border Horse between June 1915 and November 1916.

The Division first concentrated in Sussex and in June 1915 moved to Aldershot for its final intensive training. On 3 September an advance party left for France. The remainder of the Division followed over

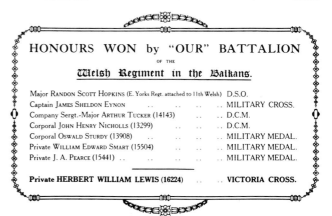

*Cover of magazine published by the 11th Bn, Welsh Regt, Feb 1917.* Welch Regt Museum

*9th Bn, East Lancashire Regt in Sussex, 1915.* D. Barnes

*Members of the Sgts' Mess, 8th Bn, King's (Shropshire Light Infantry) 1915.*   D. Barnes

*Member of the 8th Bn, South Wales Borderers outside his billet in Hastings, 1915.*   B. Nevison

the next few days, and by 9 September all units were positioned around Flesselles, north of Amiens and under the command of Maj-Gen The Hon F. Gordon. On 18 September the Division took over from French units, part of the front line on the Amiens-St Quentin Road.

The Division retained these positions until 23 October when, as a result of orders received on the 20th, it began to make ready for a move to the Macedonian theatre of war.

Embarkation for Salonika began on 27 October. Some units did not leave France until quite late, however, and the last artillery brigade did not arrive until 13 December. Between 8-13 December, part of Divisional Headquarters, the 65th Brigade, the pioneers and 68th Field Ambulance, were engaged in the operations that took place during the retreat from Serbia.

Things remained relatively quiet in Macedonia until mid-August 1916 when an attack made on positions at Horseshoe Hill, two-and-a-quarter miles south-west of Doiran, involved the 22nd Division in some fierce hand-to-hand fighting.

On 13-14 September a further action was fought at Machukovo. Later, on 22-23 October, a party from the 11th Welsh Regiment carried out a successful raid on the enemy's positions at the Dorsale Heights. Again, some intense fighting took place and one of the battalion, Private Hubert Lewis, gained the Victoria Cross for his gallantry.

British troops took little part in the fighting on the Macedonian front during 1917. The 22nd Division were engaged at the Doiran battles, 24-25 April and 8-9 May and in the following year fought in the same area on 18-19 September. On 18 September Lt-Col Daniel Burges, an officer of the Gloucestershire Regiment

then commanding the 7th South Wales Borderers, gained the Victoria Cross for his gallantry and leadership that day. The Division was further honoured when the French Government awarded the *Croix de Guerre* to both the 12th Cheshires and 7th South Wales Borderers.

In June 1918, due to the heavy casualties incurred during the German offensive on the Somme, three battalions were withdrawn from the 22nd Division and moved to the Western Front.

On 22 September, the Division advanced and occupied the line between Lake Doiran and 'P' Ridge. The advance continued and on 30 September an armistice with Bulgaria brought hostilities to a close.

On 11 October the Division began to move southward to Stavros where it proceeded to Dede Agach to take up operations against the Turks. However, the Armistice with Turkey came into force at noon on 31 October and no further activity took place.

Demobilisation began in January 1919 and the existence of the 22nd Division eventually came to a close in the following March. The total losses of the 22nd Division were 7,728 killed, wounded and missing.

*Advertisement for souvenir badge produced in order to raise funds for the 11th Bn, Welsh Regt.*   Welch Regt Museum

*11th Bn, Welsh Regt, Salonika 1916.*   Welch Regt Museum

# 23rd
## DIVISION

**23rd Division**

Divisional sign: A red Maltese Cross within a red circle.

The 23rd Division of the Third New Army was formed during September 1914 and first assembled in the Aldershot area under the command of Maj-Gen J. M. Babington. The three infantry brigades were numbered 68th, 69th, 70th and were organised as follows:

*68th Brigade*

10th and 11th Bns The Northumberland Fusiliers. Formed at Newcastle.

12th and 13th Bns The Durham Light Infantry. Formed at Newcastle. The 13th Battalion returned to France on 14 September 1918 where it joined the 25th Division.

*69th Brigade*

11th Bn The Prince of Wales's Own (West Yorkshire Regt). Formed at York.

8th and 9th Bns Alexandra, Princess of Wales's Own (Yorkshire Regt). Formed at Richmond. The 9th Battalion returned to France in September 1918 where it joined the 25th Division.

10th Bn The Duke of Wellington's (West Riding Regt). Formed at Halifax.

*70th Brigade*

11th Bn The Sherwood Foresters (Nottinghamshire and Derbyshire Regt). Formed at Derby. Returned to France in September 1918 where it joined the 25th Division.

8th Bn The King's Own (Yorkshire Light Infantry). Formed at Pontefract.

8th and 9th Bns The York and Lancaster Regt. Formed at Pontefract.

*Pioneers*

9th Bn The South Staffordshire Regt. Formed at Lichfield and became the Division's pioneer battalion in December 1914.

The four artillery brigades were numbered 102nd to 105th and the engineer field companies were 101st,

*Pte J. Woodcock, 10th Bn, Northumberland Fusiliers.* D. Barnes

102nd and 128th. When the Division was formed, the engineers were 89th and 90th. However, these companies were transferred to the 14th and 9th Divisions respectively. The divisional train consisted of the 190th-193rd Companies, Army Service Corps and the three field ambulances were 69th, 70th and 71st. Other units of the Division included the 35th Mobile Veterinary Section and part of the 1/1st Duke of Lancaster's Own Yeomanry which was attached between June 1915 and April 1916.

The Division was inspected by Field-Marshal Earl Kitchener on 22 January 1915. A move was made to the Shorncliffe area at the end of February, and in May final intensive training for war began at Bordon and Bramshott.

Orders to move to France were received on 20 August and nine days later the Division was complete around Tilques, north-west of St Omer. Before entering its first major battle in July 1916, a member of the Division – Pte Thomas Kenny of the 13th Durhams – won the Victoria Cross while on patrol near La Houssoie on 4 November 1915.

The 23rd Division entered the 1916 Somme Offensive on 4 July and subsequently fought in the Battle of Albert. On 10 July it captured the stronghold at Contalmaison and until October fought on the Somme at Pozières Ridge, Flers-Courcelette, Morval, the Transloy Ridges and Le Sars. During this period three more Victoria Crosses were gained by men of the Division.

Between 18 October 1915 and 16 July 1916, the 70th Infantry Brigade served with the 8th Division. This was done in an exchange for the 24th Brigade which contained the following Regular Army battalions: 1st Worcestershire, 2nd East Lancashire, 1st Notts and Derby and 2nd Northamptonshire. After the Division's success at Contalmaison it is recorded that the Commander-in-Chief asked General Babington what he would like. He replied: 'Give me back my 70th Brigade.' The 70th were back with the 23rd Division within a week.

From 7 June to 12 October 1917, the 23rd Division were engaged at Messines (7-14 June), the Menin Road Ridge (20-24 September), Polygon Wood (28 September-2 October) and at the First Battle of Passchendaele on 12 October. Yet another Victoria Cross, that of 2/Lt Frederick Youens, 13th Durhams, was gained by the Division during these operations.

The Division came out of the line on 23 October 1917 and on the 31st was informed that it was to move to the Italian Front. Entrainment began later and on 16 November the 23rd Division was concentrated between Mantua and Marcaria. The Division moved forward on 19 November and on 4 December took over the front line on the Montello, behind the River Piave.

On 14 March 1918 the Division was relieved by the 51st (Italian) Division. It then moved westward and on 23 March took over positions on the line of the Asiago Plateau. The Austrian offensive opened on 15 June along the Piave. The 23rd Division held strong defensive positions and was able to repulse the assault by the next day.

In September one battalion from each brigade was ordered back to France where they were to join up and serve with the 25th Division. The final operations of the Italian campaign began with the opening of the Battle of Vittorio Veneto in October. The 23rd, together wtih the 7th Division fought at the Passage of the Piave (26-28 October) and then on 29 October at the Passage of the Monticano. Four Victoria Crosses were gained during the Italian operations.

The Division was put into reserve on 2 November 1918 and at 3pm on the 4th an Armistice with Austria was signed, bringing hostilities to a close on the Italian front. In February 1919 the Army of Occupation in Italy was reduced to a mixed brigade and later the 23rd Division had ceased to exist. During the war the 23rd Division lost 23,574 killed, wounded and missing.

*An artist's impression (J. F. Campbell) of Temporary 2/Lt Donald Simpson Bell, 9th Yorkshire Regt, winning the VC at Horseshoe Trench, 5 July 1916.*

# 24th
## DIVISION

**24th Division**

Divisional sign: Four red triangles inside four white triangles.

The 24th Division formed part of the Third New Army. It began to assemble around Shoreham, Sussex in September 1914 and at first contained the following infantry brigades:

*71st Brigade*
9th Bn The Norfolk Regt. Formed at Norwich.
9th Bn The Suffolk Regt. Formed at Bury St Edmunds.
8th Bn The Bedfordshire Regt. Formed at Bedford.
11th Bn The Essex Regt. Formed at Warley.

*72nd Brigade*
8th Bn The Queen's (Royal West Surrey Regt). Formed at Guildford. Transferred to 17th Brigade in February 1918.

8th Bn The Buffs (East Kent Regt). Formed at Canterbury. Transferred to 17th Brigade in exchange for the 1st North Staffs in October 1915.
9th Bn The East Surrey Regt. Formed at Kingston-on-Thames.
8th Bn The Queen's Own (Royal West Kent Regt). Formed at Maidstone.
1st Bn The Prince of Wales's (North Staffordshire Regt). A Regular Army battalion which transferred from 17th Brigade in October 1915 as an exchange for 8th Buffs.

*73rd Brigade*
12th Bn The Royal Fusiliers (City of London Regt). Formed at Hounslow. Transferred to 17th Brigade in October 1915.

*Drums and Bugles, 7th Bn, Northamptonshire Regt, March 1915.* D. Barnes

*An artist's impression (J. F. Campbell) of Sgt A. F. Saunders, 9th Bn, Suffolk Regt, winning his VC near Loos on 26 Sept 1915. His officer having been wounded, Sgt Saunders took charge of two machine guns and, although severely wounded in the thigh, closely followed the last four charges of another battalion and later covered its retirement.*

*Pte R. W. Estaugh, 9th Bn, East Surrey Regt. This photograph was taken in Germany while Pte Eastaugh was a prisoner of war. He wears the usual service dress jacket with trousers probably issued by his captors.*

9th Bn The Royal Sussex Regt. Formed at Chichester.
7th Bn The Northamptonshire Regt. Formed at Northampton.
13th Bn The Duke of Cambridge's Own (Middlesex Regt). Formed at Mill Hill.
2nd Bn The Prince of Wales's Leinster Regt (Royal Canadians). A Regular Army battalion which transferred from 17th Brigade in October 1915. Transferred to the 16th Division in February 1918.

On 11 October 1915, 71st Brigade was exchanged for the 17th Brigade of the 6th Division. This move was in consequence of the new scheme for the merging of Regular Army battalions into New Army divisions. At this time 17th Brigade contained four Regular Army battalions: 1st Royal Fusiliers, 1st North Staffordshire,

*Staff and Band, 9th Bn, Royal Sussex Regt, March 1915.*

2nd Leinster, 3rd Rifle Brigade, and one Territorial Force battalion, the 2nd London Regiment. In February 1916 the 2nd Londons left the Division. The remaining battalions, by this time, had been reorganised and the eventual 17th Brigade was made up as follows:

*17th Brigade*
8th Bn The Queen's (Royal West Surrey Regt). Transferred from 72nd Brigade in February 1918.
8th Bn The Buffs (East Kent Regt). Transferred from 72nd Brigade in October 1915 and disbanded in February 1918.
1st Bn The Royal Fusiliers (City of London Regt). A Regular Army battalion with the original 17th Brigade.
12th Bn The Royal Fusiliers (City of London Regt). Transferred from 73rd Brigade in October 1915 and disbanded in February 1918.
3rd Bn The Rifle Brigade (The Prince Consort's Own). A Regular Army battalion with the original 17th Brigade.

*Pioneers*
12th Bn The Sherwood Foresters (Nottinghamshire and Derbyshire Regt). Formed at Derby.

The four field artillery brigades were numbered 106th to 109th and the engineer companies 103rd, 104th and 129th. The original field companies were 91st and 92nd but these were transferred to the 15th and 18th Divisions respectively at the beginning of 1915. The divisional train contained the 194th-197th Companies, Army Service Corps, the three field ambulances were 72nd, 73rd and 74th and the mobile veterinary section was numbered 36th. 'A' Squadron, 1/1st Royal Glasgow Yeomanry formed part of the 24th Division between June 1915 and April 1916.

The Division moved from Shoreham to the Aldershot training area in June 1915. Field-Marshal Earl Kitchener inspected the Division on 19 August and this was followed by a visit from HM The King on the 20th. Orders to move overseas were received on 21 August, the troops began to entrain on 28 August and concentration was complete between St Pol and Etaples on 4 September.

Having reached France, the 24th Division was not afforded the usual months of trench warfare training and gradual initiation into active service conditions. Plans were already well advanced for an attack on the enemy's positions around the coal-mining area of Loos and on the night of 25 September the 24th advanced, as part of XI Corps, across the Lens-La Basssée Road towards Hulluch. During the next hours the Division suffered heavy casualties, some 4,178 all ranks, and was subsequently withdrawn from the battle on 26 September. However, on the 26th the Division gained its first Victoria Cross when Sgt A. F. Saunders of the 9th Suffolks showed great bravery and leadership during an attack.

On 14 February 1916, near Hooge, Capt Eric McNair of the 9th Royal Sussex also gained the Victoria Cross for his courage and leadership after the enemy had exploded a mine below his position. The best part of two platoons were killed and although he himself was wounded, Capt McNair quickly organised a party which manned the lip of the crater and subsequently held back the advancing enemy.

In March 1916 the Division was sent to the Wulverghem sector where on 30 April it was subjected to large-scale gas attacks from the enemy. Having moved south in June, the 24th Division entered the Somme offensive on 11 August. It fought at Delville Wood until 2 September and then on 3, 4 and 5 September saw action at Guillemont.

After a period of rest and reorganisation, the Division found itself in the area around Vimy Ridge, where it fought between 9-14 April 1917. The Battle of Messines followed on 7-14 June and then between 31 July-18 August the Division was engaged at the great Ypres battles at Pilckem Ridge and Langemarck. The last action of 1917 took place between 30 November-3 December and involved the 24th Division in the counter-attacks made by the Germans at Cambrai.

When the long expected German attack on the Somme began on 21 March 1918, the 24th Division was in the 'forward zone' around St Quentin and became subject to tremendous bombardment. An attack of great force followed which resulted in most units suffering heavy losses. One member of the Division, L/Cpl John William Sayer, 8th Queen's, was mortally wounded while holding a position at Le Verguier. He was later awarded the Victoria Cross for his bravery and determination that day.

On 24-25 March 1918 the Division was in action around Fonches where the enemy had forced its way across the Somme and was pressing forward. During the following two days the Division fought at Rosières and on 4 April it took part in the Battle of the Avre.

With the Somme battles over, the 24th Division moved into positions around Lens and throughout July, August and September fought a number of minor actions in the area. During this period another two Victoria Crosses were gained when both Lt D. J. Dean, 8th Royal West Kents, and Cpl John McNamara, 9th East Surreys, performed gallantly while holding important positions.

A new British offensive on the Hindenburg Line began on 12 September 1918. The 24th Division entered the Battle of Cambrai on 8 October and between 9-12 October was involved in the pursuit of the enemy to the River Selle. The Division fought at the Battle of the Sambre on 4 November and on the 11th had advanced to one-half mile to the east of the Maubeuge-Mons Road.

For the remainder of November and into December, the Division was employed on salvage work and training. Demobilisation began in January 1919 and by March all men were back in England. Throughout the war the 24th Division lost 35,362 killed, wounded and missing.

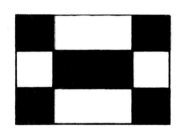

# 25th
## DIVISION

## 25th Division

Divisional sign: The 25th Division had two signs – a red horseshoe was worn on the uniforms, while an oblong of red and white check was painted on vehicles and signboards.

The 25th Division began to assemble around the Salisbury area in September 1914. It contained battalions from Lancashire, Cheshire, Cumberland, Wales and Shropshire and at first contained the following infantry brigades:

*74th Brigade*
11th Bn The Lancashire Fusiliers. Formed at Codford and disbanded in August 1918.
13th Bn The Cheshire Regt. Raised at Port Sunlight by Gershom Stewart, MP. Disbanded in February 1918.
8th Bn The Loyal North Lancashire Regt. Formed at Preston and transferred to 7th Brigade in October 1915.
9th Bn The Loyal North Lancashire Regt. Formed at Preston and transferred to the 50th Division in June 1918.
2nd Bn The Royal Irish Rifles. A Regular Army

battalion which joined from 7th Brigade in October 1915 as an exchange for 8th Loyals. Transferred to the 36th Division in November 1917.
3rd Bn The Worcestershire Regt. A Regular Army battalion which transferred from 7th Brigade in November 1917 as a replacement for 2nd Royal Irish Rifles. Transferred to the 19th Division in June 1918.

*75th Brigade*
10th Bn The Cheshire Regt. Formed at Chester and transferred to 7th Brigade in October 1915.
11th Bn The Cheshire Regt. Formed at Chester. Reduced to a cadre in June 1918 and later disbanded while attached to the 39th Division.
8th Bn The Border Regt. Formed at Carlisle and transferred to the 50th Division in June 1918.
8th Bn The Prince of Wales's Volunteers (South Lancashire Regt). Formed at Warrington and disbanded in February 1918.
2nd Bn The Prince of Wales's Volunteers (South Lancashire Regt). A Regular Army battalion which transferred from 7th Brigade as an exchange for 10th Cheshires in October 1915. Transferred to the 30th Division in June 1918.

*6th Bn, South Wales Borderers, 1915. While waiting for its badges to be issued, this Battalion wore for identification a tin badge bearing the number '6' over the letters 'S.W.B'. The badge can be seen here being worn on the collar.*

*Tin badge worn by 6th Bn, South Wales Borderers in lieu of regimental issue.*

*Charles H. Barr, 155th Brigade, Royal Field Artillery, aged 16 years. Charles Barr joined the RFA at Wetherby, Yorkshire in spring 1915. He went on to spend the next 30 years in the Army and retired as Regimental Sergeant Major of 85th Anti-Tank Regt in 1946. He was taken prisoner by the Japanese at Singapore in Feb 1942.* S. Barr

*76th Brigade*
8th Bn The King's Own (Royal Lancaster Regt). Formed at Lancaster.
13th Bn The King's (Liverpool Regt). Formed at Seaforth, Liverpool.
10th Bn The Royal Welsh Fusiliers. Formed at Wrexham.
7th Bn King's (Shropshire Light Infantry). Formed at Shrewsbury.

On 15 October 1915 the 76th Brigade was exchanged for the 7th Brigade, 3rd Division. The 7th was a Regular Army Brigade and at the time of the exchange contained the following battalions: 3rd Worcestershire, 2nd South Lancashire, 1st Wiltshire and 2nd Royal Irish Rifles. The 2nd South Lancs and 2nd Royal Irish Rifles were, within a few days, transferred to 75th and 74th Brigades respectively. The reorganised 7th Brigade was as follows:

*7th Brigade*
3rd Bn The Worcestershire Regt. Transferred to 74th Brigade in November 1917.
10th Bn The Cheshire Regt. Joined from 75th Brigade in October 1915. Reduced to a cadre in June 1918 and later absorbed into the 15th Battalion, South Wales Borderers.
8th Bn The Loyal North Lancashire Regt. Transferred from 74th Brigade in October 1915 and disbanded in February 1918.
1st Bn The Duke of Edinburgh's (Wiltshire Regt). Transferred to the 21st Division in June 1918.
4th Bn The South Staffordshire Regt. An Extra Reserve battalion which joined in November 1917 as a replacement for 3rd Worcesters. The battalion left the Division in June 1918 and was later disbanded.

*Pioneers*
6th Bn The South Wales Borderers. Formed at Brecon and transferred to the 30th Division in July 1918.

Other units which formed part of the 25th Division included 110th-113th Field Brigades, Royal Field Artillery; 105th, 106th and 130th Field Companies, Royal Engineers. The original engineers were 93rd and 94th and, these were transferred to the 17th and 19th Divisions respectively in January 1915. The Army

*Band, 8th Loyal North Lancashire Regt.*

Service Corps companies were 198th to 201st; medical units were 75th, 76th and 77th Field Ambulances and the mobile veterinary section was the 37th. Part of the 1/1st Lothians and Border Horse joined the Division in England and served until May 1916.

During its early months the Division underwent the usual difficulties in obtaining arms and equipment. A number of red coats were issued to half of the men, who paraded in these coats, drab trousers and civilian head-gear.

Having moved to Aldershot for its final training in May, full equipment and transport soon arrived, but service rifles were not received until August. The Division was inspected by Field-Marshal Earl Kitchener on 12 August. Shortly after, notice to move overseas was received and by 30 September the Division was complete around Nieppe.

After the usual months of war training, patrols and tours of duty at the front, the 25th Division saw its first major action on 21 May 1916 when, as part of XVII Corps, it was involved in the German attack on Vimy Ridge. During this operation Lt Richard Jones of the 8th Loyals was in charge of a platoon holding a recently captured position. Having been cut off, the platoon was then attacked in great numbers. Lt Jones set a fine example to his men and shot fifteen of the enemy before his ammunition ran out. He was just about to throw a bomb when he was hit in the head. For his gallantry and leadership Lt Jones was awarded the Victoria Cross.

The Somme offensive began on 1 July 1916 and two days later the 25th Division entered the Battle of Albert. It remained in action until October and took part in the following engagements: Bazentin Ridge,

*Silk bookmark showing both of the 25th Div signs and commemorating the Div involvement at Messines in June 1917.* S. Barr

*Christmas card (1917) produced by 106th Field Company, Royal Engineers, 25th Div.* S. Barr

*Members of 8th Bn, Border Regt, Codford, November 1914.*

*Part of the programme for a 25th Division Fête held in the area of Allovagne, near Bethune, 26 Sept 1917.*   S. Barr

## PROGRAMME OF EVENTS.

### Part I : Horse Show.

#### JUDGES.

Major-General E. G. T. BAINBRIDGE, C.B.
Brig.-General H. K. BETHELL, D.S.O.
Brig.-General H. B. D. BAIRD, D.S.O.
Colonel Sir S. HILL CHILD, Bart., M.V.O., D.S.O.
Lieut.-Col. H. C. MALET, D.S.O.
Lieut.-Colonel F. J. L. HOWARD, D.S.O.
Lieut.-Colonel O. H. L. NICHOLSON, D.S.O.
Lieut.-Colonel R. F. LEGGE, D.S.O.
Lieut.-Colonel R. M. DODINGTON.
Lieut.-Colonel J. de V. BOWLES, D.S.O.
Major J. P. B. ROBINSON, D.S.O.
Major W. LUDGATE.
Capt. S. C. GRANT.

#### STARTERS.

Major The Hon. W. E. GUINNESS, D.S.O.
Capt. E. K. B. FURZE.

| Officer i/c | Ring " A " | ... | ... | Capt. J. S. FULTON. |
| ,, | Ring " B " | ... | ... | Major N. M. MacLEOD, M.C. |
| ,, | Ring " C " | ... | ... | Capt. S. HAWKINS, M.C. |

The Assembly call will be sounded for each Class by a Bugler.

|  | Result. |  |
|---|---|---|
| CLASS 1.—GRETNA GREEN RACE. RING " A " | Off. | 1 |
| Conditions :—To ride a distance of 300 yards over 3 hurdles, dismount, pick up a dummy, mount and return over hurdles to starting point | | 2 |
| | O.R. | 1 |
| Officer i/c, Capt. N. G. HAY-WILL, M.C. | | 2 |
| | | 3 |

---

A Commemorative Badge
Will be presented to all Ranks on arrival at the Fête ground.

### Field " A."

COCOA-NUT AND " FRIGHTFUL FRITZ " SHIES.
Open from 12 noon to 7 p.m.

### Field " B."

THE DIVISIONAL " PIERROTS."
Performances : 2 p.m. ; 3.30 p.m. ; 6 p.m.

### The Divisional Band and a Massed Band
Drawn from the Units of the Division,
will be in attendance.

### Refreshments
Can be obtained throughout the afternoon.
Tea will be served at 4.30 p.m.

### The Divisional Orchestra
will be in attendance at the Officers' Marquee.

### Prize Distribution.
The prizes will be distributed in FIELD " B " (from an enclosure in front of the Chateau), by the G.O.C. of THE DIVISION at the conclusion of the sports. This distribution will be preceded by A GRAND MARCH, played by the combined bands.

### The Massed Bands
will play at the close of the Fête—
" THE MARSEILLAISE."
" GOD SAVE THE KING."

---

# 25th Divisional Fête.

IN THE FIELD.                    26th SEPTEMBER, 1917.

### COMMENCING AT NOON.

#### PRESIDENT.

Major-General E. G. T. BAINBRIDGE, C.B.

#### VICE-PRESIDENTS.

Brigadier-General H. K. BETHEL, D.S.O.
Brigadier-General K. J. KINCAID-SMITH, C.M.G., D.S.O.
Brigadier-General H. B. D. BAIRD, D.S.O.
Brigadier-General C. J. GRIFFIN, D.S.O.

#### COMMITTEE.

Lieut.-Colonel F. J. L. HOWARD, D.S.O.
Lieut.-Colonel O. H. L. NICHOLSON, D.S.O.
Lieut.-Colonel R. F. LEGGE, D.S.O.
Lieut.-Colonel R. J. DONE, D.S.O.
Major J. P. B. ROBINSON, D.S.O.
Major W. LUDGATE.
Captain F. J. NEY, M.C.
Captain A. REISS.

HARRISON AND SONS,
Printers in Ordinary to His Majesty,
ST. MARTIN'S LANE, LONDON, W.C. 2.

*Members of the 8th Bn, Loyal North Lancashire Regt with their friends and families. A special arm band is being worn denoting the men's battalion and regiment.* M. Ingrey

Pozières Ridge, Mouquet Farm, the Ancre Heights, Stuff Redoubt and Regina Trench.

The Division fought as part of II Anzac Corps at the Battle of Messines between 7-14 June 1917. Six weeks later the Third Battle of Ypres began and the 25th was involved in the main British attack at Pilckem Ridge between 31 July-2 August and the capture of Westhoek on 10 August.

With the opening in March of the 1918 German offensive on the Somme, the Division went into action at St Quentin and on 24-25 March fought gallantly at Bapaume. After a lull in the fighting a new attack, which was to last for just over a fortnight, was started by the enemy on 9 April in Flanders. During this period, which became known as the Battle of The Lys, the Division took part in the following operations: Estaires (74th Brigade), Messines (less 74th Brigade), Hill 63 (7th Brigade), Bailleul, Kemmel Ridge and the Scherpenberg.

After the Battle of the Aisne (27 May-6 June) the 25th Division, due to severe losses, was ordered back to England. On 30 June 1918 the remnants of the Division crossed the Channel and made for Mytchett Camp, Aldershot. Shortly after, the 75th Brigade was reformed with 17th King's Liverpools, 6th and 13th Yorkshire and 11th Royal Sussex. The Brigade was

then renumbered as 236th and on 9 September 1918 it left the 25th Division for service in North Russia.

While in England the 25th Division was reconstituted. It moved back to France on 14 September and between 16-19 September was joined by nine battalions withdrawn from divisions then serving in Italy (7th, 23rd and 48th).

The reconstituted 25th Division was organised as follows:

7th Brigade: 9th Devonshire, 20th and 21st Manchester
74th Brigade: 9th Yorkshire, 11th Notts & Derby and 13th Durhams
75th Brigade: 1/8th Royal Warwicksd, 1/5th Glosters and 1/8th Worcesters
*Pioneers:* 11th South Lancashire

Having returned to the Western Front and containing none of its original battalions, the 25th Division took over part of the front line south of Gouy. The Division was later engaged on the Hindenburg Line throughout the early weeks of October and then, until the end of the war, took part in the final advance in Picardy.

After the Armistice had brought hostilities to a close the Division moved back to Le Cateau where it was employed on salvage work. Demobilisation began in January 1919 and by March the 25th Division had ceased to exist. During the war the 25th Division lost 48,289 killed, wounded and missing.

# 26th
## DIVISION

**26th Division**
Divisional sign: A blue bar.

The 26th Division was the last to be formed within the Third New Army. It began to assemble in Wiltshire during September 1914 and contained the following infantry brigades:

*77th Brigade*
8th Bn The Royal Scots Fusiliers. Formed at Ayr.
11th Bn The Cameronians (Scottish Rifles). Formed at Hamilton.
10th Bn The Black Watch (Royal Highlanders). Formed at Perth. Left the Brigade in July 1918 and later became part of the 66th Division.
12th Bn Princess Louise's (Argyll and Sutherland Highlanders). Formed at Stirling.

*78th Brigade*
9th Bn The Gloucestershire Regt. Formed at Bristol and transferred to the 66th Division in July 1918.
11th Bn The Worcestershire Regt. Formed at Worcester.
7th Bn The Oxfordshire and Buckinghamshire Light Infantry. Formed at Oxford.
7th Bn Princess Charlotte of Wales's (Royal Berkshire Regt). Formed at Reading.

*79th Brigade*
10th Bn The Devonshire Regt. Formed at Exeter.
8th Bn The Duke of Cornwall's Light Infantry. Formed at Bodmin.
12th Bn The Hampshire Regt. Formed at Winchester.
7th Bn the Duke of Edinburgh's (Wiltshire Regt). Formed at Devizes and transferred to the 50th Division in July 1918.

*Pioneers*
8th Bn The Oxfordshire and Buckinghamshire Light Infantry. Formed at Oxford.

The four field artillery brigades were numbered 114th to 117th and the engineer field companies 107th, 108th, 131st. At first, the engineers were 95th and 96th; however, these were transferred to the 16th and 20th Divisions respectively in the early weeks of 1915. The divisional train was made up from the 202nd to 205th Companies, Army Service Corps and field ambulances were numbered 78th, 79th and 80th. The mobile veterinary section attached to the Division was the 38th and between June 1915 and November 1916 'A' Squadron, 1/1st Lothians and Border Horse Yeomanry was attached.

As with other divisions of the New Armies, the 26th in its early months had little or no equipment. Civilian clothing was worn for quite some time and records show that battalions wore coloured cloth patches for identification.

In July 1915 divisional training began and final preparations for overseas service were undertaken. Embarkation orders were received on 10 September and by the 23rd the Division had completed its concentration around Guignemicourt, west of Amiens.

Shortly after arriving in France, brigades and units were attached to other divisions for training and battle experience. However, in October the 26th Division was informed that it was to be moved from the Western Front to the Macedonian theatre.

The Division began to arrive at Salonika on 23 November and by the end of the year was located at the Happy Valley Camp. While en route to Salonika the vessel *Norsemen*, with the divisional train on board, was torpedoed. No loss of life was incurred, but half (some 500) of the Division's mules were lost.

Between 10-18 August 1916 the Division fought its first major engagement of the war. This was the operation at Horseshoe Hill, south-west of Doiran. It was not until April 1917, after the winter of 1916-17 had brought the Allied forces to a standstill, that the Division was again involved in any action.

For the spring, a great attack using the British 22nd and 26th Divisions had been planned. The artillery commenced a bombardment on the enemy's wire and trenches on 21 April and on 24 April the 26th Division made a direct attack across the Jumeaux Ravine. In two days of fighting the Division suffered greatly, both from a severe artillery barrage and a series of counter-attacks by the Bulgarians.

Having withdrawn from the area, the 26th Division went into reserve and for the following two weeks rested and refitted. A new attack was to be made across the Jumeaux Ravine on the night of 8 May. Again the Division was involved in a two-day engagement, and once more it was unable to make much headway.

Operations having closed down due to the intense

heat of the Macedonian summer, the Division saw little action for the remainder of 1917. Likewise, during the first nine months of 1918, little of great importance happened to the British Army in Macedonia. However, in July one battalion from each brigade (10th Black Watch, 9th Gloster, 7th Wiltshire) was withdrawn, and transferred to France.

Further fighting took place at Doiran on 18-19 September, the Division once more being heavily involved. Unlike the operations in this area of the previous year, the new offensive was a great success. The enemy in retreat, a general advance was then ordered towards the Strumica Valley.

The Armistice bringing hostilities to an end with Bulgaria was signed at noon on 30 September 1918. The following month the Division began to move towards the Turks at Adrianople, but on 31 October operations in that theatre of war were also brought to a close. During the war the 26th Division lost 8,022 killed, wounded and missing.

# 30th
## DIVISION

**30th Division**
Divisional sign: The Derby Crest.

This division was at first numbered as 37th and comprised the 110th, 111th and 112th infantry brigades. When the original Fourth New Army was broken up in April 1915, the 37th Division was renumbered as 30th. At the same time its 110th and 111th Brigades became 89th and 90th respectively, while the 112th was transferred to the 35th Division (new) in exchange for that division's 126th Brigade. Upon joining the 30th Division, 126th Brigade was renumbered 91st. In December 1915, 91st Brigade was then exchanged for 21st Brigade, 7th Division.

The 30th was the first of the Pals Divisions. One brigade (the 89th) consisted entirely of men from Liverpool, while the other two were made up of seven battalions from Manchester and one from Oldham.

*89th Brigade*
17th Bn The King's (Liverpool Regt) (1st City). Raised in Liverpool by Lord Derby and transferred to the 25th Division in June 1918.
18th Bn The King's (Liverpool Regt) (2nd City). Raised in Liverpool by Lord Derby. Transferred to 21st Brigade in December 1915 but returned to the 89th in February 1918. Moved to the 66th Division in June 1918.
19th Bn The King's (Liverpool Regt) (3rd City).

*21st Bn, Manchester Regt (6th City) at Belton Park Camp, Grantham, June 1915.* D. Barnes

*Civilians constructing huts for the Liverpool Pals.* D. Barnes

Raised in Liverpool by Lord Derby and transferred to the 66th Division in June 1918.

20th Bn The King's (Liverpool Regt) (4th City). Raised in Liverpool by Lord Derby and disbanded in February 1918.

2nd Bn The Bedfordshire Regt. A Regular Army battalion which joined from 21st Brigade in December 1915. Transferred to 90th Brigade in February 1918.

*90th Brigade*
16th Bn The Manchester Regt (1st City). Raised by the Lord Mayor and City of Manchester and transferred to the 14th Division in June 1918.

17th Bn The Manchester Regt (2nd City). Raised by the Lord Mayor and City of Manchester and transferred to 21st Brigade in February 1918.

18th Bn The Manchester Regt (3rd City). Raised by the Lord Mayor and City of Manchester and disbanded in February 1918.

19th Bn The Manchester Regt (4th City). Raised by the Lord Mayor and City of Manchester and transferred to 21st Brigade in December 1915.

2nd Bn The Royal Scots Fusiliers. A Regular Army battalion which joined from 21st Brigade in exchange for the 19th Manchesters in December 1915. Moved to the 9th Division in April 1918.

2nd Bn The Bedfordshire Regt. A Regular Army battalion which transferred from 89th Brigade in February 1918 and moved to the 18th Division in the following May.

*91st Brigade*
20th, 21st, 22nd Bns The Manchester Regt (5th City), (6th City), (7th City). Raised by the Lord Mayor and City of Manchester.

24th Bn The Manchester Regt (Oldham). Raised by the Mayor and Town of Oldham.

Upon being transferred in December 1915, 21st Brigade comprised four Regular Army battalions: 2nd Bedford, 2nd Yorkshire, 2nd Royal Scots Fusiliers and 2nd Wiltshire. Two of these battalions were exchanged, one each, with battalions of 89th and 90th Brigades.

*21st Brigade*
18th Bn The King's (Liverpool Regt) (2nd City). Joined from 89th Brigade in December 1915 and in September 1917 absorbed 1/1st Lancashire Hussars, assuming the title 18th (Lancashire Hussars Yeomanry) Battalion. The battalion returned to 89th Brigade in February 1918.

2nd Bn Alexandra, Princess of Wales's Own (Yorkshire Regt). Moved to the 11th Division in May 1918.

2nd Bn The Duke of Edinburgh's (Wiltshire Regt). Moved to the 19th Division in May 1918.

19th Bn The Manchester Regt (4th City). Joined from 90th Brigade in December 1915 and disbanded in February 1918.

17th Bn The Manchester Regt (2nd City). Joined from 90th Brigade in February 1918 and moved to the 66th Division in June 1918.

*Pioneers*
11th Bn The Prince of Wales's Volunteers (South Lancashire Regt) (St Helen's Pioneers). Raised by Lord Derby and transferred to the 25th Division in June 1918.

6th Bn The South Wales Borderers. Joined the reconstituted division in July 1918.

The artillery and engineer units were all recruited in

*20th Bn, Manchester Regt (5th City) at Morecambe, Feb 1915.* D. Barnes

Lancashire and bore the additional designation 'County Palatine'. Field artillery brigades were numbered 148th to 151st while the three engineer companies were 200th, 201st and 202nd. The original divisional train consisted of the 213th-216th Companies, Army Service Corps but these were replaced in November 1915 by the 186th-189th. The 96th, 97th and 98th Field Ambulances and 40th Mobile Veterinary Section also formed part of the Division, as did 'D' Squadron, 1/1st Lancashire Hussars between October 1915-May 1916.

The Earl of Derby, who played an important role in raising the original units for the 30th Division, allowed his family crest to be used as its divisional sign. This device, an eagle, was also worn as a cap badge by the Liverpool Pals (17th-20th King's), and as a special incentive Lord Derby gave a silver badge to each man who joined before 16 October 1914.

The Division began to assemble towards the end of April 1915 at Grantham, where by the beginning of September it was complete. Having undergone its final preparation for the field at Larkhill, Salisbury Plain, the Division received orders to move overseas at the end of October. An inspection by Lord Derby took place on 4 November, and by the 12th the 30th Division was concentrated to the north of the Somme at Ailly le Haut Clocher (north-north-west of Amiens).

For the remainder of 1915 and the early months of the following year, the Division spent its time training and getting accustomed to active service conditions. It performed its share of front line duty and was active on numerous raids and patrols.

*L/Cpl Albert Walker, 16th Bn, Manchester Regt (1st City). Albert Walker was later promoted to sergeant and won the MM in France at the beginning of 1918. He died of wounds on 8 April 1918.* D. Barnes

On 1 July 1916, the first day of the Somme offensive, the 30th Division was holding the line just north of Maricourt. It attacked at zero hour and was later involved in the capture of Montauban. In action until 12 July, the Division fought throughout the Battle of Albert, and from 7 July at Trônes Wood.

On 30 July, during an attack on Guillemont, five runners from the 18th Manchesters were killed while attempting to take back an important message. Company Sergeant Major George Evans then volunteered and was subsequently successful in covering the 700yd journey. Although wounded, he then insisted on returning to his company, but on the way he was overcome by the enemy and taken prisoner. CSM Evans was later awarded the Victoria Cross for his conspicuous bravery and devotion duty.

After a period in reserve the Division, on the night of 10-11 October, relieved the 41st Division in the front line north-west of Flers. During the following day, orders were received informing the Division that it was to be included in an attack at Le Transloy. A number of attempts to take enemy positions in this area had commenced on 7 October, but no real advance had been made. Throughout the following week, the Division was engaged but, again, due to appalling conditions and deadly machine-gun fire, little ground was gained.

By March 1917 the 30th Division was serving as part of VII Corps, Third Army, and with that formation took part in operations between 14 March-5 April during the German retreat to the Hindenburg Line. Still with VII Corps, the Division entered the Battle of Arras on 9 April and subsequently fought at both Battles of the Scarpe (9-13 April, 23-24 April).

Having moved to II Corps, Fifth Army – then in the Ypres Sector – the Division fought its last major engagement of 1917 between 31 July-2 August at Pilckem Ridge.

With the opening on 21 March 1918 of the German offensive in Picardy, the Division went into action around St Quentin, and until the end of March was involved in the operations at the Somme Crossings (24-25) and at the Battle of Rosières (26-27). On 21 March another Manchester Regiment man, this time the

*One of the Manchester Pals. The special shoulder title has a '3' in the centre and indicates that the wearer is a member of the 18th Bn, Manchester Regt (3rd City).*

*Pte Sydney Kelly, 18th Manchester Regt. Died of wounds received during the fighting at Trônes Wood, 7-13 July 1916.*
D. Barnes

*19th Bn, King's (Liverpool Regiment) (3rd City), Knowsley Park 1915.* D. Barnes

*The eight Manchester City Bns en route for inspection by Lord Kitchener in March 1915.* D. Barnes

temporary commander of the 16th Battalion – Wilfrith Elstob, received the Victoria Cross. The Colonel, who also held the Distinguished Service Order and Military Cross, was killed during operations at the Manchester Redoubt near St Quentin.

On 7 April 1918 the Germans began their offensive in Flanders, heavily bombarding the British line with gas and high-explosive shells from Lens to Armentières. At this time, due to the heavy casualties suffered during the preceding weeks, only remnants of battalions existed within the Division. In the First Battle of Kemmel Ridge (17-19 April) only the 89th Brigade took part. Then, during the second action in the area (25-26 April) and the Battle of Scherpenberg (29 April) the 89th was joined by a composite brigade made up from the other two.

Between May-July 1918 what was left of the Division's infantry was reduced to cadre strength and transferred to other formations in France. The 30th Division was then reconstituted with two Irish battalions, one each from Cheshire and Lancashire and five from the London Regiment. For the remainder of the war the 30th Division was organised as follows:

*21st Brigade:*
7th Bn Royal Irish Regt.
1/6th Bn Cheshire Regt.
2/23rd Bn London Regt.

*89th Brigade:*
7th/8th Bn Royal Inniskilling Fusiliers.
2nd Bn South Lancashire Regt.
2/17th Bn London Regt.

*90th Brigade:*
2/14 Bn London Regt.
2/15th Bn London Regt.
2/16th Bn London Regt.

*Special Brass shoulder titles worn by the 17th and 18th Bns, King's (Liverpool Regiment) (1st and 2nd City). The 19th and 20th Bns (3rd and 4th City) wore the same pattern, but with the relevant number in the centre.*

*Shoulder title worn by the 24th Bn, Manchester Regt (Oldham).*

*Cap badge worn by the Liverpool Pals.*

*One of the Liverpool Pals (2nd City Bn). Both the special cap badge and shoulder title are seen clearly.* D. Barnes

After reconstruction the new 30th Division played a major role in the advance to victory and the final advance in Flanders. The 89th Brigade distinguished itself at the capture of Neuve Église on 1 September and then on the following day, 21st Brigade was involved in another successful action when it took Wulverghem.

The Division later fought at the Battle of Ypres (28 September-2 October) and between 14-19 October at Courtrai. On 9 November 89th Brigade forced the passage of the Schelde; the Division then advanced through Anseroeuil and reached Renaix by the end of the day. By 11 November, advance parties of 89th Brigade were in positions holding a line from Ghoy-La Livarde (north-west of Lassines).

In January 1919 the Division took over duties at the Base Ports of Dunkirk, Calais and Boulogne. Demobilisation began in the same month but it was not until September that the 30th Division ceased to exist. During the war the 30th Division lost 35,182 killed, wounded and missing

# 31st
## DIVISION

### 31st Division

Divisional sign: Two roses, one red and one white. The Division was made up from Yorkshire and Lancashire units and, in the case of the latter, the red rose overlapped the white. The Yorkshire men, however, wore their sign showing the roses as white over red.

This division was at first known as the 38th and its infantry brigades numbered 113th, 114th and 115th. When the original Fourth New Army was broken up in April 1915, the 38th Division was renumbered as 31st. At the same time the three infantry brigades became 92nd, 93rd and 94th.

In the 92nd Brigade, all four battalions were formed in Hull. The 93rd contained the Leeds and Bradford Pals, together with men from the County of Durham; and the 94th comprised Pals battalions from Accrington, Sheffield and Barnsley.

### 92nd Brigade

10th Bn The East Yorkshire Regt (1st Hull). Raised in Hull by Lord Nunburnholme and the Territorial Force Association of Yorks (East Riding).

11th Bn The East Yorkshire Regt (2nd Hull). Raised in Hull by Lord Nunburnholme and the Territorial Force Association of Yorks (East Riding).

12th Bn The East Yorkshire Regt (3rd Hull). Raised in Hull by Lord Nunburnholme and the Territorial Force Association of Yorks (East Riding). Disbanded in February 1918.

13th Bn The East Yorkshire Regt (4th Hull). Raised in Hull by Lord Nunburnholme and the Territorial Force Association of Yorks (East Riding). Disbanded in February 1918.

11th Bn The East Lancashire Regt (Accrington). Transferred from the 94th Brigade in February 1918.

### 93rd Brigade

15th Bn The Prince of Wales's Own (West Yorkshire Regt) (1st Leeds). Raised by the Lord Mayor and City of Leeds. Amalgamated with the 17th West Yorks from the 35th Division to form the 15/17th Battalion in December 1917.

*Accrington Pals – 11th Bn, East Lancashire Regt at Cannock Chase, May 1915.* D. Barnes

16th Bn The Prince of Wales's Own (West Yorkshire Regt) (1st Bradford). Raised by the Lord Mayor and City of Bradford. Disbanded in February 1918.

18th Bn The Prince of Wales's Own (West Yorkshire Regt) (2nd Bradford). Raised by the Lord Mayor and City of Bradford. Disbanded in February 1918.

18th Bn The Durham Light Infantry (1st County). Raised by Col R. Burdon in the County of Durham.

13th Bn The York and Lancaster Regt (1st Barnsley). Transferred from 94th Brigade in February 1918.

### 94th Brigade

11th Bn The East Lancashire Regt (Accrington). Raised by the Mayor and Town of Accrington. Transferred to 92nd Brigade in February 1918.

12th Bn The York and Lancaster Regt (Sheffield). Raised by the Lord Mayor and City of Sheffield. Disbanded in February 1918.

13th Bn The York and Lancaster Regt (1st Barnsley). Raised by the Mayor and Town of Barnsley. Transferred to 93rd Brigade in February 1918.

14th Bn The York and Lancaster Regt (2nd Barnsley). Raised by the Mayor and Town of Barnsley. Disbanded in February 1918.

The 94th Brigade was broken up and ceased to exist with effect from 17 February 1918. It was replaced by the 4th Guards Brigade containing – 4th Grenadier, 3rd Coldstream and 2nd Irish until 20 May. Later in the same month a new brigade designated 94th (Yeomanry) was formed from three battalions of the 74th (Yeomanry) Division – 12th Norfolk Regiment, 12th Royal Scots Fusiliers and 24th Royal Welsh Fusiliers.

### Pioneers

12th Bn The King's Own (Yorkshire Light Infantry) (Miners (Pioneers)). Raised in Leeds by the West Yorkshire Coalowners Association.

The original artillery brigades were designated 155th (West Yorkshire), 161st (Yorkshire), 164th (Rotherham) and 168th (Huddersfield). However, these units did not go overseas with the 31st Division and later became part of the 32nd Division in France. The eventual field brigades of the Division were numbered 165th, 169th, 170th, 171st and were raised by the Earl of Derby at Lytham and St Anne's-on-Sea with the sub-title 2nd County Palatine.

*Cap badge of 15th Bn, Prince of Wales's Own (West Yorkshire Regt) (1st Leeds). The Arms of Leeds.*

*Leeds Pals – 15th Bn, West Yorkshire Regt, 1915.* D. Barnes

*12th Bn, The King's Own Yorkshire Light Infantry (Miners (Pioneers)), Farnley Park, Otley, June 1915.*
D. Barnes

Engineer field companies, 210th, 211th, 223rd, and the divisional signals were recruited in Leeds. Medical units were 93rd, 94th, 95th Field Ambulances and the mobile veterinary section was numbered 41st. The original service companies of the Division were 217th-220th but these remained in Egypt when the Division left for France in March 1916. A new train was allotted in France which consisted of the 221st, 222nd, 223rd and 279th Companies. Also forming part of the Division, between November 1915-May 1916 was part of the 1/1st Lancashire Hussars.

Until early in 1915 the men of most units were billeted in their own homes, their training being carried out locally. To one battalion of the Division, the 18th Durham Light Infantry, goes the distinction of being the first of the New Army to come under fire. By October 1914 the 18th Durhams were up to strength and on 16 November sent two companies to Hartlepool to assist with coastal defence. On 15 December word was received that enemy warships might raid the East Coast. The following morning the Durhams were in their positions when three vessels opened fire on the town. Some 1,500 shells were fired, causing heavy casualties among the civilian population. The 18th Durhams themselves had six men killed and ten wounded.

Local training came to an end during the last weeks of May 1915, and in the following months the 31st Division began to assemble at South Camp, Ripon. Orders to embark for France were received on 29 November and within days advance parties were arriving at Folkestone and Dover, but on 2 December new orders were issued sending the Division, instead, to Egypt.

Embarkation for the East began on 7 December, and by the 24th Divisional Headquarters had reached Port Said. The following month the Division moved to Qantara where, until 1 March 1916, it served in No 3 Section, Suez Canal Defences.

The 31st Division was eventually called to France during late February 1916, a build-up in strength on the Western Front taking place for the planned summer offensive. By the middle of March 1916, the 31st Division had completed its concentration south of the Somme, around Hallencourt in VIII Corps area.

After a short period of war training and trench duty, the 31st Division entered the Somme offensive on 1 July and that day took part in the attack at Serre. From their positions directly in front of the village, the 93rd and 94th Brigades attacked at zero hour, the 92nd being held in reserve throughout the day. Within moments of leaving their trenches, the leading waves were cut down by the enemy's machine guns. However, a little success was gained in the early stages, but soon the two brigades were driven back, having suffered terrific losses.

No further operations were carried out until November, when between 13-18 November the Division fought at the Battle of the Ancre. It was on the

Wood on 28 June. It was at Oppy, on 3 May, that 2/Lt John Harrison, 11th East Yorks, was killed while attempting to knock out an enemy machine gun which was holding up the advance of his unit. He was later awarded the Victoria Cross for his bravery and self-sacrifice.

In February 1918 all divisions on the Western Front were reduced in strength from twelve battalions down to nine, this being a necessary move due to the severe British losses that had been incurred in France throughout the previous months. In consequence, the 31st Division lost its 94th Brigade, the Accrington and 1st Barnsley Pals being transferred to the 92nd and 93rd Brigades respectively, while the Sheffield and 2nd Barnsley Battalions were disbanded. For the remainder of the war the third brigade of the 31st Division did not contain any of the original Pals volunteers.

In March 1918 the Division fought in the Battle of St Quentin on the 23rd, Bapaume on 24th and 25th, and at Hamelincourt on the 26th, where Sgt Albert Mountain of the 15th/17th West Yorks won the Victoria Cross. In the Lys operations of April 1918 action was seen at Estaires, Hazebrouck, and at the defence of Nieppe Forest. On 28 June the Division under XI Corps fought at La Becque.

*31st Div Christmas card for 1917. The four cartoons shown in the inside of the card illustrate the Division's training and service in Egypt and France.* P. Blagojevic

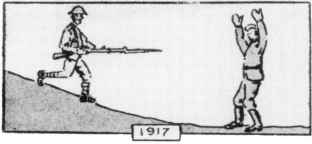

first day of these engagements that Pte John Cunningham of the 12th East Yorks won the Victoria Cross for his brave conduct while bombing an enemy communication trench opposite the Hebuterne Sector.

The 31st Division was again involved in operations on the Ancre River between 22 February and 12 March 1917. The following May it joined the Arras offensive and subsequently fought successful engagements on the Scarpe (3rd and 4th), and at the capture of Oppy

During the 1918 Advance To Victory the Division captured Vieux Berquin on 13 August, and in September and October fought at Ypres and Tieghem. Having crossed the Schelde on 9 November, the Division was located at Renaix at the time of the Armistice. Demobilisation had commenced by the end of 1918 and the last men left for England in May 1919. Casualties throughout the war amounted to 30,091 killed, wounded and missing.

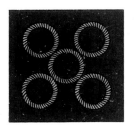

# 32nd
## DIVISION

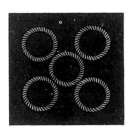

### 32nd Division
Divisional sign: A design representing four eights (thirty-two).

This Division was originally numbered 39th and its infantry brigades 116th, 117th and 118th. On 27 April 1915 the 39th became the 32nd Division and at the same time the 116th and 117th Brigades became 95th and 97th respectively. The 118th was transferred to the 33rd Division (new) and became 98th Brigade. To replace the 118th the 122nd Brigade from the 34th Division (new) joined and received the number 96th.

The battalions of the Division were recruited over much of England and in Scotland. In the West, Bristol formed a battalion, while over in the Midlands, Birmingham supplied three battalions of Pals. Newcastle and Gateshead formed a committee that was successful in providing a battalion of the Northumberland Fusiliers. The Lancashire Fusiliers received three battalions from Salford and the Border Regiment were given men from Carlisle, Kendal and

Workington. North of the border, three battalions from Glasgow, which included workers from the City's public transport, members of the Boys Brigade and business men, joined the Highland Light Infantry.

On 26 December 1915 the four battalions of the 95th Brigade were transferred in exchange for the Staff of 14th Brigade, along with four battalions of the 5th Division. The battalions which joined from the 5th Divisions were all Regulars – 2nd Royal Inniskilling Fusiliers, 1st Dorset, 2nd King's Own Yorkshire Light Infantry and 2nd Manchester. In January 1916 two of these battalions were allotted, one each, to 96th and 97th Brigades in exchange for two New Army units. At first the new brigade was known as 95th but on 7 January 1916 it was designated 14th Brigade, 32nd Division.

*95th Brigade*
14th, 15th, 16th Bns The Royal Warwickshire Regt (1st

*right.*
*Lapel badge worn in civilian clothes by 14th, 15th and 16th Bns, Royal Warwickshire Regt.*

*Band, 16th Bn, Royal Warwickshire Regt (3rd Birmingham), Malvern 1915.*

*The first Church Parade of the 14th Bn, Royal Warwickshire Regt (1st Birmingham), led by their Colonel, Sir John Barnsley. The battalion, in civilian clothes, march behind a police band. Note lapel badges.*

Birmingham), (2nd Birmingham), (3rd Birmingham). The three battalions were raised by the Lord Mayor and City of Birmingham.

12th Bn The Gloucestershire Regt (Bristol). Raised by the Citizen's Recruiting Committee of Bristol.

*96th Brigade*
16th Bn The Northumberland Fusiliers (Newcastle). Raised by the Newcastle and Gateshead Chamber of Commerce and disbanded in February 1918.

15th Bn The Lancashire Fusiliers (1st Salford). Raised by Montague Barlow, MP and the Salford Brigade Committee.

16th Bn The Lancashire Fusiliers (2nd Salford). Raised by Montague Barlow, MP and the Salford Brigade Committee.

19th Bn The Lancashire Fusiliers (3rd Salford). Raised by Montague Barlow, MP and the Salford Brigade Committee. Transferred to 14th Brigade in January 1916.

2nd Bn The Royal Inniskilling Fusiliers. A Regular Army battalion which joined from 14th Brigade in January 1916 as an exchange for 19th Lancashire Fusiliers. Transferred to the 36th Division in February 1918.

2nd Bn The Manchester Regt. A Regular Army battalion which joined from the 14th Brigade in February 1918.

*97th Brigade*
11th Bn The Border Regt (Lonsdale). Raised by the Earl of Lonsdale at Penrith. Reduced to a training cadre in May 1918 and later transferred to the 66th Division.

15th Bn The Highland Light Infantry (1st Glasgow). Raised by the Lord Provost and City of Glasgow. The Battalion was recruited mainly from employees of the Glasgow Tramways. Transferred to the 14th Brigade in January 1916.

16th Bn The Highland Light Infantry (2nd Glasgow). Raised by the Lord Provost and City of Glasgow. The Battalion was recruited mainly from the Glasgow Boys Brigade and on 22 February 1918 became the divisional pioneer battalion.

17th Bn The Highland Light Infantry (3rd Glasgow). Raised by the Glasgow Chamber of Commerce and disbanded in Febaruary 1918.

2nd Bn The King's Own (Yorkshire Light Infantry). A Regular Army battalion which joined from 14th Brigade in January 1916 as an exchange for 15th HLI.

*17th Bn Highland Light Infantry (3rd Glasgow). Some men at the rear are still wearing civilian clothes, whilst the bulk of this company are in the original blue emergency uniform.*   B. Nevison

*One of the Salford Bns, Lancashire Fusiliers training at Conway, North Wales, 1915. Note the two colours of uniform.*   B. Nevison

1/5th (Cumberland) Bn The Border Regt. A Territorial Force battalion which joined the 66th Division in May 1918 as a replacement for 11th Border Regiment.

10th Bn Princess Louise's (Argyll and Sutherland Highlanders). Joined from the 9th Division in February 1918.

*14th Brigade*

19th Bn The Lancashire Fusiliers (3rd Salford). Joined from 96th Brigade in January 1916 and in the following August became the pioneer battalion of the 49th Division.

1st Bn The Dorsetshire Regt. A Regular Army battalion.

*Part of the Cyclist Section from one of the Birmingham Bns, Royal Warwickshire Regt.*

*Guard from one of the Birmingham Bns, Royal Warwickshire Regt.* B. Nevison

2nd Bn The Manchester Regt. A Regular Army battalion. Transferred to 96th Brigade in February 1918.

15th Bn The Highland Light Infantry (1st Glasgow). Transferred from 97th Brigade in January 1916.

5th/6th Bn The Royal Scots (Lothian Regt). A battalion of the Territorial Force which joined the Brigade in July 1916.

*Pioneers*

17th Bn The Northumberland Fusiliers (NER, Pioneers). Raised by the North Eastern Railway. The battalion served as railway construction troops from 19 October 1916 to 2 September 1917 then between 15 November 1917 and 31 May 1918. The battalion later trasferred to the 52nd Division.

16th Bn The Highland Light Infantry (2nd Glasgow).

*14th Bn Royal Warwickshire Regt (1st Birmingham), marching past saluting base in Victoria Square, Birmingham, 13 March 1915.*   D. Barnes

*16th Bn, Royal Warwickshire Regt (3rd Birmingham) at Malvern 1915. The battalion's distinctive shoulder titles are clearly seen.*   D. Barnes

*16th Bn, Northumberland Fusiliers (Newcastle). The Battalion sign – a red triangle over a red bar, can be seen worn at the top of the left arm.* G. Stewart

*Member of one of the Birmingham Bns, Royal Warwickshire Regt. A special blue uniform was worn by the Birmingham Bns.*

Became the pioneer battalion, from the 97th Brigade, in February 1918.

The original divisional artillery was raised at Lytham and St Anne's-on-Sea by the Earl of Derby. It was designated 2nd County Palatine and in December 1915 transferred to the 31st Division for service in Egypt. The original artillery of the 31st Division, which was 155th (West Yorkshire), 161st (Yorkshire), 164th (Rotherham) and 168th (Huddersfield), remained in England and later joined the 32nd Division in France.

The three engineer field companies allotted to the Division were recruited in Glasgow and numbered 206th, 218th, 219th, and the signals were from Reading. The original field ambulances – 96th, 97th, 98th, were replaced by the 90th, 91st, 92nd in November 1915. At this time the original train – 221st-224th Companies, also left the Division and their place taken by 202nd-205th Companies. Other units associated with the 32nd Division included 'B' Squadron, South Irish Horse and the 42nd Mobile Veterinary Section.

Recruiting went exceptionally well in the 32nd Division. One Glasgow battalion, the 15th Highland Light Infantry, completing within sixteen hours. In the early days the men were billeted at home and, until uniforms were issued, various coloured shoulder cords and armlets were used to distinguish the personnel of different units.

Having previously spent time training at various locations, the 32nd Division eventually collected at Codford, Salisbury Plain in August 1915, where final preparations for the field were carried out. Embarkation for France began in November.

At the commencement of the 1916 Somme offensive on 1 July, the 32nd Division was under X Corps, Fourth Army. It fought at the Battle of Albert until 3 July and then, after a period out of the line, was involved in the operations at Bazentin Ridge on 14-15 July. In October the final 1916 assault on the Somme began at the northern end of the front along the River Ancre. The 32nd Division fought in these operations between 23rd October-19 November.

By the New Year the Division was still in positions

*Cap badge of 11th Bn Border Regt (Lonsdale). The Crest of the founder of the Bn, the Earl of Lonsdale.*

*Cap badge of the 15th Bn, Royal Warwickshire Regt (2nd Birmingham). The 1st and 3rd Birmingham Bns (14th and 16th Royal Warwickshire) had similar badges, but with the relevant title scrolls.*

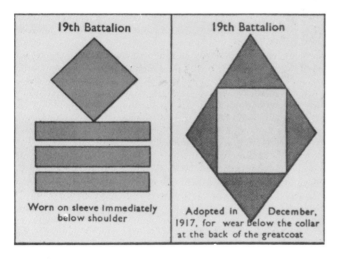

*Two cloth signs worn by the 19th Bn, Lancashire Fusiliers. The colours used are red for the sleeve patch and yellow on dark red for the greatcoat sign.*

*Special shoulder title worn by the Salford Bns of the Lancashire Fusiliers.*

by the Ancre, where between 11 January-15 February further fighting took place. Four weeks later a successful attack on Bapaume was launched which was then followed, until 5 April, by the enemy's retreat to the Hindenburg Line. Throughout the summer and autumn of 1917 the 32nd Division was involved in operations on the Flanders Coast, including the defence of Nieuport on 10 and 11 July.

On 28 March 1918 the 97th Brigade, while attached to the 31st Division, fought at Arras. The 3 April saw the 14th and 96th Brigades at the capture of Ayette and on 5 April the Division once again fought around the Ancre River.

On 8 August a great allied asault began on the Somme. The 32nd, along with Canadian troops, broke through at Amiens and before the end of the month fought side by side with Australians at Albert and Bapaume.

As the final advance continued, the 32nd Division fought at the St Quentin Canal between 29 September-2 October, and then on 3 and 4 October at the Beaurevoir Line. On 2 November Sgt James Clarke of the 15th Lancashire Fusiliers was awarded the Victoria Cross for his gallant action during an attack on Happegarbes. Two days later, three more Victoria Crosses were won by members of the Division at the Sambre-Oise Canal.

The advance eastward continued. Le Grande Fayt was taken on 6 November, and on the 11th the 32nd Division occupied Avesnes. The Division took part in the advance on the Rhine and by the end of 1918 was acting as part of the reserve to the Army in Germany. Losses throughout the war amounted to 34,226 killed, wounded and missing.

# 33rd
## DIVISION

**33rd Division**
Divisional sign: A double-three domino.

This division was formed in December 1914 and was at first known as 40th with infantry brigades numbered 119th, 120th and 121st. On 27 April 1915, the 40th became 33rd. At the same time, 120th Brigade was renumbered 99th and 119th Brigade became 100th. The 121st Brigade was transferred to the 39th Division (new) and its place taken in the 33rd by 118th Brigade (from new 32nd Division), which upon joining received the number 98th.

The Division consisted almost entirely of Londoners and comprised battalions from the Royal Fusiliers, Essex and Middlesex Regiments, and the King's Royal Rifle Corps. In one case, a whole brigade was formed by the Universities and Public Schools. Other battalions were raised in the London Boroughs of Kensington and West Ham, and the Middlesex Regiment managed a complete battalion of footballers.

Sportsmen, as well as trappers, planters and big-game hunters from all over the world, also formed the basis of two battalions of the Royal Fusiliers – the 23rd and 24th. These were raised by Mrs E. Cunliffe-Owen who subsequently quartered and planned the menu for some 1,500 men. Mrs Cunliffe-Owen also took a keen interest in the fitness of her recruits and could often be seen drilling them in the street outside headquarters. When the first of the Sportsmen's battalions was ready, Mrs Cunliffe-Owen sent the following telegram to Lord Kitchener:

'Will you accept complete battalion of upper and middle class men, physically fit, able to shoot and ride, up to the age forty-five?'

*98th Brigade*
The original 98th Brigade was formed on 11 September 1914 by the Public Schools and University Men's Force. The four battalions were designated 18th, 19th, 20th and 21st Royal Fusiliers and bore the addition titles 1st, 2nd, 3rd and 4th Public Schools. On 27 November 1915 the 20th Battalion (3rd Public Schools) was transferred to the 19th Brigade. In the following February the remaining three battalions came under GHQ Troops and on 24 April 1916 were all disbanded. Most of the personnel were commissioned. After February 1916, the 98th Brigade was organised as follows:

*23rd Bn, Royal Fusiliers (1st Sportsmen's) leaving Hyde Park, 1914.* B. Nevison

*Lt-Col F. C. Maitland, 23rd Bn, Royal Fusiliers (1st Sportsmen's).*  B. Nevison

*Barrack hut of 21st Bn, Royal Fusiliers (4th Public Schools), Epsom 1915.*  B. Nevison

4th Bn The King's (Liverpool Regt). An Extra Reserve battalion.

1/4th Bn The Suffolk Regt. A Territorial Force battalion. Transferred to the 58th Division as pioneers in February 1918.

1st Bn The Duke of Cambridge's Own (Middlesex Regt). A Regular Army battalion from 19th Brigade.

2nd Bn Princess Louise's (Argyll and Sutherland Highlanders). A Regular Army battalion from 19th Brigade.

*99th Brigade*

17th Bn The Royal Fusiliers (City of London Regt) (Empire). Raised in London by the British Empire Committee.

22nd Bn The Royal Fusiliers (City of London Regt) (Kensington). Raised by the Mayor and Borough of Kensington.

23rd Bn The Royal Fusiliers (City of London Regt) (1st Sportsmen's). Raised at the Hotel Cecil, Strand, London by Mrs E. Cunliffe-Owen.

24th Bn The Royal Fusiliers (City of London Regt) (2nd Sportsmen's). Raised by Mrs E. Cunliffe-Owen in London.

*100th Brigade*

13th Bn The Essex Regt (West Ham). Raised by the Mayor and Borough of West Ham. Transferred to the 2nd Division in December 1915.

16th Bn The Duke of Cambridge's Own (Middlesex Regt) (Public Schools). Raised in London by Lt-Col J. J. Mackay. Came under GHQ Troops in February 1916 and later joined the 29th Division.

17th Bn The Duke of Cambridge's Own (Middlesex Regt) (1st Football). Raised in London by The Rt Hon W. Joynson-Hicks, MP. Transferred to the 2nd Division in December 1915.

16th Bn The King's Royal Rifle Corps (Church Lads Brigade). Raised at Denham by Field-Marshal Lord Grenfell from past and present members of the CLB.

1st Bn The Queen's (Royal West Surrey Regt). A Regular Army battalion which joined from the 2nd Division in December 1915. Transferred to 19th Brigade in February 1918.

2nd Bn The Worcestershire Regt. A Regular Army battalion which joined from the 2nd Division in December 1915.

1/6th Bn The Cameronians (Scottish Rifles). Joined from the 51st Division as a replacement for the 16th Middlesex Regiment in February 1916. Transferred to 19th Brigade and amalgamated with 1/5th Scottish Rifles in May 1916.

1/9th Bn The Highland Light Infantry. A Territorial Force battalion which joined the Brigade in May 1916 as a replacement for 1/6th Scottish Rifles.

On 25 November 1915, 99th Brigade was transferred in exchange for the 19th of the 2nd Division. The 19th Brigade consisted of four Regular Army battalions – 2nd Royal Welsh Fusiliers, 1st Scottish Rifles, 1st Middlesex Regiment, 2nd Argylls – and one Territorial, 1/5th Scottish Rifles. Upon joining the 33rd Division, 19th Brigade was reorganised: two of its battalions were transferred to 98th Brigade, and at the same time, 20th Royal Fusiliers joined.

*19th Brigade*

20th Bn The Royal Fusiliers (City of London Regt)

*Pipers, 16th Bn, Middlesex Regt (Public Schools). Perham Down, August 1915. The pipers for the 16th Middlesex, one of the few English battalions to have them, were recruited in Glasgow.*

*17th Bn, Middlesex Regt (1st Football), Clipstone, July 1915.*
D. Barnes

*Band, 24th Bn, Royal Fusiliers (2nd Sportsmen's), Clipstone, June 1915.*

(3rd Public Schools). Joined from 98th Brigade in November 1915 and disbanded in February 1918.

2nd Bn The Royal Welsh Fusiliers. A Regular Army battalion which transferred to the 38th Division in February 1918.

1st Bn The Cameronians (Scottish Rifles). A Regular Army battalion.

1/5th Bn The Cameronians (Scottish Rifles). A Territorial Force battalion. Amalgamated with 1/6th Scottish Rifles from 100th Brigade on 29 May 1916 and designated 5th/6th Battalion.

1st Bn The Queen's (Royal West Surrey Regt). A Regular Army battalion which joined from 100th Brigade in February 1918.

*Pioneers*
18th Bn The Duke of Cambridge's Own (Middlesex Regt) (1st Public Works Pioneers). Raised in London by Lt-Col John Ward, MP.

The artillery was raised in the South London borough of Camberwell and was numbered 156th, 162nd, 166th and 167th Brigades. The engineer field companies, 212th, 222nd and 226th, were all from Tottenham. The 226th Field Company was exchanged for the 11th of the 2nd Division on 2 December 1915. The divisional train at first comprised 225th, 226th, 227th, 228th Companies, Army Service Corps, but these later transferred to the 29th Division. New companies joined in France and these were 170th, 171st, 172nd, 173rd. Royal Army Medical Corps units

were originally the 99th, 100th and 101st Field Ambulances, but in November 1915 the 100th went to the 2nd Division in exchange for their 19th. Other units included 43rd Mobile Veterinary Section and part of the North Irish Horse.

The Division began to assemble at Clipstone Camp, Notts, on 1 July 1915 and within two weeks all the infantry units had arrived. In the following month the infantry moved to Wiltshire where the battalions were joined by the remainder of the Division for final intensive training on Salisbury Plain.

Orders to move overseas were received on 4 November. HM The Queen inspected the Division at Figheldean Down on 8 November and within a few days entrainment for France began. The 33rd Division completed its concentration around Morbecque on 21 November.

The Division entered the 1916 Somme offensive on 12 July, having been brought down from the Bethune area three days previously. Under XV Corps, Fourth Army, the Division spent its first day or so in reserve. Then, moving from its bivouacs at the edge of the valley just north of Fricourt, the Division commenced an attack at Bazentin Ridge on 14 July. In its advance through gas clouds, heavy casualties were incurred from the enemy's shelling and machine-gun fire. The Division was engaged in this area until 17 July.

Before the end of the month the 33rd Division saw

*Brass shoulder title, 23rd Bn, Royal Fusiliers (1st Sportsmen's).*

*Cap badge of the 18th Bn, Middlesex Regt (1st Public Works, Pioneers). The badge is that of the Middlesex Regt, but with the addition of a scroll at the bottom bearing the name of the battalion.*

action at High Wood. It then withdrew from the line until 25 October, when a series of actions until 7 November brought about the capture of the Dewdrop and Boritska Trenches.

The first major action of 1917 involving units of the 33rd Division was that of 14 April, when 19th Brigade,

*HQ Staff, 33rd Bn, Machine Gun Corps, 4 Aug 1918. The group includes a French officer (standing left) serving as interpreter, and an American Medical Officer (standing right).*

which had been placed under the orders of the 21st Division, was engaged during the First Battle of the Scarpe. Two battalions attacked north of Fontaine-les-Croisilles and made a little ground by bombing along the Hindenburg Line.

The Second Battle of the Scarpe took place later in April. These operations were to cover a front of nine miles from Croisilles, across the river to Gavrelle. The 33rd Division made two separate attacks. one was a flanking assault by 98th Brigade moving up the Hindenburg Line from west of the River Sensee; the other, by 100th Brigade, was a frontal attack down the eastern bank of the river.

On 20 May a series of actions on the Hindenburg Line began. The main feature of these operations was an attack made by the 33rd Division between Bullecourt and the Sensee River at Croisilles. From their start positions at the Chalk Pit, two brigades (98th and 100th) attacked at 5.15am and successfully took the enemy's front-line trenches. These were later gallantly defended, with great loss, against a series of counter-attacks by the enemy.

At the end of July the Division moved to the Flanders coast for rest and training. At this time the Division came under XV Corps, Fourth Army, and operated in the Nieuport Sector.

The training period on the coast came to an end on 15 September, the 33rd Division having received orders to make its way to the Ypres Salient. Here it came under X Corps, Second Army area, where on 24-27 September, it fought in the great battles of the Menin Road Ridge and Polygon Wood.

At the beginning of 1918 the Division moved to IX Corps and throughout April took part in the battles of Messines, Hazebrouck, Bailleul and Kemmel Ridge. The Bailleul operations on 13-15 April included a gallant defence by the 100th Brigade of Neuve Église.

On 18 September the Division took part in the Battle of Epéhy. Operations on the St Quentin Canal followed between 29 September-2 October, and 8-9 October by action at Cambrai. This was followed up by the Pursuit to the Selle until 12 October.

In its final advance through Picardy the Division fought at the Battle of the Selle, 23-25 October and on the 26th captured the village of Englefontaine. The Division was relieved by the 38th (Welsh) Division during the evening and did not take part in any major actions until 6 November, when it fought its last battle of the war at Leval.

By January 1919 the Division was located on the French coast at Quiberville. Demobilisation soon began and the Division had ceased to exist by the end of June. Total casualties throughout the war were 37,404.

# 34th
## DIVISION

### 34th Division

Divisional sign: A chequered pattern of twenty-five black and white squares.

This Division was at first numbered 41st and its infantry brigades 122nd, 123rd and 124th. On 27 April 1915 it was renumbered 34th and at the same time 123rd and 124th Brigades became 102nd and 103rd respectively. The 122nd Brigade was transferred to the 32nd Division (new) and was renumbered 96th. To replace this a new brigade was formed which received the number 101st.

The 34th Division, in one brigade, included two battalions from Edinburgh, one from Cambridgeshire and the 10th Lincolns, who were known as the Grimsby Chums. In the other two, all battalions were raised in Newcastle-on-Tyne for the Northumberland Fusiliers. The 102nd Brigade was the Tyneside Scottish, while those battalions of 103rd Brigade were known as the Tyneside Irish.

### 101st Brigade

15th Bn The Royal Scots (Lothian Regt) (1st Edinburgh). Raised by the Lord Provost and City of Edinburgh. Reduced to a training cadre in May 1918 and later attached to the 39th Division.

16th Bn The Royal Scots (Lothian Regt) (2nd Edinburgh). Raised in Edinburgh by Col Sir G. McCrae, MP. Reduced to a training cadre in May 1918 and later transferred to the 39th Division.

10th Bn The Lincolnshire Regt (Grimsby). Raised by the Mayor and Town of Grimsby. Transferred to the 103rd Brigade in February 1918.

11th Bn The Suffolk Regt (Cambridgeshire). Raised in Cambridgeshire by the Cambridge and Isle of Ely Territorial Force Association. Transferred to the 61st Division in May 1918.

### 102nd Brigade

20th Bn The Northumberland Fusiliers (1st Tyneside Scottish). Raised by the Lord Mayor and City of

*Band of one of the Tyneside Irish Bns.*

*L/Cpl, Tyneside Scottish. The headdress is the Tam-O'-Shanter bonnet and the badge has a tartan backing of Black Watch pattern.*

Newcastle. Disbanded in February 1918.

21st Bn The Northumberland Fusiliers (2nd Tyneside Scottish). Raised by the Lord Mayor and City of Newcastle. Disbanded in October 1918.

22nd Bn The Northumberland Fusiliers (3rd Tyneside Scottish). Raised by the Lord Mayor and City of Newcastle. Reduced to a cadre in May 1918 and later transferred to the 16th Division.

23rd Bn The Northumberland Fusiliers (4th Tyneside Scottish). Raised by the Lord Mayor and City of Newcastle. Reduced to a cadre in May 1918 and later attached to the 39th Division.

25th Bn The Northumberland Fusiliers (2nd Tyneside Irish). Joined from 103rd Brigade in February 1918. Reduced to a cadre in May and later attached to the 39th Division.

*103rd Brigade*

24th Bn The Northumberland Fusiliers (1st Tyneside Irish). Raised by the Lord Mayor and City of Newcastle. Amalgamated with the 27th Battalion to form 24th/27th in August 1917. Disbanded in February 1918.

25th Bn The Northumberland Fusiliers (2nd Tyneside Irish). Raised by the Lord Mayor and City of Newcastle. Transferred to 102nd Brigade in February 1918.

26th Bn The Northumberland Fusiliers (3rd Tyneside Irish). Raised by the Lord Mayor and City of Newcastle. Disbanded in February 1918.

27th Bn The Northumberland Fusiliers (4th Tyneside Irish). Raised by the Lord Mayor and City of Newcastle. Amalgamated with the 24th Battalion in August 1917.

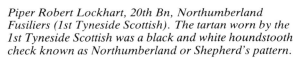

*Piper Robert Lockhart, 20th Bn, Northumberland Fusiliers (1st Tyneside Scottish). The tartan worn by the 1st Tyneside Scottish was a black and white houndstooth check known as Northumberland or Shepherd's pattern.*

*Sgt, Tyneside Irish. Small harp badges are worn on the collar and crossed rifles, indicating the wearer to be a marksman, on the lower left arm. The cloth shamrock badge, worn above the chevrons, denotes the Sgt's battalion – 1st (red), 2nd (greyish blue), 3rd (violet) and 4th (black).* G. Stewart

*right*
*Maj-Gen Sir Lothian Nicholson, KCB, DSO. The General was a regular soldier with the East Lancashire Regt and became GOC, 34th Div, in July 1916. The chevrons worn on the lower right arm (one red and four blue) indicate his service on the Western Front from 1914 to the end of the war.*

9th Bn The Northumberland Fusiliers. Joined from the 17th Division in August 1917 as a replacement for 27th Northumberland Fusiliers. Absorbed 2/1st Northumberland Hussars in September 1917 and assumed title of 9th (Northumberland Hussars Yeomanry) Battalion. Transferred to the 61st Division in May 1918.

10th Bn The Lincolnshire Regt (Grimsby). Joined from 101st Brigade in February 1918. Reduced to a training cadre in May 1918 and later attached to the 39th Division.

*Recruiting poster, Tyneside Scottish.*  G. Stewart

The four artillery brigades were raised in Nottingham (152nd), Sunderland (160th), Staffordshire (175th) and Leicestershire (176th). All of the Division's engineer units, 207th, 208th, 209th Field Companies and Signals, were raised in Norwich and the divisional train contained 229th-232nd Companies, Army Service Corps. The three field ambulances were numbered 102nd, 103rd, 104th and the mobile veterinary section was 44th. 'E' Squadron, North Irish Horse also formed part of the Division until transferring to VII Corps Cavalry Regiment in May 1916.

The Division concentrated at Salisbury Plain between 28-31 August 1915, its headquarters at first being set up at Cholderton but moving to Sutton Veny on 30 September. Embarkation orders were received on 3 January 1916. Entrainment began on the 7th and on the 15th, the 34th Division completed its concentration around La Crosse, east of St Omer.

After several months of war training and tours of duty in the front line, the 34th Division, on 1 July 1916, was positioned in III Corps, Fourth Army area opposite La Boisselle on the Somme. This was the first day of the great offensive in that area and at zero hour the men of the Division went into the attack. All twelve battalions were involved in the initial assault. None were held in reserve, the battle formation being four

*Sgt, 34th Bn, Machine Gun Corps. He wears the Corps badge, consisting of crossed Vickers machine guns, the brass shoulder title – 'MGC' and the 34th divisional sign on the upper arm.*  C. Lewis

1st Bn The East Lancashire Regt. A Regular Army battalion which joined from the 4th Division in February 1918. Transferred to the 61st Division in May 1918.

The 34th Division suffered heavy casualties during the early months of 1918, and by May its infantry battalions had either been disbanded or reduced to cadre strength and transferred. The Division was reconstituted between 19 June-1 July 1918 and until the end of the war its infantry consisted of Territorial Force battalions and one Regular Battalion (2nd Loyals).

101st Brigade: 2/4th Queen's, 1/4th Royal Sussex, 2nd Loyal North Lancs.
102nd Brigade: 1/4th Cheshire, 1/7th Cheshire, 1/1st Hereford.
103rd Brigade: 1/5th KOSB, 1/8th Cameronians, 1/5th Argylls.

*Pioneers*
18th Bn The Northumberland Fusiliers (1st Tyneside Pioneers). Raised by the Lord Mayor of Newcastle. Reduced to a training cadre in May 1918 and later attached to the 39th Division.
2/4th Bn Prince Albert's (Somerset Light Infantry). A Territorial Force battalion which joined the reconstituted division in June 1918.

columns, each with three battalions deep on a frontage of 400yds.

From their positions at the Tara-Usna Ridge, 1st, 3rd and 4th Tyneside Irish moved down the slopes into open ground. The battalions advanced at a steady rate but from the very moment that the men left their trenches they were cut down by the enemy's machine guns. Within ten minutes some 80% of the three battalions were casualties.

On the right, the main part of 101st Brigade had to advance up the steep convex slope of the western side of the Fricourt spur, through Sausage Valley and towards Contalmaison. At zero hour, part of the 15th Royal Scots were in position within 200yds of the German front line. With the pipe-major playing the men over the top, the leading wave attacked and soon

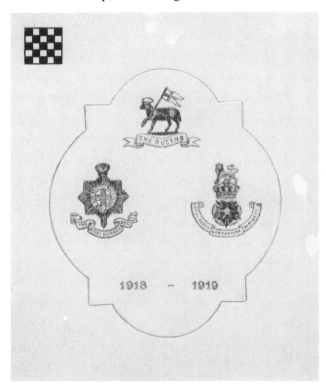

overran the enemy's front trench. However, the following companies of the 15th, together with those of the 16th Royal Scots, met heavy machine-gun fire from Sausage Valley and La Boisselle and suffered heavily. Likewise, the Lincolns and Suffolks were raked by deadly fire, their lines being reduced to isolated small groups.

Very heavy losses were also incurred by the Tyneside Scottish on the left of the attack. The leading line rose from their trenches at 7.28am at the same time that the huge Lochnagar mine was blown. Moving north of the crater and crossing the 200yds of No Man's Land, the Tyneside Scottish then succeeded in taking the enemy's positions at Schwaben Hohe.

The fortified village of La Boisselle was one of the most important areas of the battle front on 1 July 1916. This was the 34th Division's objective on the day, but the deadly machine-gun fire put up by the enemy prevented any great advance being made. In its attempt the 34th Division lost some 6,380 casualties, the most incurred by any division on the First Day of the Somme.

On 2 July, the Division captured both the Scots and Sausage Redoubts. Two important battles were fought at Bazentin and Pozières Ridges later in July and August, and on 15 September the 103rd Brigade, while attached to the 15th Division, fought at the battle of Flers-Courcelette.

As part of XVII Corps, Third Army, the Division fought in the Arras operations of April to August 1917. During this period two gallant Tyneside Irishmen won the Victoria Cross. The first, L/Cpl Thomas Bryan of the 25th Northumberland Fusiliers, put out of action single-handed an enemy machine-gun post which was

*34th Div Christmas card from Germany, 1918-19. The divisional sign is seen in the top left-hand corner, and the three badges are those of the regiments in the reconstituted 101st Bde – Queen's, Royal Sussex and Loyal North Lancashire.*

*102nd Bde, comprising the four Tyneside Scottish Bns, being reviewed by Honorary Col The Duke of Northumberland, ICG, at Alnwick, 18 May 1915.*

*Three members of the 27th Bn, Northumberland Fusiliers (4th Tyneside Irish) with medic from the Tyneside Scottish.*

*Senior NCOs from 'B' Coy, 18th Bn, Northumberland Fusiliers (1st Tyneside Pioneers), France 1916.* G. Stewart

inflicting great losses on his unit. Later, Pte Ernest Sykes, 27th Battalion, showed the utmost courage attending wounded men while under incessant machine-gun and rifle fire.

On 26 August a third VC was won for the Division during the operations at Hargicourt. On this occasion Cpl Sidney Day of the 11th Suffolks gallantly led a bombing party and cleared a maze of trenches held by the enemy. He later showed great courage when a stick bomb fell into an occupied trench. The corporal seized the bomb and threw it over the trench, where it immediately exploded. A move to the XIV Corps area in October subsequently saw the 34th Division in action in the Ypres Sector.

The Division fought in the 1918 battles of the Somme and the Lys throughout March and April. It again suffered heavy losses after engagements at St Quentin, Estaires, Bailleul and Kemmel Ridge, and on 21 April withdrew from the line to positions behind Poperinghe. Here it was subsequently employed in the training of American troops until all battalions were either disbanded or transferred.

Having been reconstituted between 19 June-1 July 1918, the 34th Division with its new infantry fought on the Marne between 22 July-3 August. It then took part in the final advance in Flanders from 28 September. After the Armistice the 34th Division advanced into Germany where it remained until demobilisation. Throughout the war the Division lost 41,183 killed, wounded and missing.

*Special shoulder designation worn by the 24th Bn, Northumberland Fusiliers (1st Tyneside Irish). The Harp badge is often taken by collectors to be a cap badge; the Tyneside Irish wore the usual Northumberland Fusiliers pattern. Other Tyneside Irish Bns wore a similar shoulder badge, but with the relevant number.* D. Wood

*Gilt and silver shoulder title worn by officer's of the Tyneside Scottish. The four battalions in the Tyneside Scottish Bde wore a similar title, but with the relevant battalion number replacing the silver grenade.* D. Wood

*Cap badges of the Tyneside Scottish. Four patterns of cap badge were worn throughout the First World War, each incorporating the cross of St Andrew, thistles and the Scottish lion. The circular badge (1) was the first to be worn and bore the motto of the Northumberland Fusiliers* Quo Fata Vocant *(wherever fate calls). This was followed by a larger badge which appeared with slight variations (2), (3), (4). As a collar badge, the Tyneside Scottish wore just the lion standing on the tower and carrying the pennant.* D. R. Wood

# 35th DIVISION

## 35th Division

Divisional sign: At first, a bantam cock was used, but after the reorganisation in December 1916, a change was made to seven fives (35) arranged in a circle.

This Division was at first numbered 42nd, and its infantry brigades 125th, 126th and 127th. On 27 April 1915, the 42nd was renumbered 35th.

At the same time, 125th Brigade became 105th, and 126th Brigade was renumbered 91st and transferred to the 30th Division (new). The 126th was then replaced by the 112th Brigade from the 30th Division, which upon joining the 35th assumed the number 104th. At the time of renumbering, no 127th Brigade had yet been formed. When a third brigade was eventually raised, this received the number 106th.

### 104th Brigade

17th Bn The Lancashire Fusiliers (1st South-East Lancashire). Raised at Bury by Lt-Col G. E. Wike.
18th Bn The Lancashire Fusiliers (2nd South-East Lancashire). Raised at Bury by Lt-Col G. E. Wike.
20th Bn The Lancashire Fusiliers (4th Salford). Raised

*Brass shoulder title worn by 18th Bn Highland Light Infantry (4th Glasgow).*

*'B' Coy, 17th Bn Lancashire Fusiliers (1st South-East Lancashire), March 1915.*

*Cpl R. Riley, 23rd Bn Manchester Regt (8th City). A special oval title was worn with the battalion number '8' in the centre.* D. Barnes

at Salford by Mr Montague Barlow, MP. Disbanded in February 1918.

23rd Bn The Manchester Regt (8th City). Raised by the Lord Mayor and City of Manchester. Disbanded in February 1918.

19th Bn The Durham Light Infantry (2nd County). Transferred from 106th Brigade in February 1918.

### 105th Brigade

15th Bn The Cheshire Regt (1st Birkenhead). Raised at Birkenhead by Alfred Bigland, MP.

16th Bn The Cheshire Regt (2nd Birkenhead). Raised at Birkenhead by Alfred Bigland, MP. Disbanded in February 1918.

14th Bn The Gloucestershire Regt (West of England). Raised by the Bristol Citizens' Recruiting Committee. Disbanded in February 1918.

15th Bn The Sherwood Foresters (Nottinghamshire and Derbyshire Regt) (Nottingham). Raised by the Mayor and Recruiting Committee of Nottingham.

4th Bn The Prince of Wales's (North Staffordshire Regt). An Extra Reserve battalion which joined from 106th Brigade in February 1918.

### 106th Brigade

17th Bn The Royal Scots (Lothian Regt) (Rosebury). Raised in Edinburgh by Lord Rosebery.

17th Bn The Prince of Wales's Own (West Yorkshire Regt) (2nd Leeds). Raised by the Lord Mayor and City of Leeds. Left the Division on 16 Novemebr 1917 to work on railways for XIX Corps and then amalgamated with 15th West Yorkshire Regiment of the 31st Division to form the 15th/17th Battalion.

19th Bn The Durham Light Infantry (2nd County). Raised by the Durham Parliamentary Recruiting Committee in Durham. Transferred to the 104th Brigade in February 1918.

18th Bn The Highland Light Infantry (4th Glasgow). Raised by the Lord Provost and City of Glasgow. Redesignated 18th (Royal Glasgow Yeomanry) Battalion upon amalgamation in September 1917.

4th Bn The Prince of Wales's (North Staffordshire Regt). An Extra Reserve battalion which joined from the 56th Division in November 1917 as a replacement for 17th West Yorks. Transferred to 105th Brigade in February 1918.

12th Bn The Highland Light Infantry. Joined from the 15th Division in February 1918.

### Pioneers

19th Bn The Northumberland Fusiliers (2nd Tyneside Pioneers). Raised by the Lord Mayor and City of Newcastle.

The 35th Divisional Artillery was recruited: Aberdeen (157th Brigade), Accrington and Burnley (158th Brigade), Glasgow (159th Brigade), West Ham, London (163rd Brigade), and Lancashire (Ammunition Column). Engineer field companies were 203rd (Cambridge), 204th (Empire) and 205th (Dundee) and the signal company came from Reading. The three field ambulance units were numbered 105th, 106th, 107th and the mobile veterinary section was the 45th. The divisional train consisted of 233rd-236th Companies, Army Service Corps. 'C' Squadron, 1/1st Lancashire Hussars formed part of the Division until moving to VIII Corps Cavalry Regiment in May 1916.

The 35th Division was a 'Bantam' division and the history of the Cheshire Regiment tells how, in 1914, four miners walked from Durham to Birkenhead in answer to the regiment's call for recruits. When the men were medically examined it was found that they did not come up to the required standard in height, although in every other respect they were healthy sturdy men determined to serve their country.

Later, the Member of Parliament for Birkenhead, Alfred Bigland, who saw the rejection of these men as a waste of manpower, managed to obtain from the War Office permission to form a battalion of Bantams. Within a few days of notice being given, some 3,000 men from all over the United Kingdom came forward and offered themselves for enlistment. These men were subsequently formed into the 1st and 2nd Birkenhead Battalions (15th and 16th Cheshires) and were to be the foundation for a complete Bantam division.

Soon, other regiments began to recruit special battalions of Bantams. Three were provided by the Lancashire Fusiliers which, with the 8th City Battalion from Manchester, provided the 104th Brigade. The Birkenhead battalions, together with one each from Bristol and Nottingham, formed the 105th Brigade, while the 106th was completed by Lord Rosebury's 17th Royal Scots, the 17th West Yorks from Leeds, a battalion of miners from Durham and the 18th Highland Light Infantry from Glasgow.

With its twelve battalions of Bantams – there were none enrolled into the artillery, engineers and pioneers – the 35th began to collect around Masham in June 1915. Later, in August, the Division moved to Salisbury Plain where the final stages of its training for war were carried out.

Before the end of 1915 the Division received orders to prepare for service in Egypt, tropical uniforms and pith helmets being issued to all ranks. However, after a short time fresh orders were issued which took the Bantams to France.

The Division began to leave England at the end of January 1916 and by the morning of 6 February was complete east of St Omer. Throughout the following months the Bantams gained experience in the trenches, each unit serving a period attached to an already battle-hardened division at the front.

The 35th Division was located around Bethune when it received orders to be prepared to move at any time and take part in the 1916 Somme offensive. Having moved into reserve under XIII Corps area, the

*Drums and Bugles, 23rd Bn Manchester Regt (8th City), Morecambe 1915.* D. Barnes

Division fought its first major engagements at Bazentin Ridge from 15 July through to 26 August. At this time 105th Brigade was attached to the 18th Division, and 106th Brigade to the 9th. From 19 July until 30 July, the Division was involved in the fighting at Arrow Head Copse and Maltzhorn Farm. It then fought its last battle of 1916 at Falfemont Farm between 19-26 August.

After moving to Arras in September 1916, the 35th Division began to receive replacements to make up for the heavy losses incurred on the Somme. Although the drafts being sent out from England were of the required height for a Bantam unit, it was the opinion of the GOC, 35th Division, Maj-Gen H. J. S. Landon, that the men were merely undersized and not 'real Bantams'. They were, he submitted, 'physically underdeveloped and unfit men of low moral standard'.

Between 9-15 December 1916 an inspection of the Division's twelve infantry battalions was carried out and, subsequently, 1,439 men were rejected. Later, an additional number were withdrawn, bringing the total to 2,784, and Brigade Commanders were informed that no more Bantams were to be accepted.

The 35th Division had now lost its Bantam status, but a considerable number of the original men remained and were to serve throughout the remainder of the war. The strength of the Division was made up by men drawn from dismounted yeomanry regiments and the cavalry training depot.

The Division was engaged 14-18 March 1917 during the German retreat to the Hindenburg Line. It was later taken out of the line and used for pioneering duties in the area, which had been devastated during the enemy's withdrawal.

After returning to duty at the front and a number of minor actions, two remarkable Victoria Crosses were won by members of the Division. On 6 August 1917, Pte William Boynton Butler, who joined the 17th West Yorks in January 1915, was in charge of a Stokes Mortar in trenches at Lempire. As his position was being heavily shelled, suddenly one of the fly-off levers of a Stokes shell came off and fired the shell. Pte Butler then picked up the shell and jumped to the entrance of his emplacement, which at that moment a party of infantry were passing. He shouted to them to hurry past, as the shell was going off. He then turned around, placed himself between the party of men and the live shell, and so held it till they were out of danger. He then threw the shell on to the parados and took cover in the bottom of the trench. The shell exploded almost on leaving his hand.

Two weeks after Pte Butler's heroic action, an officer attached to the 14th Glosters, 2/Lt Hardy Falconer Parsons, lost his life as a result of a gallant single-handed stand during an attack on his position near Epéhy on the night of 20-21 August. Although severely burnt by liquid fire, he continued to hold up the enemy's advance until a bombing party could be organised, which succeeded in driving them back. 2/Lt Parsons received severe and fatal wounds as a result of his great courage and devotion to duty.

The Division entered its first major battle of the 1917 operations at the Ypres Salient on 22 October. While under XIV Corps the 35th took part in the fighting at the Houthulst Forest (22 October) and between 26 October-4 November, took part in the Second Battle of Passchendaele.

The Division was engaged in the first stages of the

*17th Bn Lancashire Fusiliers (1st South East Lancashire) parading in civilian clothes, Dec 1914.*

*Special shoulder title worn by the 20th Bn Lancashire Fusiliers (4th Salford).*

18th Battalion

Worn at back of jacket

Worn on both sleeves just below shoulder.

*Blue identification signs worn by the 18th Bn, Lancashire Fusiliers.*

March 1918 German offensive, fighting under VII Corps at Bapaume on the 24 and 25 March. On the 25th, the Commanding Officer of the 12th Highland Light Infantry, Lt-Col William Herbert Anderson, was killed while leading his men in a counter-attack at Bois Favières near Maricourt. This was the second occasion that Lt-Col Anderson had shown great courage and leadership that day and was later awarded the Victoria Cross.

Throughout the final advance in Flanders, the 35th fought at Ypres (28 September-2 October), Courtrai (14-19 October) and Tieghem (31 October). On 11 November the Division entered Grammont and on the following day went into Corps Reserve. At the beginning of December billets were taken over north-west of St Omer. That same month the Division was used to control a series of riots at Calais.

Demobilisation was complete by the end of April 1919. The 35th Division's casualties for the First World War amounted to 23,915 killed, wounded and missing.

# 36th
## (ULSTER)
# DIVISION

### 36th (Ulster) Division
Divisional sign: The Red Hand of Ulster.

It was several weeks after war was declared that permission to form an Ulster Division was granted. The Ulster Volunteer Force, a Protestant organisation created by Sir Edward Carson as a force to counter the threat of the Home Rule Bill, was already in existence and its members were as eager as any to join the war. However, due to the political situation in Ireland, things were held up. Many volunteers refused to wait and either crossed to England to enlist, or joined the 10th or 16th Divisions already forming in Ireland.

With over 80,000 members, it was clear that the UVF was in a position to make an important contribution to the recruitment of the New Army. Lord Kitchener met with Sir Edward Carson in London who, although eager to help, was concerned as to how the situation in Ireland might turn while his force was away at war. The Government were not able to give any guarantees that might put Sir Edward's mind at rest. However, he later agreed to raise a division, without any conditions, and within days had placed an order for 10,000 uniforms with a London firm of outfitters.

The formation of the Division began in September 1914 and at first the three brigades were numbered 1st, 2nd and 3rd. The designation 36th (Ulster) Division was received on 28 October and in the following November the brigades took the numbers 107th, 108th and 109th.

In 107th Brigade all battalions were formed in Belfast, while in the 108th three were raised in Antrim and Down, with a fourth coming from Armagh, Monaghan and Cavan. In 109th Brigade there were three battalions of the Royal Inniskilling Fusiliers:

from Tyrone, Derry, Donegal and Fermanagh: along with the 14th Royal Irish Rifles which were formed by the Young Citizens' Volunteers of Belfast. The pioneers were from County Down.

*107th Brigade*
8th Bn The Royal Irish Rifles (East Belfast). Formed in Belfast and amalgamated with the 9th Battalion to form 8th/9th in August 1917. Disbanded in February 1918.
9th Bn The Royal Irish Rifles (West Belfast). Formed in Belfast and amalgamated with the 8th Battalion in August 1917.
10th Bn The Royal Irish Rifles (South Belfast). Formed in Belfast and disbanded in February 1918.
15th Bn Royal Irish Rifles (North Belfast). Formed in Belfast.
1st Bn Princess Victoria's (Royal Irish Fusiliers). A Regular Army battalion which joined from the 4th Division as a replacement for 9th Royal Irish Rifles in August 1917. Transferred to 108th Brigade in February 1918.
1st Bn The Royal Irish Rifles. A Regular Army battalion which joined from the 8th Division in February 1918.
2nd Bn The Royal Irish Rifles. A Regular Army battalion which transferred from 108th Brigade in February 1918.

For a brief period between November 1915 and February 1916, 107th Brigade was transferred in exchange for 12th Brigade, 4th Division.

*108th Brigade*
11th Bn The Royal Irish Rifles (South Antrim). Formed in County Antrim and amalgamated with the

a

b

c

d

e

f

g

h

i

j

k

l

**Divisional Signs**

*In addition to the brassard, units of the Ulster Volunteer Force wore special badges (usually incorporating the Red Hand of Ulster) in civilian clothing, military caps where worn, and uniform.*   Ulster Museum, Belfast

*(a)  Proposed cap and collar badges, made by S. D. Neill of Belfast, for officers of the 36th (Ulster) Div. There is no evidence that these were worn, photographs showing the normal regimental badges.*

*(b)  Cap badge and shoulder title, Ulster Special Service Force.*

*(c)  Officer's silver cap and collar badges, Young Citizens' Volunteers of Ireland.*

*(d)  2nd Bn, North Down Regt.*

*(e)  Cap badge, shoulder title and buttons, Young Citizens' Volunteers of Ireland. This unit continued to wear these items after becoming 14th Bn, Royal Irish Rifles in 1914.*

*(f)  1st Bn Armagh Regt.*

*(g)  Proficiency badge, 3rd Fermanagh Regt.*

*(h)  Cloth badge (red hand on a royal blue ground) worn by 150 Field Coy, Royal Engineers.*

*(i)  4th Bn, East Belfast Regt.*

*(j)  Badge worn by soldiers of the 36th (Ulster) Div until regimental patterns were available.*

*(k)  Irish National Volunteers, Belfast Regt.*

*(l)  5th South Belfast Regt.*

*Officer, 2nd West Belfast Regt, Ulster Volunteer Force.*
Ulster Museum Belfast

13th Battalion as 11th/13th in November 1917. Disbanded in February 1918.

12th Bn The Royal Irish Rifles (Central Antrim). Formed in County Antrim.

13th Bn The Royal Irish Rifles (1st Co Down). Formed in County Down and amalgamated with the 11th Battalion in November 1917.

9th Bn Princess Victoria's (Royal Irish Fusiliers) (Co Armagh). Raised in the Armagh, Monaghan and Cavan areas. Absorbed 'B' and 'C' Squadrons, 2nd North Irish Horse in September 1917 and redesignated 9th (North Irish Horse) Battalion.

2nd Bn The Royal Irish Rifles. A Regular Army battalion which joined from the 25th Division in November 1917 as a replacement for 13th Royal Irish Rifles. Transferred to 107th Brigade in February 1918.

1st Bn Princess Victoria's (Royal Irish Fusiliers). A Regular Army battalion which transferred from the 107th Brigade in February 1918.

*109th Brigade*
9th Bn The Royal Inniskilling Fusiliers (Co Tyrone). Raised in Omagh.

10th Bn The Royal Inniskilling Fusiliers (Derry). Raised in Omagh and disbanded in February 1918.

11th Bn The Royal Inniskilling Fusiliers (Donegal and Fermanagh). Raised in Omagh and disbanded in February 1918.

14th Bn The Royal Irish Rifles (Young Citizens). Raised in Belfast and disbanded in February 1918.

1st Bn The Royal Inniskilling Fusiliers. A Regular Army battalion which joined from the 29th Division in February 1918.

2nd Bn The Royal Inniskilling Fusiliers. A Regular Army battalion which joined from the 32nd Division in February 1918.

*Pioneers*
16th Bn The Royal Irish Rifles (2nd Co Down). Raised at Lergan.

Included in the mounted troops of the Division was a unit formed at Enniskillen in November 1914 and designated 1st Service Squadron, 6th (Inniskilling) Dragoons. The unit became part of X Corps Cavalry Regiment in June 1916 but later, in 1917, became part of the 9th Royal Irish Fusiliers.

There were no artillery units raised in Ireland for the 36th (Ulster) Division. Two brigades were raised in Croydon (153rd, 154th) one in East Ham (172nd) and one in West Ham (173rd). When the Division went overseas in 1915, its artillery was not fully trained and, instead, the 1st London Divisional Artillery of the Territorial Force accompanied the 36th to France. However, the 36th Divisional Artillery joined by the end of the year.

The three engineer field companies were numbered 121st, 122nd and 150th and were formed largely from workers in the Belfast Shipyards. Field ambulances were 108th, 109th and 110th and their motor ambulances were bought with funds raised by local areas or associations. Each vehicle bore the name of the town or organisation which had paid for it. The veterinary section was the 48th.

Unlike the majority of other New Army divisions, who spent a considerable amount of time waiting for their uniforms, the 36th (Ulster) was fortunate in that its men received their kit upon enrolment. Recruits were sent to training camps at Clandeboye, Ballykinlar, Newtownards and Finner.

The Division left Ireland for England in July 1915 and concentrated at Seaford in Sussex where Field-Marshal Earl Kitchener made an inspection on 20 July. Early in September the whole Division moved to

*The majority of units in the Ulster Volunteer Force did not have uniforms and for identification the men wore a brassard on their left arm. The following are examples.* Ulster Museum Belfast

*(a) Yellow on blue, worn by lieutenants.*

*(d) Young Citizens Volunteers.*

*(b) Black on khaki, worn by sergeants.*

*(e) Ulster Signalling & Despatch Rider Corps.*

*(c) Black on khaki, worn by corporals.*

*(f) Black on khaki.*

Bordon and Bramshott for its final training and preparations for the field.

The 36th (Ulster) Division, under the command of Maj-Gen O. S. W. Nugent, crossed to France between 3-6 October 1915, and by the 9th was concentrated around Flesselles, north of Amiens. The following months were spent in positions on the Somme, north of the River Ancre, where the Division was to gain its first experiences of war conditions.

During the night of the 30 June-1 July, the Division was in its assembly trenches at Thiepval Wood. Here it was in readiness for the start, on the following morning, of the great 1916 Somme offensive. As equipment was being checked and the ammunition

prepared, a box of Mills Bombs fell, and several pins dropped out. At this point, and without hesitation, Pte William McFadzean of the 14th Royal Irish Rifles threw himself on top of the grenades. The bombs exploded, blowing him to pieces, but only one other man in the crowded trench was injured. For his most conspicuous bravery, Pte McFadzean was awarded the Victoria Cross.

On 1 July the 36th (Ulster) Division came under X Corps and was holding part of the line around Thiepval and Hamel. The main objective set for the Ulstermen was an enemy stronghold known as the Schwaben Redoubt. These positions were heavily fortified with concrete gun emplacements and protected by several rows of wire.

With the redoubt featuring in the centre of the attack, the 11th, 13th and 15th Royal Irish Rifles were set the task of assaulting its north side while, to their left, two battalions of 108th Brigade advanced along the north bank of the River Ancre to take the railway station at Beaucourt. The 109th Brigade, on the right of the Division's battle-front, had the job of clearing the enemy from its position known as the Crucifix.

At two minutes before zero, the 12th Royal Irish Rifles and 9th Royal Irish Fusiliers left their trenches and began to cross the 600yds of No Man's Land between them and the enemy. Almost immediately, heavy machine-gun fire cut down the leading waves, and many were dead before the battalions could pass through the gaps in their own wire.

After several attempts to advance had failed, what was left of the two battalions returned to their lines. Having reached his trench, Pte Robert Quigg, Royal Irish Rifles, found that his officer, Lt Sir Harry Macnaghton, was missing and, it was thought, could be

*King's Colour, 1st South Belfast Regt, Ulster Volunteer Force.* Ulster Museum Belfast

*A North Down Bn receiving Colours in 1913.*
Ulster Museum Belfast

*The Ulster Tower, shortly after its opening in 1921. Erected by public subscription in memory of the 36th (Ulster) Div, the monument stands on the Somme battlefield of 1 July 1916. The Tower is a facsimile of Helen's Tower at Clandeboyn, Co. Down, where the Division carried out much of its training prior to going to France.* S. Barr

out in No Man's Land lying wounded. Pte Quigg had worked for Sir Harry prior to the war and was now his servant in the Army. During a seven-hour period, Pte Quigg made seven attempts to locate the officer, who was never in fact found. Nonetheless, on each return to his line he brought back a wounded man. Pte Robert Quigg was later awarded the Victoria Cross.

The assaults on the Schwaben Redoubt and Crucifix met with greater success than that to the left along the river bank. After severe hand-to-hand fighting, in which another two VCs were won, the Ulstermen by late morning had achieved all their objectives. The 36th (Ulster) Division was relieved during the night of 2 July and returned through Thiepval Wood to billets in Martinsart.

After its first roll-call, the 36th (Ulster) Division became aware of the price it had paid during its first days of battle. Out of the 9,000 or so that had attacked on 1 July, more than 5,000 had become casualties, either killed, wounded, missing or taken prisoner. In one battalion, all the officers had been lost and only eighty other ranks remained.

The 36th (Ulster) Division was not the only formation from Northern Ireland to suffer heavily on the Somme in July 1916. Several other battalions which took part in the battle were formed from Ulstermen and, in consequence, hardly a home in the nine counties was left unaffected by grief. As a mark of respect, the traditional Orange Day parade on 12 July was cancelled, and on that day a five-minute tribute, in which all business was suspended, traffic came to a standstill, blinds were drawn and flags were flown at half-mast, was paid to those who had fallen.

The Division moved back to Rubempre on 5 July and, later on, to the training area west of St Omer where replacements were received. It was not until 7

*Irish National Volunteers.* Ulster Museum Belfast

July 1917 that the Division took part in another major engagement. Their successful offensive at Messines lasted two days, during which time the Ulstermen fought gallanty alongside the 16th (Irish) Division at the capture of Wytschaete. The Battle of Langemarck followed on 16-17 August and in November the Division took part in the great tank attack at Cambrai followed by the capture of Bourlon Wood.

The German offensive on the Somme began in March 1918. The Division fought at the Battle of St Quentin on 21-23 March, during which time Lt Knox of the 150th Field Company received the Victoria Cross, and later at the Somme Crossings and Rosières.

Having once again suffered heavy casualties (over 7,000 since 21 March), the 36th Division moved to

*Young Citizens' Volunteers, Review at Balmoral Showgrounds, 27 Sept 1913. The uniforms are grey with Prussian blue collars, cuffs and piping.* Ulster Museum Belfast

Ypres in April 1918. Throughout this month the 108th Brigade fought at Messines, Baillieul and Kemmel Ridge. During the closing stages of the war the 36th Division took part in the last advance through Flanders and fought at Ypres, Courtrai and Ooteghem.

The 36th (Ulster) Division took over billets around Mouscron after the Armistice was signed on 11 November. Demobilisation began in January 1919 and finally, on 29 June, the Division ceased to exist. Total losses during the war were 32,186 killed, wounded and missing.

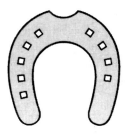

# 37th
## DIVISION

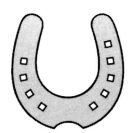

### 37th Division
Divisional sign: A golden horseshoe.

This Division was formed in March 1915 and was at first numbered 44th with 131st, 132nd and 133rd Infantry Brigades. On 12 April it was decided that the 16th (Irish) Division, then far behind in its training, should be replaced in the Second New Army by another division. The 44th Division was to be its replacement. Its thirteen infantry battalions had been in existence

for some months serving as Army Troops attached to the first three New Armies, and therefore were at an advanced stage of training. In April, the 44th Division was renumbered 37th and at the same time its brigades became 110th, 111th and 112th.

*110th Brigade*
6th Bn The Leicestershire Regt. Formed at Leicester and attached as Army Troops to the 9th Division.
7th Bn The Leicestershire Regt. Formed at Leicester

and attached as Army Troops to the 15th Division.
8th Bn The Leicestershire Regt. Formed at Leicester and attached as Army Troops to the 23rd Division.
9th Bn The Leicestershire Regt. Formed at Leicester and attached as Army Troops to the 23rd Division.

### 111th Brigade

10th Bn The Royal Fusiliers (City of London Regt). Raised by the Lord Mayor and City of London. The Battalion was recruited from businessmen of the City and was unofficially known as the 'Stockbrokers'. Originally attached as Army Troops to the 18th Division.
13th Bn The Royal Fusiliers (City of London Regt). Formed at Hounslow and attached as Army Troops to the 24th Division. Transferred to the 112th Brigade in February 1918.
13th Bn The King's Royal Rifle Corps. Formed at Winchester and attached as Army Troops to the 21st Division.
13th Bn The Rifle Brigade (The Prince Consort's Own). Formed at Winchester and attached as Army Troops to the 21st Division.

*Members of the 13th Bn, Royal Fusiliers, with souvenirs taken after an attack at La Boisselle in July 1916. The battalion was on loan, with 111th Bde, to the 34th Div during the early weeks of the 1916 Somme Offensive. Among the identifiable trophies can be seen a cap cover of the 190th Regt (centre), this regiment was part of the German 185th Div, and a Luger pistol (top right).* Imperial War Museum

### 112th Brigade

11th Bn The Royal Warwickshire Regt. Formed at Warwick and attached as Army Troops to the 24th Division. Disbanded in February 1918.
6th Bn The Bedfordshire Regt. Formed at Bedford and attached as Army Troops to the 9th Division. Reduced to a cadre in May 1918 and later transferred to the 39th Division.
8th Bn The East Lancashire Regt. Formed at Preston and attached as Army Troops to the 25th Division. Disbanded in February 1918.
10th Bn The Loyal North Lancashire Regt. Formed at Preston and attached as Army Troops to the 22nd Division. Disbanded in February 1918.
13th Bn The Royal Fusiliers (City of London Regt). Transferred from 111th Brigade in February 1918.
1st Bn The Essex Regt. A Regular Army battalion which joined from the 29th Division in February 1918.
1/1st Bn The Hertfordshire Regt. A Territorial Force battalion which joined from the 39th Division in May 1918 as a replacement for 6th Bedfords.

In July 1916, 110th Brigade was transferred to the 21st Division and at the same time was replaced by 63rd Brigade from the 21st.

### 63rd Brigade

8th Bn The Lincolnshire Regt.
8th Bn Prince Albert's (Somerset Light Infantry).
4th Bn The Duke of Cambridge's Own (Middlesex Regt). A Regular Army battalion.

10th Bn The York and Lancaster Regt. Disbanded in February 1918.

*Pioneers*

9th Bn The Prince of Wales's (North Staffordshire Regt). Formed at Lichfield and attached as Army Troops to the 22nd Division.

The four artillery brigades, 123rd, 124th, 125th, 126th, were originally raised for the 31st and 32nd Divisions (original Fourth New Army). Engineer field companies were numbered 152nd, 153rd, 154th and the divisional train consisted of 288th-291st Companies, Army Service Corps. The three field ambulances, 48th, 49th, 50th, were transferred from the 16th Division in June, 1915. Other units of the 37th Division included the 28th Mobile Veterinary Section and part of the 1/1st Yorkshire Dragoons which served between June 1915 and May 1916.

Divisional Headquarters moved from Andover to Cholderton on 21 April 1915 and, before long, intensive training began. On 25 June HM The King inspected the Division at Sidbury Hill. The following month orders were received to move to France and on 2 August concentration was complete around Tilques, north-west of St Omer.

On 22 December 1915 the Division was in positions east of Fonquevillers, when a sergeant of the 8th East Lancashires was wounded just outside the battalion's sector at Trench 51. At once, Pte William Young made his way to the NCO and began to bring him in to safety. This task was eventually accomplished but not before Pte Young had himself been wounded in the jaw and chest. For his gallantry, Pte Young was later awarded the Victoria Cross. He died from his wounds, however, on 28 August 1916.

Between 6 July and 22 August 1916, the 111th and 112th Brigades, together with the pioneers, were attached to the 34th Division. During this period these units fought on the Somme at the battles of Albert and the Bazentin and Pozières Ridges.

Since the failed attempt in July to take the enemy's positions along the banks and north of the River Ancre, the Germans had spent a considerable amount of time in improving and adding to their defences in this area. The villages of St Pierre Divion, Beaucourt and Beamont Hamel were now almost fortresses and posed an important obstacle in the way of any intended advance.

On 11 November a preliminary bombardment of the area commenced. This lasted for two days, until the morning of 13 November, when seven British divisions went into the attack. As a division, the 37th was not directly involved in the battle. However, throughout the Ancre operations (13-18 November) the 63rd and 111th Brigade were placed under the orders of the 63rd (Royal Naval) Division while the 112th served with the 2nd.

The 63rd (Royal Naval) Division, together with the two brigades from the 37th, attacked north of the Ancre and were fortunate in reaching all of their objectives. This was to include the capture of

13th (S) BATTALION
THE RIFLE BRIGADE O.C.A.

THIRTY-THIRD

A n n u a l

REUNION
DINNER

SATURDAY, 7th MAY 1960
at the

HEADQUARTERS CLUB,
DUKE OF YORK'S T. A. H. Q.
KINGS ROAD, CHELSEA, S.W.3

BEFORE DINNER IS SERVED A TWO
MINUTES' SILENCE WILL BE OBSERVED
IN MEMORY OF
OUR FALLEN COMRADES

*Menu card from the Thirty-Third Annual Reunion Dinner of the 13th Bn, Rifle Bde Old Comrades Association, 7 May 1960. Over 100 members attended.*

Beaucourt, which had remained out of reach of the 36th (Ulster) Division and cost the lives of so many Ulstermen on 1 July.

Also on the north side of the river, 112th Brigade was involved in an attack around the village of Serre, its orders being to take the two trenches known as Munich and Frankfurt. This attack failed and on the night of 16-17 November the Brigade was relieved and rejoined the 37th Division at Englebelmer.

On 9 April 1917 two parallel attacks began on an area east of Arras. The southern advance was along the River Scarpe and involved the 37th Division in heavy fighting until 11 April when Monchy Le Preux was captured. The Division was also engaged during the second battle of the Scarpe (23-24 April) and before the end of the month fought at Arleux.

Moving to the Ypres Sector, after a period of rest and training, the Division was placed under IX Corps, Second Army. It subsequently fought at Pilckem Ridge between 31 July-2 August; and from 22-25 September, 112th Brigade, under 19th and 39th Divisions, was engaged during the Menin Road Ridge operations.

Later battles involving the 37th Division during the remainder of 1917 were: Polygon Wood (27 September-3 October); Broodseinde (4 October), where Private Thomas Sage, 8th Somerset Light Infantry, won the Victoria Cross; Poelcappelle (9

*Regimental Police, 10th Bn Royal Fusiliers. Note the L/Cpl
seated in the centre who is wearing a small brass '10' on the
right lapel of the collar. This custom, practised by the NCOs
of the 10th Royal Fusiliers, is believed to be unique to this
battalion.*

*The Rev Theodore Bayley Hardy, VC, DSO, MC,
Temporary Chaplain to the Forces, attached to 8th Bn,
Lincolnshire Regt.*   Imperial War Museum

October); and Passchendaele (12 October) and (26th
October-10 November).

In the weeks prior to the 1918 German offensive on
the Somme, another Victoria Cross was added to the
Division's list. On this occasion, L/Cpl Charles
Robertson of the 10th Royal Fusiliers held an
important position just west of Polderhoek Chateau.
During the night of 8-9 March, and although alone and
cut off from his unit for most of the time, L/Cpl
Robertson successfully repelled the enemy's advance,
killing a large number with his Lewis gun. Having
received severe wounds and exhausted all his
ammunition, he then crawled with the gun to his line.

The Division did not move from the Ypres Sector
until the end of March, and therefore was not involved
in any German attack on the Somme until the
beginning of April.

The Division again fought around the Ancre River

in April 1918 when, on the 5th, the 8th Lincolns and 8th Somersets attacked at Rossignol Wood. A little ground was gained in this operation but at the cost of high casualties.

Before the end of April, another of the 37th Division's heroes was recognised and awarded the Victoria Cross. The Rev Theodore Bayley Hardy, a man of over 50 years of age, was Chaplain attached to the 8th Lincolns, and at numerous times had shown great courage in tending the wounded while under fire. On three occasions during April 1918, near Bucquoy and east of Gommecourt, Rev Hardy again displayed great bravery and devotion to duty. Following a raiding party into action Mr Hardy put his own life at risk several times in order to administer comfort and aid to the wounded. He was also responsible for freeing, with his bare hands, a number of men who had been buried alive. Rev Hardy was killed on 18 October 1918, having received the Victoria Cross, Distinguished Service Order and Military Cross during his service on the Western Front.

Between 4 and 10 May 1918, the 13th Rifle Brigade was in line at Bucquoy, during which time a number of daring raids were carried out. On one such operation Sgt Gregg and Rifleman Beesley of the Battalion won the Victoria Cross.

With a high casualty rate incurred during April 1918, the 6th Bedfords were reduced to a training cadre in the following May and subsequently attached to the 39th Division. Many members of the battalion, however, were to join the 1/1st Hertfordshire Regiment, the replacement for the Bedfords in 112th Brigade. While on its way to join the Division, the 1st Herts suffered over 500 casualties when it entered an area that had just been infected by a German gas-shell bombardment.

The Division fought in the Somme operations of 21-23 August 1918 and later, during September and October, on the Hindenburg Line at Havrincourt, the Canal du Nord and Cambrai. The enemy were pursued to the Selle between 9-12 October and, having strengthened its defences along the river, put up great resistance until 25 October. The 37th Division was relieved after its action on the Sambre River on 4 November, having suffered throughout the First World War 29,969 killed, wounded and missing.

# 38th
## (WELSH)
# DIVISION

**38th (Welsh) Division**
The Red Dragon of Wales.

In the middle of September 1914, a project in which a force raised under the same conditions as those locally raised units in England and Scotland was proclaimed by the then Chancellor of the Exchequer, David Lloyd George.

To administer this venture, a committee, the Welsh National Executive Committee (WNEC), was formally established at a meeting held in Cardiff on 29 September, its task being to recruit a 'Welsh Army Corps' of two or more divisions.

In its recruiting campaign, the WNEC set great emphasis on national pride and made every effort to create a totally Welsh formation. Even on the question of uniforms, the committee took advantage of the general shortage of clothing among the New Armies and chose not to clothe recruits in the emergency blue uniform then in use by most divisions. Instead, a homespun grey cloth known as 'Brethyn Llwyd' was taken into use. Although this uniform was primarily issued as a temporary measure, it was desired by the WNEC that the Welsh Army Corps should go to war in the homespun. However, as regulation khaki began to arrive, what grey had been given out was gradually discarded and subsequently used up by the reserve battalions.

Also, in the Welsh Army Corps, the use of the Welsh language within its units was encouraged by the WNEC. Many of its recruiting posts and leaflets appearing in both English and Welsh, *viz*:

I'R FYDDIN
FECHGYN
GWALIA!

Cas gwr nid cas ganddo
elyn ei wlad

CYMRU AM BYTH!

(To the Army, lads of Wales! Hateful is the man who does not hate his country's enemy. Wales for Ever!)

Although the initial response was tremendous, and enough men had come forward to form in excess of a division, the Welsh Army Corps was confined to a

*15th Bn, Welsh Regt (Carmarthenshire) at Rhyl, 1915.*

*below*

*15th Bn, Royal Welsh Fusiliers (1st London Welsh), Goat Major, 1915.*

single division, the surplus infantry, all Bantam battalions, being allotted to the 40th Division as its 119th Brigade.

Not all of the battalions intended for the Welsh Army Corps were directly recruited by the WNEC. A number were already under formation prior to its conception, but the administration and responsibility of these was, in the main, transferred to the committee.

On 10 December 1914 the 43rd Division was formed out of the units intended for the Welsh Army Corps, its three infantry brigades at first being numbered 1st, 2nd and 3rd but, later on, 128th, 129th and 130th. The use of the additional title 'Welsh' was also permitted, the Division being the only complete Welsh formation in the New Army and, along with the 36th (Ulster), one of only two in the Third, Fourth and Fifth New Armies to bear a sub-title. On 29 April 1915 the 43rd Division was renumbered 38th, and at the same time its infantry brigades became 113th, 114th and 115th.

The senior brigade comprised four battalions of the Royal Welsh Fusiliers and, with the exception of one that was formed from Welshmen living in London, were recruited throughout North Wales. In the Rhondda Valleys, two battalions were raised; another Glamorganshire battalion was formed in Swansea and these, together with a fourth from the County of Carmarthenshire, provided 114th Brigade – all Welsh Regiment. In the last brigade, one battalion of the Royal Welsh Fusiliers, two from the South Wales Borderers, and a fourth from the Welsh Regiment at Cardiff, made up the order of battle.

### 113th Brigade
13th Bn The Royal Welsh Fusiliers (1st North Wales). Raised at Rhyl by the Denbigh and Flint Territorial Force Associations.
14th Bn The Royal Welsh Fusiliers. Raised by the WNEC at Llandudno.

15th Bn The Royal Welsh Fusiliers (1st London Welsh). Raised in London. Disbanded in February 1918.

16th Bn The Royal Welsh Fusiliers. Raised by the WNEC at Llandudno.

*114th Brigade*

10th Bn The Welsh Regt (1st Rhondda). Raised throughout the Rhondda Valleys. Disbanded in February 1918.

13th Bn The Welsh Regt (2nd Rhondda). Raised in Cardiff.

14th Bn The Welsh Regt (Swansea). Raised by Mayor and Corporation with the Swansea Football and Cricket Club.

15th Bn The Welsh Regt (Carmarthenshire). Raised by the Carmarthenshire County Committee.

*115th Brigade*

17th Bn The Royal Welsh Fusiliers (2nd North Wales). Raised at Llandudno.

10th Bn The South Wales Borderers (1st Gwent). Raised at Brecon by the WNEC.

11th Bn The South Wales Borderers (2nd Gwent). Raised at Brecon by the WNEC. Disbanded in February 1918.

16th Bn The Welsh Regt (Cardiff City). Raised by the Lord Mayor and Corporation of Cardiff. Disbanded in February 1918.

2nd Bn The Royal Welsh Fusiliers. A Regular Army battalion which transferred from the 33rd Division in February 1918.

*Pioneers*

19th Bn The Welsh Regt (Glamorgan Pioneers). Formed at Colwyn Bay.

In the artillery, one battery was formed at Cardiff

*10th Bn, South Wales Borderers (1st Gwent), Colwyn Bay, 1915.* D. Barnes

*16th Bn, Welsh Regiment (Cardiff City), Goat Major, 1915. Note the special 'Arms of the City of Cardiff' collar badges worn by the battalion.* C. Lewis

*Collar badge of the 16th Bn Welsh Regt (Cardiff City).*

*16th Bn Welsh Regt (Cardiff City). Note the special 'Arms of Cardiff' brass collar badge.*   J. Lowe

which later, in January 1915, joined three others at Porthcawl. From Porthcawl, the batteries then moved to Pwellheli, where each received instructions to duplicate. In March and April and now comprising eight batteries, the artillery was divided into two, and in this way provided the nucleus of four brigades, each of four batteries. To make up the extra personnel required, 119th, 120th and 121st Brigades were transferred complete from the original 30th Division in England. In the same way, 122nd Brigade from the original 31st Division also joined. The original numbers, 119th-122nd, were retained, and these brigades formed part of the 38th (Welsh) Division.

The Divisional Field Companies, Royal Engineers were 123rd and 124th, both formed from some 650 skilled craftsmen originally included in the 13th Welsh Regiment. The third field company, the 151st, was formed later at Abergavenny.

The Royal Army Medical Corps Field Ambulances received the numbers 129th, 130th and 131st, the 130th being raised from members of the St John's Ambulance Association and being permitted to include the sub-title 'St John's' in its title. In addition, the association's insignia was worn on the men's uniforms and used as a vehicle marking.

Other divisional units included 330th-333rd Companies, Army Service Corps, 49th Mobile Veterinary Section and, for a period up to May 1916, part of 'D' Squadron, Royal Wiltshire Yeomanry.

Divisional Headquarters opened at Colwyn Bay on 19 January 1915, and in the following June the Division began to collect at Winchester. The Division was reviewed at Crawley Down by HM The Queen on 29 November, by which time advance parties were already on their way to France. Concentration was complete, minus the artillery which was still training in England, west of Aire in XI Corps area by 6 December.

The 38th Division spent the early months of 1916 training for trench warfare and gaining experience under actual battle conditions in the line around Givenchy. While under instruction from the Guards Division, a number of small raids were carried out, the 15th Royal Welsh Fusiliers being the first battalion in the Division to attack the enemy's line.

In preparation for the 1916 offensive on the Somme, the 38th Division left the Givenchy area on 10 June. It then moved to the neighbourhood of St Pol for additional training, and on 5 July relieved the 7th Division in front of Mametz Wood.

In 1916, Mametz Wood lying due north of Mametz Village, east of Contalmaison and south-west of Bazentin, posed a tremendous obstacle in the way of any planned advance in the Somme region. Mametz was a dense, dark and hostile wood, carpeted with a thick undergrowth, cluttered with broken trees, and heavily defended with machine-gun posts. Its capture, General Haig believed, was essential – a salient being formed in the Allied lines would be avoided, and the British left flank secured.

After spending two days in reconnaissance, the 38th (Welsh) Division eventually attacked the wood on 7 July. The Brigade chosen to lead the assault was the 115th who, upon leaving their trenches at 8.30am immediately encountered heavy machine-gun fire. During the day several attempts to reach their objective failed and the Brigade, having got no closer to the wood than 250yds, was forced to retire.

*RSM, 14th Bn Welsh Regt, France 1917.*  C. Lewis

1916 – 'The flower of young Wales stood up to machine guns with success that astonished all those who knew the ground.'

It was to be just over a year before the Division was engaged in another major battle. On 31 July 1917, the first day of the Third Battle of Ypres, the 38th Division under XIV Corps, Fifth Army, was sent into attack at Pilckem Ridge. The objective set before the Division was to take the ridge and pass on 700yds to the Steenbeeke, where it would secure a crossing.

In this engagement, two brigades, 114th on the right with 113th on the left, successfully captured the German line east of Ypres Canal, the ridge itself and a further position east of Pilckem known as Iron Cross. The 115th Brigade then passed through and, after great loss, made good the crossing of the Steenbeeke.

On the 38th Division's front at Pilckem it was estimated that there were some 280 pill-boxes – concrete structures usually housing one or more machine guns. It was these obstacles that posed the greatest threat to the leading battalions and were to account for most of the high casualties incurred on 31 July. During the fighting both Cpl J. L. Davies (13th

*Officers, 13th Bn Royal Welsh Fusiliers, France, Feb 1917. The Bn badge was a red cloth triangle, seen on the upper arm of the officer on the left.*  C. Lewis

Casualties within 115th Brigade throughout 7 July amounted to over 400 and included the death of Col J. S. Wilkinson, Commanding Officer of the 10th South Wales Borderers.

Fresh attacks were launched towards the wood during the next day. This time the remaining brigades of the 38th Division (113th and 114th) were used, but they, like the 115th on the previous days, could make no headway. Likewise, on 9 July, no progress was made and the main attack planned for that day was postponed until the following morning.

At 4.15am on 10 July the 38th Division again attacked Mametz Wood. This time all three brigades were involved – 113th attacking the western side of the wood, 114th the eastern flank, with 115th in reserve. Once more the murderous journey across the valley towards the enemy's front line claimed many casualties. However, advance parties on this day managed to enter the outskirts of the wood and subsequently secured their first objective.

By the afternoon some eleven battalions were fighting in the wood, and by the evening a line had been established, which at its nearest point was just 300yds from its northern end. On 11 July further ground was taken and Mametz Wood fell even more firmly into Allied hands.

The efforts made by the 38th (Welsh) Division during the assault on Mametz have been recorded and praised many times – Graves, Sassoon, Masefield, Jones, etc. But it is surely in the words of Wyn Griffith, 15th Royal Welsh Fusiliers, that we find insight as to the supreme sacrifice made by the Welch Nation in July

RWF) and Sgt I. Rees (11th SWB) won the Victoria Cross for their courage and devotion to duty while putting out of action two pill-boxes.

After a time out of the line and a series of engagements around St Julien and Langemarck, the 38th (Welsh) Division was moved to the front around Armentières in the Lys valley. Here numerous patrols and raids were carried out including a most daring and successful assault by the 10th South Wales Borderers on the night of 7-8 November.

The Division was in reserve during the Battle of The Ancre on 5 April 1918, but was again in action throughout the Second Battle of the Somme, 21 August-3 September. In these operations, L/Cpl Henry Weale, 14th Royal Welsh Fusiliers won the Victoria Cross at Bazentin-le-Grand.

In the battles of the Hindenburg Line: Havrincourt (12 September), Epéphy (18 September), the Beaurevoir Line (5 October), and Cambrai (8 October), the Division gained another two Victoria Crosses. Its last major engagements of the war took place during 17-22 October, at the Battle of the Selle, and on 4 November at the Battle of the Sambre.

On 5 November the Division concentrated in the Mormal Forest and set up its headquarters at

*CSM Glanfrwyd Buse, 14th Bn, Welsh Regt, France 1917. Mr Buse was from Swansea and won the MM in France.* C. Lewis

*Sgt, Welsh Regt. The 38th (Welsh) Div sign is worn below the brass shoulder title 'WELSH'. The Sgt has three small blue chevrons on his lower right arm, denoting three years' service abroad after 1914, and on the other arm, a wound stripe.* C. Lewis

*CSM Jack Williams, 10th Bn, South Wales Borderers. CSM Williams was one of the most decorated men of the war. He had already won the DCM and the MM and Bar, when on the night of 7-8 Oct 1918, during an attack on Villers Outreaux, he also gained the VC.*

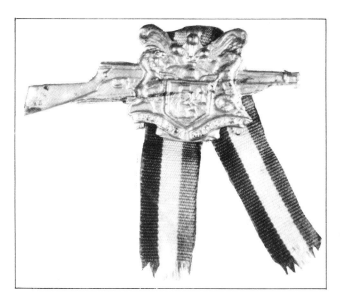

*Gilt brooch with red, white and blue ribbon and the Arms of Cardiff made for wives and sweethearts of members of the 16th Bn, Welsh Regt.*

Locquignol. It later took over from the 33rd Division, beyond the Sambre, made a steady advance, and on 11 November its leading brigade was located at Wattignies la Victoire.

In December some 3,000 miners were demobilised and left France. Drafts were sent to Germany throughout the early months of 1919 but by June all units had been disbanded. The 38th (Welsh) Division lost throughout the war 28,635 killed, wounded and missing.

*The Mametz Wood Memorial to the 38th (Welsh) Div. This splendid memorial looks across towards the wood and was erected in July 1987 as a result of a fund set up by the South Wales Branch of the Western Front Association.*  B. Owen

# 39th
## DIVISION

**39th Division**
Divisional sign: A white square with three light-blue stripes.

Winchester was the first headquarters of the 39th Division, its units beginning to concentrate there in early August 1915. By September, however, only one infantry brigade, the pioneers, and one Army Service Corps company had arrived; on 28 September these units moved to Aldershot.

The Division was up to strength by November and that month moved to Witley. The three infantry brigades were numbered 116th, which originally had been raised for the 33rd Division (new), 117th and 118th. The latter brigade had been formed in London during July 1915 and at first included the 10th and 11th Battalions, Queen's Own Royal West Kents. However, these units were transferred to other brigades on 16 October. With two replacement battalions, the 118th Brigade was then made up as follows: 13th East Surreys, 20th and 21st Middlesex, and 14th Argylls. When the Division received its orders to move to France, the 118th Brigade was not yet ready for service and had to be left behind. The battalions were later transferred and their places taken in the 39th Division by four Territorial Force battalions, then serving in France.

### 116th Brigade
11th Bn The Royal Sussex Regt (1st South Down). Raised by Lt-Col C. Lowther, MP, at Bexhill. Reduced to a cadre in May 1918 and later transferred to 75th Brigade, 25th Division, absorbing the 13th West Kents (formed 1 June) in July.
12th Bn The Royal Sussex Regt (2nd South Down). Raised by Lt-Col C. Lowther, MP, at Bexhill. Disbanded in February 1918.

### 117th Brigade
13th Bn The Royal Sussex Regt (3rd South Down). Raised by Lt-Col C. Lowther, MP, at Bexhill. Reduced to a cadre in June 1918 and disbanded in the following August.
14th Bn The Hampshire Regt (1st Portsmouth). Raised by the Mayor and Town of Portsmouth. Disbanded in February 1918.
1/1st Bn The Hertfordshire Regt. Joined from 118th Brigade in February 1918. Transferred to the 37th Division in the following May.
16th Bn The Sherwood Foresters (Nottinghamshire and Derbyshire Regt) (Chatsworth Rifles). Raised by the Duke of Devonshire at Derby. Reduced to a cadre in May 1918 and later transferred to the 66th Division.
17th Bn The Sherwood Foresters (Nottinghamshire and Derbyshire Regt) (Welbeck Rangers). Raised by the Mayor and Recruiting Committee of Nottingham. Disbanded in February 1918.
17th Bn The King's Royal Rifle Corps (British Empire League). Raised by the BEL in London. Reduced to a cadre in May 1918 and later transferred to the 66th Division.
16th Bn The Rifle Brigade (The Prince Consort's Own) (St Pancras). Raised by the Parliamentary Recruiting Committee of the London Borough of St Pancras. Reduced to a cadre in May 1918 and later transferred to the 66th Division.

### 118th Brigade
1/6th Bn The Cheshire Regt. Transferred to the 25th Division in May 1918.
4th/5th Bn The Black Watch (Royal Highlanders). The 4th and 5th Battalions, Black Watch were amalgamated on 15 March 1916. Transferred to the 15th Division in May 1918.
1/1st Bn The Cambridgeshire Regt. Transferred to the 12th Division in May 1918.
1/1st Bn The Hertfordshire Regt. Transferred to the 116th Brigade in February 1918.

### Pioneers
13th Bn The Gloucestershire Regt (Forest of Dean Pioneers). Formed by Lt-Col H. Webb, MP, at Malvern. Transferred to the 66th Division in May 1918.

The 39th Divisional Artillery was raised by the Thames Ironworks in London, 174th Brigade at

Greenwich, 179th and 184th Brigades at Lee Green, and 186th Brigade at Deptford. The ammunition column also came from the Deptford works. The three engineer field companies were formed at Marton Hall, Yorkshire and were designated 225th 227th and 234th (Stockton-on-Tees). The signal company was from Norbury and bore the sub-title (Empire). The three field ambulances were numbered 132nd, 133rd, 134th and the mobile veterinary section, 50th, 284th-287th Companies, Army Service Corps, all formed at Pangbourne, made up the divisional train. 'E' Squadron, South Irish Horse also formed part of the Division until May 1916, when it was transferred to I Corps Cavalry Regiment.

The Division began to move to France at the end of February 1916, and was complete around Blaringhem in First Army area by 17 March. During the next months the Division gained experience of trench warfare. It took its turn in the line and was active on numerous raids and patrols. On 30 June the Division was in positions at the 'Boar's Head', Richebourg l'Avoue. An attack was made and one company of the 12th Royal Sussex Regiment led by Company Sergeant Major Nelson Carter, managed to reach the enemy's second-line trench. Whilst under constant fire, CSM Carter inflicted heavy casualties with bombs. He was then responsible for bringing in a number of wounded before he himself was killed. CSM Carter was awarded the Victoria Cross for his bravery that day.

Throughout August 1916 the 39th Division moved south from the Bethune area. The 1916 Allied

July 1917, when under XVIII Corps it fought at Pilckem Ridge. This was the first engagement of the 1917 Ypres battles and added another Victoria Cross, that of 2/Lt D. G. W. Hewitt of the 14th Hampshires, to the Division's list.

Subsequent operations throughout 1917 involving the 39th Division were at Langemarck (16-18 August); the Menin Road Ridge (20-25 September) where Cpl Ernest Egerton of the 16th Sherwood Foresters won the Victoria Cross on the 20th; Polygon Wood (26-27 September); and Passchendaele (29 October-10 November).

The Division left the Ypres sector at the end of January 1918, moving south to positions east of Amiens. The German offensive in Picardy began on 21 March 1918 and during that evening 116th Brigade was placed temporarily under the command of 16th Division, holding a line between Epéhy and St Emilie. On the following day 16th Division, under great pressure from the enemy's attack, was forced to retire. During this withdrawal, 116th Brigade fought a heroic rearguard action in which it suffered high casualties.

Throughout 22 and 23 March the Division took part in the heavy fighting around St Quentin. On 24 and 25 March, both 117th and 118th Brigades were involved during a series of vital operations on the Somme River, in which important crossing points were defended, while at the same time 116th Brigade was involved north of the Somme during the Battle of Bapaume. The last of the enemy's March attacks on the Somme, involving the 39th Division, took place at Rosières on the 26 and 27 March.

On 9 April the enemy's attention turned towards Flanders and during the next twenty days the Battles of the Lys took place. Due to the heavy casualties incurred throughout March, the 39th Division was reduced to a composite brigade on 10 April. As such, the 39th served under XXII Corps and took part in the following operations: Wytschaete Ridge (16 April), the First and Second Battles of Kemmel Ridge (17-19 and 25-26 April) and in reserve at the Battle of the Scherpenburg on 29 April.

The composite brigade returned to divisional headquarters at Eperlecques, north-west of St Omer on 6 May, having fought its last active operations of the war. However, the artillery and elements of other divisional units remained in the line and fought on until the Armistice. The Division was reduced to a cadre by 1 June and thereafter it was engaged in the instruction and training of American Troops.

Divisional headquarters moved to Varengeville, on the coast by Dieppe. On 15 August and on 16 November orders were received to disband the 117th and 118th Brigades. At the same time, the 39th Division was reconstituted by taking over a brigade then at the camp for malarial convalescents at Martin Église, and the 197th Brigade formerly of the 66th Division. Losses throughout the First World War were 27,869 killed, wounded and missing.

offensive on the Somme had begun on 1 July and the Division was heading for its first major engagement of the war. Having reached positions in the line west of Thiepval, a divisional attack was ordered on 3 September, north-west of the River Ancre. Operations around this part of the Somme battle-front had been suspended since the initial attack of 1 July. The autumn attempt, like those of two months previous, also failed and severe casualties were once again incurred.

Before the end of 1916 and the ceasing of operations on the Somme in November, the 39th Division were engaged in a number of important, and successful, engagements. The Battle of Thiepval Ridge between 26-28 September was followed, on 14 and 21 October respectively, by the capture of two of the enemy's heaviest defended positions – the Schwaben Redoubt and Stuff Trench. Still in the region of the Ancre, the 39th Division, on 13 November, advanced northwards from the Schwaben Redoubt towards St Pierre Divion and the German Hansa Line, which ran from the Thiepval Ridge to the river near Beaucourt. During 13 November and the following day, and in appalling conditions, the Division took all of its objectives, including some 1,000yds of the Hansa.

The great Somme offensive came to an end on 18 November 1916, by which time the 39th Division had suffered heavy casualties. The percentage of reinforcements by 10 November being: officers 50%, and other ranks 66%.

The 39th was withdrawn from the line in November 1916 and did not take part in any major action until 31

# 40th
## DIVISION

### 40th Division
Divisional sign: A diamond bearing an acorn and oak leaves superimposed upon a bantam cock.

The 40th Division was formed at Aldershot in September 1915 and included units recruited in England, Wales and Scotland. At first the four Welsh battalions of the 119th Brigade were composed entirely of Bantams, men below the regulation height for an infantry soldier. These units had been raised by the Welsh National Executive Committee and had originally been intended for the Welsh Army Corps (later 38th (Welsh) Division). The other two brigades, 120th and 121st, were mixed in height but contained a fair proportion of Bantams. In consequence, the 40th Division was considered to be a Bantam Division.

Although the 119th Brigade was made up of small but hardy men, the other two brigades included many that were considered to be underdeveloped and unfit for active service. For this reason large-scale medical examinations were carried out, and in the case of one battalion which arrived at Aldershot 1,000 strong, over 800 were later rejected.

The 119th Brigade encountered littled reduction as a result of the inspection. However, both the 120th and 121st were reduced in such great numbers that each required two battalions to bring it up to war establishment. To achieve this, those men of each brigade regarded as fit for war service were amalgamated into two battalions. The remaining two required for each brigade were added when four battalions were transferred from the 39th Division.

The four battalions which ceased to exist as a result of the 40th Division's reorganisation were: 13th Cameronians and 12th South Lancashire from 120th Brigade, and 18th Notts & Derby and 22nd Middlesex, 121st Brigade. The new units transferred from the 39th Division were 13th East Surreys, 20th and 21st Middlesex, and 14th Argyll and Sutherland Highlanders.

### 119th Brigade
19th Bn The Royal Welsh Fusiliers. Disbanded in February 1918.
12th Bn The South Wales Borderers (3rd Gwent). Raised at Newport and disbanded in February 1918.
17th Bn The Welsh Regt (1st Glamorgan). Disbanded in February 1918.

18th Bn The Welsh Regt (2nd Glamorgan). Reduced to a cadre in May 1918 and later transferred to the 16th Division.
13th Bn The East Surrey Regt (Wandsworth). Joined from 120th Brigade in February 1918. Reduced to a cadre in May 1918 and later transferred to the 25th Division.

*17th Bn Welsh Regt (1st Glamorgan), Rhos 1915. The 17th was a Bantam Bn and displays a bantam cock above the Prince of Wales's Plumes on the Mascot's coat. Note also the alternative spelling 'WELCH' being used in the title. The more widely used 'WELSH' was standardised to 'WELCH' for both the Royal Welsh Fusiliers and Welsh Regt in Army Order 56 of 1920.* Welch Regt Museum

21st Bn The Duke of Cambridge's Own (Middlesex Regt) (Islington). Joined from 121st Brigade in February 1918. Reduced to a cadre in May 1918 and in June left the Division and returned to England where it absorbed the 20th Queen's Regiment which had been formed on 21 June 1918.

### 120th Brigade

11th Bn The King's Own (Royal Lancaster Regt). Formed at Lancaster as a Bantam battalion and disbanded in February 1918.

13th Bn The East Surrey Regt (Wandsworth). Raised by the Mayor and Borough of Wandsworth. Transferred to 119th Brigade in February 1918.

14th Bn The Highland Light Infantry. Formed as a Bantam battalion. Reduced to a cadre in May 1918 and later transferred to the 34th Division.

14th Bn Princess Louise's (Argyll and Sutherland Highlanders). Reduced to a cadre in May 1918 and later transferred to the 14th Division.

10th/11th Bn The Highland Light Infantry. Joined from the 15th Division in February 1918. Reduced to a cadre in May 1918 and later transferred to the 14th Division.

### 121st Brigade

12th Bn The Suffolk Regt (East Anglian). Formed at Bury St Edmunds as a Bantam battalion. Reduced to a cadre in May 1918 and later transferred to the 14th Division.

13th Bn Alexandra, Princess of Wales's Own (Yorkshire Regt). Formed as a Bantam battalion at Richmond in July 1915. Reduced to a cadre in May 1918 and later transferred to the 75th Brigade, 25th Division absorbing the 23rd Yorkshire Regiment which had been formed in June.

20th Bn The Duke of Cambridge's Own (Middlesex Regt) (Shoreditch). Raised by the Mayor and Borough of Shoreditch. Reduced to a cadre in May 1918 and later transferred to the 14th Division.

21st Bn The Duke of Cambridge's Own (Middlesex Regt) (Islington). Raised by the Mayor and Borough of Islington. Transferred to 119th Brigade in February 1918.

### Pioneers

12th Bn Alexandra, Princess of Wales's Own (Yorkshire Regt) (Tees-side Pioneers). Formed by the Mayor and Town of Middlesbrough. Reduced to a cadre in May 1918 and the following month was absorbed into the 17th Worcestershire Regiment.

Due to heavy losses throughout the March and April 1918 German offensives, the Division was reconstituted in June, and until the end of the war was organised as follows:

119th Brigade: 13th Royal Inniskilling Fusiliers, 13th East Lancashire, 12th North Staffordshire.

120th Brigade: 10th King's Own Scottish Borderers, 15th King's Own Yorkshire Light Infantry, 11th Cameron Highlanders.

*Capt J. Gwyther Jones, 18th Bn, Welsh Regt (2nd Glamorgan), France 1916.*  Welch Regt Museum

121st Brigade: 8th Royal Irish Regiment, 23rd Lancashire Fusiliers, 23rd Cheshire.

### Pioneers

17th Bn The Worcestershire Regt. Formed in June 1918 from the regiment's 17th (Garrison) Battalion and included the Division's former pioneers, the 12th Yorkshire Regiment.

The divisional artillery was formed at East Ham (178th Brigade), Ashton (181st Brigade), Tottenham (185th Brigade), Nottingham (188th Brigade), and Hammersmith (Ammunition Column). The three engineer field companies, 224th, 229th and 231st were raised at Doncaster.

The three field ambulances were numbered 135th, 136th and 137th and the mobile veterinary section was the 51st. Divisional train consisted of the 292nd-295th Companies, Army Service Corps. 'A' Squadron, 1/1st Royal Wiltshire Yeomanry formed part of the Division until moving to IX Corps Cavalry Regiment in June 1916.

Due to its early difficulties and subsequent reorganisation, the 40th Division did not complete its training until the middle of May 1916. Whilst awaiting its orders to move to France, the Division was inspected by HM The King at Laffans Plain on 25 May. Then, within days, mobilisation began, and by 9 June concentration was complete in the Lillers area, near Bethune.

In the months that followed, intensive training for trench warfare was carried out. Part of the line was taken over in the Lens area where the Division was soon to gain experience of actual war conditions.

While, according to the Divisional History, the 40th had been 'learning its trade', the 1916 allied offensive on the Somme had commenced. The Division moved south to the area at the beginning of November and while attached to the 31st Division between the 14th and 18th, 120th Brigade fought at the Battle of the Ancre.

The November operations around the Ancre River were the last of the 1916 Somme offensive. Headquarters were set up at Bray where, for their first winter in France, the Division took in reinforcements and made the best of what was considered at the time to be one of the worst areas in France.

In March 1917 the Germans began their retreat to the Hindenburg Line. On 17 March the enemy, then in front of the 40th Division, made their move. The 40th advanced immediately and on the following day had occupied Mont St Quentin and Haut Allaines. Peronne was also taken and it is claimed by the Regiment that the 13th East Surreys were the first British Troops to enter the town.

After a short period out of the line the Division, on 21 April, again went into action, this time on a front between Gouzeacourt and Gouzeacourt Wood. During the next two weeks a number of successful engagements took place: Fifteen Ravine, Villers Plouich where Cpl Edward Foster of the 13th East Surreys won the Victoria Cross, Beaucamp, and la Vacquerie. Then between 23-25 November the Division played an important role in the capture of Bourlon Wood.

After the Cambrai operations of 1917, the Division spent the winter occupying part of the Hindenburg Line around Bullecourt. On 20 March 1918, the day before the commencement of the German offensive on the Somme, the Division's three infantry brigades were moved into positions of readiness at Mercatel, Hamelincourt and Blaireville, all a few miles south of Arras. The Division was later involved in the heavy fighting around St Leger, Mory, Vrancourt and Bapaume. During this period the Division gained two

*Cap badge of 13th Bn East Surrey Regt (Wandsworth). The badge is basically that of the East Surrey Regt, but has the Arms of Wandsworth in the centre and the motto 'We Serve'.*

Victoria Crosses, those of 2/Lt Ernest Beal, 13th Yorkshire Regiment, and L/Cpl Arthur Cross, Machine Gun Corps.

At the end of March the Division was withdrawn from the line to rest and refit, the operations since 21 March having accounted for over 2,800 casualties. While at Merville, HM The King again visited the Division, and on this occasion expressed to the 40th his appreciation for their gallant behaviour during the recent fighting.

The 40th Division entered the Battles of the Lys on 9 April, and in the subsequent fighting around Estaires and Hazebrouck suffered such heavy losses that it practically ceased to exist. Having withdrawn across the river at Bac St Maur, each brigade was now fighting as a battalion, the Division was taken out of the line and retired to the St Omer area.

With each of its battalions either disbanded or moved at cadre strength to other divisions, the 40th received new infantry units throughout June 1918. These new battalions had previously been serving as 'Garrison Guard' units and were made up of all B1 men (men of low physique). Of the new personnel, a large number were considered unfit for active service. Most had done no military training for a very long time and some men had never fired a rifle.

However, the Division played its part in the final advance in Flanders, fighting at the Battle of Ypres between 28 September-2 October. The advance was continued and on 10 November cyclists of the Division had crossed the Rhosne and reached the railway north-east of Anvaing. Total losses throughout the First World War were 19,179 killed, wounded and missing.

# 41st
## DIVISION

## 41st Division

Divisional sign: Squares of various colours distinguished formations within the Division. Each square had a white diagonal band.

The 41st Division was formed as part of the Fifth New Army at Aldershot in September 1915. The majority of battalions, brigades, etc, within the Division were formed in response to Lord Kitchener's 1915 appeal for units to be raised by groups of friends associated with one locality. Except for one battalion, which was recruited in Durham, and another from East Anglia, the North of England and the Midlands, all the infantry were from the London area and the counties of Surrey, Hampshire, Kent and Essex. There was a King's Royal Rifle Corps battalion known as the 'Arts and Crafts'; the 'Footballers' of the Middlesex Regiment; a battalion raised for the Royal Fusiliers which comprised bank clerks and accountants from the City of London; and the 'Yeoman Rifles', a battalion of farmers from Yorkshire, Northumberland, Durham, Lincolnshire, Leicestershire and Norfolk.

### 122nd Brigade
12th Bn The East Surrey Regt (Bermondsey). Raised by the Mayor and Borough of Bermondsey.
15th Bn The Hampshire Regt (2nd Portsmouth). Raised by the Mayor and Borough of Portsmouth. Absorbed the 1/1st Hampshire Yeomanry during September and October 1917 and was then designated 15th (Hampshire Yeomanry) Battalion.
11th Bn The Queen's Own (Royal West Kent Regt) (Lewisham). Raised by the Mayor and Borough of Lewisham and disbanded in February 1918.
18th Bn The King's Royal Rifle Corps (Arts and Crafts). Raised at Gidea Park, Essex by Major Sir Herbert Raphael, MP.

### 123rd Brigade
11th Bn The Queen's (Royal West Surrey Regt) (Lambeth). Raised by the Mayor and Borough of Lambeth.
10th Bn The Queen's Own (Royal West Kent Regt) (Kent County). Raised by Lord Harris, Vice-Lieutenant of Kent, at Maidstone.
23rd Bn The Duke of Cambridge's Own (Middlesex Regt) (2nd Football). Raised by the Rt Hon W. Joynson-Hicks, MP, in London.

*Sgt, 23rd Bn, Duke of Cambridge's Own (Middlesex Regt) (2nd Football). Note the number '23' worn above the usual 'MIDDLESEX' shoulder title.*  B. Nevison

20th Bn The Durham Light Infantry (Wearside). Raised by the Mayor and Recruiting Committee of Sunderland. Transferred to 124th Brigade in March 1918.

### 124th Brigade
10th Bn The Queen's (Royal West Surrey Regt) (Battersea). Raised by the Mayor and Borough of Battersea.
26th Bn The Royal Fusiliers (City of London Regt) (Bankers). Raised by the Lord Mayor of the City of London from bank clerks and accountants.

32nd Bn The Royal Fusiliers (City of London Regt) (East Ham). Raised by the Mayor and Borough of East Ham and disbanded in February 1918.

21st Bn The King's Royal Rifle Corps (Yeoman Rifles). The battalion was made up from farmers and included two companies from Yorkshire; one from Northumberland and Durham; and one each from Lincoln, Leicestershire and Norfolk. Disbanded in March 1918.

20th Bn The Durham Light Infantry (Wearside). Transferred from 123rd Brigade in March 1918.

*Pioneers*

19th Bn The Duke of Cambridge's Own (Middlesex Regt) (2nd Public Works Pioneers). Raised in London by Lt-Col John Ward, MP.

The four field artillery brigades were recruited at Hampstead (183rd), Fulham (187th), Hackney (189th) and Wimbledon (190th). The divisional ammunition column was from West Ham. Engineer field companies were from Barnsley (228th), Ripon (233rd), Reading (237th), and the signals came from Glasgow.

The field ambulances were numbered 138th, 139th, 140th, the mobile veterinary section 52nd, and the service companies 296th-299th. 'B' Squadron, Royal Wiltshire Yeomanry were attached as mounted troops until May 1916.

Intensive divisional training commenced in February 1916 and on 26 April the Division was

*Regimental Police, 20th Bn, Durham Light Infantry (Wearside). Note the 'RP' arm bands and the wound stripe worn on the lower arm of the Sgt standing on the right. The Sgt (seated) has two overseas service chevrons just above his arm band.* A. Gavaghan

inspected by HM The King, accompanied by Field-Marshal Lord French and General Sir Archibald Hunter.

Having received its embarkation orders, the Division began its move to France on 1 May, disembarkation being concluded on the 6th. Two days later the 41st concentrated between Hazebrouck and Bailleul.

The first major engagement in which the 41st Division took part was during the Somme offensive of July-November 1916. On 15 September General Haig attempted a breakthrough opposite the centre of the British Line. The 41st went into action and, together with troops from New Zealand, captured the village of Flers. Casualties that day were kept to an unusually low level for an operation of this size, largely due to the use of tanks for the first time in battle. Having fought on to Courcelette, the Division retired from the line on 17 September. However, after just over two weeks they were again in action when between 4-10 October, with tanks in support, the Division took part in the Battle of the Transloy Ridges.

In 1917 the British attempted another breakthrough, this time at Ypres where the Germans held a commanding position to the south at Messines Ridge. After heavy bombardment and the detonation on 7 June of almost 500 tons of high explosive contained in mines dug under the ridge, the 41st Division, together with other divisions of the Second Army, were sent in to clear what remained of the enemy. The action on and around the ridge lasted until 14 June. Further engagements during 1917 that included the 41st Division were: Pilckem Ridge (31 July-2 August), the Menin Road Ridge (20-22 September) and the operations on the Flanders Coast (26 September-11 November).

The Division received orders on 7 November 1917 that it was to be transferred to the Italian Front. It commenced its move on 12 November and by the 18th was concentrated to the north-west of Mantua. Before the end of the month the Division had taken over part of the front line behind the Piave River, relieving the Italian 1st Division.

After four months in Italy, the 41st Division returned to France, the last of the units arriving on 9 March 1918 and forming up at Doullens and Mondicourt. As part of IV Corps, Third Army, the 41st Division took part in the following Somme actions during March: St Quentin (22-23), Bapaume (24-25) and Arras (28). Between 9-29 April the Division was involved in the actions around the River Lys in Belgium, and in September took part in the advance in Flanders.

During the last months of the war the 41st Division was engaged at the Battle of Ypres (28 September-2 October), Courtrai (14-19 October) and Ooteghem (25 October). It was relieved in the front line on 26 October and, after resting around Courtrai, linked up with the French 41st Division on 3 November. By 11am on 11 November cyclists of 124th Brigade had reached the line of the Dendre near Grammont.

During the war the 41st Division lost 32,158 killed, wounded and missing.

# 5
# RESERVE BATTALIONS

On 10 April 1915 the six divisions of the original Fourth New Army were broken up and its battalions became reserve units to the First, Second and Third New Armies. The Regular Army already had its reserve system which included the old Militia, now called Special Reserve. Consequently, in 1915, the battalions of the original 30th-35th Divisions became the 2nd Reserve and their brigades numbered 1st-18th Reserve Infantry Brigades. A number of additional 2nd Reserve battalions were formed later on.

Another type of New Army reserve battalion was created during the First World War. These were styled Local Reserve and were formed from the depot companies of the locally raised battalions which formed the bulk of the Fourth and Fifth New Armies. Again, these were organised into brigades and used to take in recruits, provide training and supply reinforcements to the parent battalions overseas.

After conscription was introduced in 1916, it was found that the large number of recruits then coming into the army could not be managed by the existing

*A Band Boy (note musician's arm badge) of the 11th (Reserve) Bn, Loyal North Lancashire Regt.*    D. Barnes

*below.*
*Band, 18th Bn, Royal Welsh Fusiliers (2nd London Welsh).*

reserve system. Subsequently, on 1 September 1916, a new organisation was created for this purpose. This was called the Training Reserve and was formed from the New Army's 2nd and Local Reserve battalions. As a result of this reorganisation, most reserve battalions discarded their designations and became numbered battalions within the Training Reserve. Others were absorbed into the battalions of their Reserve Brigades.

No 2nd Reserve battalions were formed by the Irish regiments. However, six Local Reserve units were raised for the 36th (Ulster) Division but these did not become part of the Training Reserve. Each battalion served as part of the 15th (Ulster) Reserve Infantry Brigade and in 1918 was absorbed into its regiment's 3rd (Reserve) Battalion.

The following table details the New Army reserve battalions, their origin and subsequent position in the Training Reserve:

*Four senior NCOs of the 10th Bn, South Staffordshire Regt (left to right) F. Mander, W. Bailey, W. J. Davis and W. P. Jones-Tavistock, Feb 1915. The first of these men had joined the South Staffs in 1876 and their total service in 1915 amounted to 142 years.* C. Coogan

| Battalion | Origin | Training Reserve | Battalion | Origin | Training Reserve |
|---|---|---|---|---|---|
| 14th R. Scots | 2nd Reserve from original 34th Div | 54th Bn | 29th R. Fusiliers | Local Reserve for 20th, 21st Bns | 105th Bn |
| 18th R. Scots | Local Reserve for 15th, 16th, 17th Bns | 77th Bn | 30th R. Fusiliers | Local Reserve for 23rd, 24th Bns | 106th Bn |
| 9th Queen's | 2nd Reserve from original 31st Div | Part of 5th Bde | 31st R. Fusiliers | Local Reserve for 10th, 26th Bns | 107th Bn |
| 12th Queen's | Local Reserve for 10th, 11th Bns | 97th Bn | 41st R. Fusiliers (1) | Reserve for 38th, 39th, 40th Bns | |
| 9th Buffs | 2nd Reserve from original 32nd Div | 29th Bn | 42nd R. Fusiliers (1) | Reserve for 38th, 39th, 40th Bns | |
| 10th King's Own | 2nd Reserve from original 33rd Div | 43rd Bn | 15th King's | 2nd Reserve from original 35th Div | 49th Bn |
| 12th King's Own | 2nd Reserve | 76th Bn | 16th King's | 2nd Reserve from original 35th Div | Part of 11th Bde |
| 15th North'd Fus | 2nd Reserve from original 30th Div | Part of 1st Bde | 21st King's | Local Reserve for 17th, 18th Bns | 67th Bn |
| 28th North'd Fus | Local Reserve for 18th, 19th Bns | Part of 19th Bde | 22nd King's | Local Reserve for 19th, 20th Bns | 68th Bn |
| 29th North'd Fus | Local Reserve for 20th, 21st, 22nd, 23rd Bns | 84th Bn | 10th Norfolk | 2nd Reserve from original 31st Div | 25th Bn |
| 30th North'd Fus | Local Reserve for 24th, 25th, 26th, 27th Bns | 85th Bn | 9th Lincolnshire | 2nd Reserve from original 30th Div | 11th Bn |
| 31st North'd Fus | Local Reserve for 16th Bn | 86th Bn | 11th Lincolnshire | Local Reserve for 10th Bns | 82nd Bn |
| 32nd North'd Fus | Local Reserve for 17th Bn | 80th Bn | 11th Devonshire | 2nd Reserve from original 33rd Div | 44th Bn |
| 33rd North'd Fus | Local Reserve for 20th, 21st, 22nd, 3rd Bns | Part of 20th Bde | 10th Suffolk | 2nd Reserve from original 31st Div | 26th Bn |
| 34th North'd Fus | Local Reserve for 24th, 25th, 26th, 27rd Bns | Part of 20th Bde | 13th Suffolk | Local Reserve for 11th Bn | 108th Bn |
| 12th R. Warwickshire | 2nd Reserve from original 32nd Div | Part of 8th Bde | 9th Somerset L.I. | 2nd Reserve from original 33rd Div | 45th Bn |
| 13th R. Warwickshire | 2nd Reserve from original 32nd Div | 33rd Bn | 13th W. Yorkshire | 2nd Reserve from original 30th Div | 6th Bn |
| 17th R. Warwickshire | Local Reserve for 14th, 15th, 16th Bns | 92nd Bn | 14th W. Yorkshire | 2nd Reserve from original 34th Div | Part of 3rd Bde |
| 14th R. Fusiliers | 2nd Reserve from original 32nd Div | 31st Bn | 19th W. Yorkshire | Local Reserve for 15th, 17th Bns | 88th Bn |
| 15th R. Fusiliers | 2nd Reserve from original 32nd Div | 32nd Bn | 20th W. Yorkshire | Local Reserve for 16th, 18th Bns | 89th Bn |
| 16th R. Fusiliers | 2nd Reserve from original 34th Div | 22nd Bn | 9th E. Yorkshire | 2nd Reserve from original 30th Div | 7th Bn |
| 27th R. Fusiliers | Local Reserve for 17th, 22nd, 32nd Bns | 103rd Bn | 14th E. Yorkshire | Local Reserve for 10th, 11th, 12th, 13th Bns | 90th Bn |
| 28th R. Fusiliers | Local Reserve for 18th, 19th Bns | 104th Bn | 15th E. Yorkshire | Local Reserve for 10th, 11th, 12th, 13th Bns | Part of 91st Bn |
| | | | 9th Bedfordshire | 2nd Reserve from original 31st Div | Part of 6th Bde |
| | | | 10th Bedfordshire | 2nd Reserve from original 35th Div | 27th Bn |
| | | | 10th Leicestershire | 2nd Reserve from original 32nd Div | 5th Bn |

| Battalion | Origin | Training Reserve |
|---|---|---|
| 12th Leicestershire | Local Reserve for 11th Bn | 83rd Bn |
| 11th Yorkshire | 2nd Reserve from original 30th Div | Part of 1st Bde |
| 14th Yorkshire | Local Reserve for 12th Bn | 81st Bn |
| 15th Yorkshire | 2nd Reserve | 10th Bn |
| 13th Lancashire Fus | 2nd Reserve | 15th Bn |
| 21st Lancashire Fus | Local Reserve for 15th, 16th, 19th Bns | 72nd Bn |
| 22nd Lancashire Fus | Local Reserve for 17th, 18th, 20th Bns | 73rd Bn |
| 9th R. Scots Fus | 2nd Reserve | 55th Bn |
| 14th Cheshire | 2nd Reserve from original 35th Div | 50th Bn |
| 17th Cheshire | Local Reserve for 15th, 16th Bns | 74th Bn |
| 12th R. Welsh Fus | 2nd Reserve from original 35th Div | 62nd Bn |
| 18th R. Welsh Fus | Local Reserve for 15th Bn | Part of 63rd Bn |
| 20th R. Welsh Fus | 2nd Reserve | Part of 63rd Bn |
| 21st R. Welsh Fus | 2nd Reserve | Part of 64th Bn |
| 22nd R. Welsh Fus | 2nd Reserve | Part of 64th Bn |
| 9th S.W.B. | 2nd Reserve from original 35th Div | 57th Bn |
| 13th S.W.B. | Local Reserve for 10th, 11th Bns | 59th Bn |
| 14th S.W.B. | Local Reserve for 12th Bn | 65th Bn |
| 9th K.O.S.B. | 2nd Reserve from original 34th Div | 53rd Bn |
| 12th Cameronians | 2nd Reserve from original 34th Div | 56th Bn |
| 12th R. Innis Fus | Local Reserve for 9th, 10th, 11th Bns | |
| 11th Gloucestershire | 2nd Reserve from original 35th Div | 16th Bn |
| 15th Gloucestershire | Local Reserve for 12th, 14th Bns | 93rd Bn |
| 16th Gloucestershire | Local Reserve for 13th Bn | 94th Bn |
| 12th Worcestershire | 2nd Reserve from original 33rd Div | Part of 10th Bde |
| 13th Worcestershire | 2nd Reserve from original 33rd Div | 46th Bn |
| 10th E. Lancashire | 2nd Reserve from original 33rd Div | 47th Bn |
| 12th E. Lancashire | Local Reserve for 11th Bn | 75th Bn |
| 10th E. Surrey | 2nd Reserve from original 32nd Div | 30th Bn |
| 11th E. Surrey | 2nd Reserve from original 33rd Div | 21st Bn |
| 14th E. Surrey | Local Reserve for 12th, 13th Bns | Part of 26th Bde |
| 9th D.C.L.I. | 2nd Reserve from original 34th Div | Part of 10th Bde |
| 11th D.C.L.I. | Local Reserve for 10th Bn | 95th Bn |
| 11th W. Riding | 2nd Reserve from original 30th Div | Part of 3rd Bde |
| 10th Border | 2nd Reserve | Part of 4th Bde |
| 12th Border | Local Reserve for 11th Bn | Part of 75th Bn |
| 10th R. Sussex | 2nd Reserve from original 32nd Div | 23rd Bn |
| 14th R. Sussex | Local Reserve for 11th, 12th, 13th Bns | Part of 23rd Bde |
| 13th Hampshire | 2nd Reserve from original 32nd Div | 34th Bn |
| 16th Hampshire | Local Reserve for 14th, 15th Bns | 96th Bn |
| 10th S. Staffordshire | 2nd Reserve from 33rd Div | Part of 2nd Bde |
| 11th S. Staffordshire | 2nd Reserve | 9th Bn |
| 7th Dorsetshire | 2nd Reserve from original 34th Div | 35th Bn |
| 10th S. Lancashire | 2nd Reserve from original 35th Div | 51st Bn |
| 13th S. Lancashire | Local Reserve for 11th Bn | Part of 16th Bde |
| 12th Welsh | 2nd Reserve from original 35th Div | 58th Bn |
| 20th Welsh | Local Reserve for 10th, 13th Bns | 60th Bn |
| 21st Welsh | Local Reserve for 14th, 15th, 16th, 19th Bns | 61st Bn |
| 22nd Welsh | Local Reserve for 17th, 18th Bns | 66th Bn |
| 11th Black Watch | 2nd Reserve from original 34th Div | 38th Bn |
| 9th Ox & Bucks | 2nd Reserve from original 32nd Div | 36th Bn |
| 12th Essex | 2nd Reserve from original 35th Div | Part of 6th Bde |
| 14th Essex | Local Reserve for 13th Bn | 98th Bn |
| 13th Notts & Derby | 2nd Reserve from original 33rd Div | 12th Bn |
| 14th Notts & Derby | 2nd Reserve from original 30th Div | 13th Bn |
| 19th Notts & Derby | Local Reserve for 15th, 16th, 17th Bns | Part of 19th Bde |
| 11th N. Lancashire | 2nd Reserve from original 31st Div | 17th Bn |
| 8th Northamptonshire | 2nd Reserve from original 34th Div | 28th Bn |
| 9th R. Berkshire | 2nd Reserve from original 32nd Div | 37th Bn |
| 9th R. W. Kent | 2nd Reserve from original 31st Div | Part of 5th Bde |
| 12th R. W. Kent | Local Reserve for 10th, 11th Bns | 99th Bn |
| 11th K.O.Y.L.I. | 2nd Reserve from original 30th Div | 8th Bn |
| 13th K.O.Y.L.I. | Local Reserve for 12th Bn | Part of 19th Bde |
| 9th K.S.L.I. | 2nd Reserve from original 35th Div | 48th Bn |
| 14th Middlesex | 2nd Reserve from original 31st Div | 24th Bn |
| 15th Middlesex | 2nd Reserve from original 31st Div | Part of 5th Bde |
| 24th Middlesex | Local Reserve for 16th Bn | 100th Bn |
| 25th Middlesex (2) | Local Reserve for 18th, 19th, 26th Bns | |
| 27th Middlesex | Local Reserve for 17th, 23rd Bns | 101st Bn |
| 28th Middlesex | Local Reserve for 20th, 21st Bns | 102nd Bn |
| 14th K.R.R.C. | 2nd Reserve from original 31st Div | Part of 4th Bde |
| 15th K.R.R.C. | 2nd Reserve from original 31st Div | 18th Bn |
| 19th K.R.R.C. | Local Reserve for 16th, 17th Bns | 109th Bn |
| 22nd K.R.R.C. | Local Reserve for 20th Bn | 110th Bn |
| 23rd K.R.R.C. | Local Reserve for 18th Bn | 111th Bn |
| 24th K.R.R.C. | Local Reserve for 21st Bn | Part of 21st Bde |
| 8th Wiltshire | 2nd Reserve from original 34th Div | Part of 8th Bde |
| 14th Manchester | 2nd Reserve from original 30th Div | 14th Bn |
| 25th Manchester | Local Reserve for 16th, 17th, 18th Bns | 69th Bn |
| 26th Manchester | Local Reserve for 19th, 20th, 21st Bns | 70th Bn |
| 27th Manchester | Local Reserve for 22nd, 23rd, 24th Bns | 71st Bn |
| 10th N. Staffordshire | 2nd Reserve from original 33rd Div | 3rd Bn |
| 11th N. Staffordshire | 2nd Reserve | 4th Bn |
| 11th York & Lancs | 2nd Reserve from original 30th Div | Part of 2nd Bde |
| 15th York & Lancs | Local Reserve for 12th, 13th, 14th Bns | 91st Bn |
| 16th Durham L.I. | 2nd Reserve from original 30th Div | 1st Bn |
| 17th Durham L.I. | 2nd Reserve from original 30th Div | 2nd Bn |
| 21st Durham L.I. | Local Reserve for 18th, 20th Bns | 87th Bn |
| 23rd Durham L.I. | Local Reserve for 19th Bn | Part of 20th Bde |
| 13th Highland L.I. | 2nd Reserve from original 32nd Div | 52nd Bn |
| 19th Highland L.I. | Local Reserve for 15th, 16th, 17th Bns | 78th Bn |
| 20th Highland L.I. | Local Reserve for 18th Bn | 79th Bn |
| 10th Seaforth | 2nd Reserve from original 34th Div | 39th Bn |
| 11th Gordon | 2nd Reserve | 42nd Bn |
| 8th Cameron | 2nd Reserve from original 34th Div | 40th Bn |
| 17th R. Irish Rifles | Local Reserve for 8th, 9th, 10th Bns | |
| 18th R. Irish Rifles | Local Reserve for 11th, 12th Bns | |
| 19th R. Irish Rifles | Local Reserve for 14th, 15th Bns | |
| 20th R. Irish Rifles | Local Reserve for 13th, 16th Bns | |
| 10th R. Irish Fus | Local Reserve for 9th Bn | |
| 13th A. & S.H. | 2nd Reserve from original 35th Div | 41st Bn |
| 15th A. & S.H. | 2nd Reserve | Part of 9th Bde |
| 14th Rifle Brigade | 2nd Reserve from original 31st Div | 19th Bn |
| 15th Rifle Brigade | 2nd Reserve from original 31st Div | 20th Bn |
| 17th Rifle Brigade | Local Reserve for 16th Bn | 112th Bn |

(1) See 38th, 39th, 40th Battalions, Royal Fusiliers in Miscellaneous section.
(2) Became 25th (Garrison) Battalion in September 1916.

*Musketry Staff, 29th Bn, Royal Fusiliers.*   D. Barnes

*Members of 'C' Coy, 14th Bn, West Yorkshire Regt.*

*14th Manchester Regt.* D. Barnes

*Two members of 'A' Coy, 9th Bn, South Wales Borderers.* D. Barnes

*Members of the 11th Loyal North Lancashire Regt.* D. Barnes

*above*
*Band, 14th Bn, Manchester Regt.*   D. Barnes

*Members of 'B' Coy, 9th Bn, South Wales Borderers. The round device worn as a cap badge by all but three of the party, is a general-service button (bearing the Royal Arms). These were used until regimental badges were issued.*
D. Barnes

*Member of 30th Bn, Royal Northumberland Fusiliers (Tyneside Irish). The usual Northumberland Fusiliers' cap badge is being worn, but the brass shoulder title was special to this battalion and consisted of a crowned harp badge with the battalion number above and the letters 'NF' below.*

*Lewis Gun Instructors, 41st Bn, Training Reserve, formerly 13th Bn Argyll and Sutherland Highlanders.*

*17th (Reserve) Bn, Royal Warwickshire Regt. Note the number '22' worn on the shoulder, indicating that the battalion formed part of the 22nd Reserve Bde.* M. Ingrey

# 6

# MISCELLANEOUS SERVICE BATTALIONS

In addition to those that became part of New Army divisions, a number of service battalions were formed during 1914-18 that served in other formations.

*10B Bn The Royal Fusiliers (City of London Regt).*
This Battalion had its origins in the 10th Battalion of the Regiment and was made up from men who had knowledge of other languages. In the History of the Royal Fusiliers in the First World War, the battalion is recorded as having undertaken counter-espionage work in France, Italy, Salonika, the East and Russia. The title of the battalion varies from one reference to another, being referred to as 10B, 10th (Intelligence Corps) or 10th (Intelligence Police).

*25th Bn The Royal Fusiliers (City of London Regt) (Frontiersmen).*
This unique Battalion was formed by the Legion of Frontiersmen, a self-governing military organisation which had been in existence since 1904. With branches in every part of the British Empire and throughout the British Isles, the Legion was soon to offer its services when war broke out in 1914. The War Office, however, rejected a proposal by Col Driscoll, the Commandant-General, to provide some 2,000 men who would be prepared to undertake work of a commando nature. Instead, the Legion provided the 25th Royal Fusiliers who subsequently fought with great distinction in East Africa. One of its members, Lt W. Dartnell, was posthumously awarded the Victoria Cross for his gallant action at Maktau on 3 September 1915.

*38th, 39th, 40th Bns The Royal Fusiliers (City of London Regt).*
Sanction to form a group of battalions composed of Jewish recruits was given by the War Cabinet in April 1917. At first the battalions were to be known as the Jewish Regiment of Infantry, but this was later changed to 38th, 39th and 40th Royal Fusiliers, with the 41st and 42nd Battalions as reserve. The nucleus of the battalions was formed from ex-members of the Zion Mule Corps who had come to London after disbandment of their unit in 1916. A large number of British Jews naturally joined, as well as many who had come into the country from Russia. The 39th Battalion was mobilised in January 1918 and from March served until the end of the war throughout Egypt and Palestine. During the period the Battalion was attached to the 10th and 60th Divisions, and the Australian and New Zealand Mounted Division in Chaytor's Force. Both the 39th and 40th also served in Egypt and Palestine.

*21st Bn The Prince of Wales's Own (West Yorkshire Regt) (Wool Textile Pioneers).*
Raised by the Lord Mayor and City of Leeds on 24 September 1915. The Battalion went to France in June 1916 and served throughout the war on the Western Front as the pioneer battalion of the 4th Division.

*11th Bn The Leicestershire Regt (Midland Pioneers).*
Raised by the Mayor of Leicester in October 1915. The Battalion went to France in April 1916 and served throughout the war on the Western Front as the pioneer battalion of the 6th Division.

*24th Bn The Lancashire Fusiliers.*
On 30 June 1918 the 2/7th Battalion, Lancashire Fusiliers (TF) returned to England, having been reduced to a cadre in France. Its personnel, together with new recruits, formed the 24th Battalion in the following month and remained in England.

*26th Bn The Royal Welsh Fusiliers.*
Originally formed as the 4th Garrison Battalion and redesignated in July 1918. Later served with the 59th Division on the Western Front and in Egypt.

*15th Bn The South Wales Borderers.*
Formed in June 1918 and the following month absorbed the 10th Battalion, Cheshire Regiment. The Battalion remained in England.

*10th Bn The Gloucestershire Regt.*
Formed at Bristol in September 1914 and served as Army Troops attached to the 26th Division. Became part of the 1st Division in France on 17 August 1915 and was disbanded in February 1918.

*14th Bn The Worcestershire Regt (Severn Valley Pioneers).*
Raised by Lt-Col H. Webb, MP, in Worcester on 10 September 1915. The Battalion went to France in June 1916 and served as pioneer battalion to the 63rd Division for the rest of the war.

1  2  3  4

**Top**
Members of 25th Bn, Royal Fusiliers (Frontiersmen). The officer and CSM (seated) are wearing a small version of the cap badge on their collar.

Brass cap badge worn by 38th, 39th, 40th Bns, Royal Fusiliers. As Jewish Bns, the badge was the Menorah, the ceremonial seven-branched candlestick, with the Hebrew motto Kadimah.

Cap badges, 25th Bn, Royal Fusiliers (Frontiersmen). Three patterns of cap badge are known to exist for this battalion: (1) A gilt badge bearing, in red, white and blue enamel, a Union Jack. The motto 'God Guard Thee' is placed on a small circle at centre of the Union Jack. (2) This badge is said to have been made in a local London garage by adding a scroll to a Grenadier Guard's cap badge. Two versions of the last badge exist (3 & 4).

*10th Bn The Duke of Cornwall's Light Infantry (Cornwall Pioneers).*
Raised by the Mayor of Truro on 29 March 1915. The Battalion served on the Western Front as pioneers to the 2nd Division from June 1916.

*13th Bn The Duke of Wellington's (West Riding Regt).*
Formed in July 1918 from the 13th (Garrison) Battalion, Duke of Wellington's. The Battalion served on the Western Front as part of the 59th Division.

*17th Bn The Royal Sussex Regt.*
Formed in July 1918 by the redesignation of 17th (Garrison) Battalion, Royal Sussex Regiment. The Battalion served on the Western Front as part of the 59th Division.

*L/Cpl, 25th Bn, Royal Fusiliers (Frontiersmen).*
P. Bronson.

*23rd Bn The Welsh Regt (Welsh Pioneers).*
Formed in September 1915, and in August of the following year became pioneer battalion to the 28th Division in Macedonia.

*26th Bn The Duke of Cambridge's Own (Middlesex Regt) (3rd Public Works Pioneers).*
Raised by Lt-Col John Ward, MP, in London on 9 August 1915. The Battalion served in Macedonia as pioneers to the 27th Division from August 1916.

*20th Bn The King's Royal Rifle Corps (British Empire League Pioneers).*
Raised in London by the British Empire League on 20 August 1915. The Battalion went to France in March 1916 and served as pioneers to the 3rd Division for the remainder of the war.

*25th Bn the King's Royal Rifle Corps (Pioneers).*
Formed in June 1918 by the redesignation of 25th (Garrison) Battalion, KRRC. The Battalion served on the Western Front as the pioneer battalion to the 59th Division.

*22nd Bn The Durham Light Infantry (3rd County Pioneers).*
Raised by the Durham Recruiting Committee on 1 October 1915. The Battalion went to France in June 1916 and the following month became the pioneer battalion to the 8th Division.

# BIBLIOGRAPHY

Official Publications

Army Council Instructions
Army Lists
Army Orders

General Works

Becke, Major A. F: *Order of Battle of Divisions* (HMSO 1935-44)
Chappell, Mike: *British Battle Insignia (1) 1914-18* (Osprey, 1986)
Creagh, VC, Sir O'Moore: *The Victoria Cross 1856-1920* (Hayward, 1985)
Edmonds, Brigadier-General Sir James E: *Military Operations* (Macmillan and HMSO 1922-49)
Eggenberger, David: *A Dictionary of Battles* (George Allen & Unwin, 1967)

Gaylor, J: *Military Badge Collecting* (Leo Cooper, 1971)
Gleichen, Major-General Lord Edward: *Chronology of the Great War* (Greenhill, 1988)
James, Brigadier E. A: *British Infantry Regiments in the Great War* (Samson, 1976)
James, Brigadier, E. A: *The British Armies in France and Flanders, 1914-18*
Westlake, Ray: *Collecting Metal Shoulder Titles* (Warne, 1980)
Wheeler-Holohan, V: *Divisional and Other Signs* (John Murray, 1920)

Divisional and Regimental Histories

Where available, all published histories have been consulted.

# APPENDIX

## APPENDIX I

### BRITISH INFANTRY DIVISIONS 1914-1918

*Regular Divisions*
Guards
1st
2nd
3rd
4th
5th
6th
7th
8th

*New Army Divisions*
9th (Scottish)
10th (Irish)
11th (Northern)
12th (Eastern)
13th (Western)
14th (Light)
15th (Scottish)
16th (Irish)
17th (Northern)
18th (Eastern)
19th (Western)
20th (Light)
21st
22nd
23rd
24th
25th
26th

*Regular Divisions*
27th
28th
29th

*New Army Divisions*
30th
31st
32nd
33rd
34th
35th
36th (Ulster)

37th
38th (Welsh)
39th
40th
41st

*Territorial Force Divisions*
42nd (East Lancashire)
43rd (Wessex)
44th (Home Counties)
45th (2nd/Wessex)
46th (North Midland)
47th (2nd London)
48th (South Midland)
49th (West Riding)
50th (Northumbrian)
51st (Highland)
52nd (Lowland)
53rd (Welsh)
54th (East Anglian)
55th (West Lancashire)
56th (1st London)
57th (2nd/West Lancashire)
58th (2nd/1st London)
59th (2nd/North Midland)
60th (2nd/2nd London)
61st (2nd/South Midland)
62nd (2nd/West Riding)
63rd (2nd/Northumbrian)
63rd (Royal Naval) from 19 July 1916
64th (2nd/Highland)
65th (2nd/Lowland)
66th (2nd/East Lancashire)
67th (2nd/Home Counties)
68th (2nd/Welsh)
69th (2nd/East Anglian)

*Home Service Divisions*
70th Never formed
71st
72nd
73rd

*Territorial Divisions*
74th (Yeomanry)
75th

## APPENDIX II

During the First World War the establishment of an infantry division varied and the numbers of men, guns, animals, vehicles, etc were changed on a number of occasions. The following tables show the components of a division on the Western Front at two points and are based on two authorities: War Establishment of New Armies, 1 April 1915, and War Establishment Part VII, 31 October 1918.

### Infantry Division, April 1915

Divnl H.Q.

**Infantry:**
3 Brigades
(12 Inf Battalions, with 4 machine guns each).

**Mounted Troops:**
1 Cavalry Squadron;
1 Cyclist Company.

**Artillery:**
H.Q., Divnl Artillery;
3 Field Artillery Brigades (12 batteries – 18-pdr Q.F.) and 3 B.A.C.s;
1 Field Artillery (How) Brigade (4 batteries – 4.5" How) and 1 (How) B.A.C.;
1 Heavy Battery (4, 60-pdr B.L.) and Hy Bty A.C.
1 Divnl Ammn Coln.

**Engineers:**
H.Q., Divnl Engineers;
3 Field Companies.

**Signal Service:**
1 Signal Company.

**Pioneers:**
1 Pioneer Battalion
(4 machine guns).
3 Field Ambulances.
1 Sanitary Section.
1 Mobile Veterinary Section.
1 Motor Ambulance Workshop.
1 Divnl Train.

| | |
|---|---|
| All Ranks | 19,614 |
| Horses and Mules | 5,818 |
| Guns | 68 |
| 18-pdr Q.F. | 48 |
| 4.5" How | 16 |
| 16-pdr B.L. | 4 |
| Trench Mortars | |
| Stokes | |
| Mediums | |
| Heavy | |
| Machine Guns | 52 |
| Vickers | 52 |
| Lewis | |
| Carts and Vehicles | 958 |
| Cycles | 538 |
| Motor Cycles | 19 |
| Motor Cars | 11 |
| Motor Lorries | 4 |
| Motor Ambulance Cars | 21 |

### Infantry Division, October 1918

Divnl H.Q.

**Infantry:**
3 Brigades
(9 Inf Battalions, with 36 Lewis guns each);
3 Light Trench-Mortar Batteries
(8, 3" Stokes mortars each).

**Artillery:**
H.Q., Divnl Artillery;
2 Field Artillery Brigades
(8 batteries – 6, 18-pdr Q.F. and 2, 4.5" How);
2 Medium Trench-Mortar Batteries
(6, 2" mortars each);
1 Divnl Ammn Coln.

**Engineers:**
H.Q., Divnl Engineers;
3 Field Companies.

**Signal Service:**
1 Signal Company.

**Pioneers:**
1 Pioneer Battalion
(12 Lewis guns).

**Machine Gun Unit:**
1 Machine Gun Battalion
(4 Companies, with 16 Vickers M.G.s each).

3 Field Ambulances.
1 Mobile Veterinary Section.
1 Divnl Employment Company.
1 Divnl Train.

| | |
|---|---|
| All Ranks | 16,035 |
| Horses and Mules | 3,838 |
| Guns | 48 |
| 18-pdr Q.F. | 36 |
| 4.5" How | 12 |
| 16-pdr B.L. | |
| Trench Mortars | 36 |
| Stokes | 24 |
| Mediums | 12 |
| Heavy | |
| Machine Guns | 400 |
| Vickers | 64 |
| Lewis | 336 |
| Carts and Vehicles | 870 |
| Cycles | 341 |
| Motor Cycles | 44 |
| Motor Cars | 11 |
| Motor Lorries | 3 |
| Motor Ambulance Cars | 21 |

# INDEX